'This book is a balanced assessment from authors who are experienced in the practice of meditation and who can shed light on the range and scope of the often over-enthusiastic claims made regarding the positive benefits of meditation. It is a provocative read, wise, balanced and fair even in its treatment of the dark side of meditation. If you meditate or wonder if you should, this is the one book you must read.'
Ralph W. Hood, Jr., Ph.D., Former President of the Society for the Psychology of Religion and Spirituality, American Psychological Association

'To change a human being – that is power. Whoever has it has got the key to a timeless want, to be able to free, or control, people. Farias and Wikholm give us a readable, thoughtful, and in-depth look at the promises and pitfalls of meditation as a human change procedure. It is imported to the West as a simple but powerful method to relieve suffering and promote compassion. Does it work? The answer turns out to be complicated. From real-world encounters with prison convicts combined with research on mindfulness in psychotherapy, and examination of the roots of Buddhism, the notion that meditation heals is given honest, in-depth examination. This book keeps your attention; you don't want to put it down. It provides an accurate record what mindfulness can and cannot do for depression, suffering, compassionate behavior, and a whole gambit of helpful, helpless, and harmful human behaviors. It helps us make wise decisions about it.'
Raymond F. Paloutzian, Ph.D., editor of the *International Journal for the Psychology of Religion*

'Much has been written about meditation, some of it making wild claims about how it can bring about personal change. But this is a book with a difference. Entertainingly written and always with an eye to the scientific and human evidence, it examines the good and the bad of meditation. An excellent read.'
Gordon Claridge, Emeritus Professor of Abnormal Psychology at the University of Oxford and author of *Sounds from the Bell Jar: Ten Psychotic Authors* and *Schizotypy: Implications for Health and Illness*

'In this excellent book, Dr Farias and Wikholm develop an account that shows the ambiguity of meditation and its effects on people's lives which can be positive but also, perhaps to our surprise, negative. All those interested in meditation and public health should read this book.'
Gavin Flood FBA, Professor of Hindu Studies and Comparative Religion, University of Oxford, and author of *The Blackwell Companion to Hinduism* and *The Tantric Body*

'This is a book bound to ruffle many feathers among advocates of meditation. It turns out that the evidence of benefit is not as unequivocal as many of us suppose. This is a highly readable, nontechnical and entertaining book that takes a closer look at the science behind the claims made about meditation.'
Stephen Law, provost of the Centre for Inquiry, UK, senior lecturer in philosophy at Heythrop College, University of London, and author of *The Philosophy Gym* and *Believing Bullshit: How Not to Get Sucked into an Intellectual Blackhole*

THE BUDDHA PILL

CAN
MEDITATION
CHANGE
YOU?

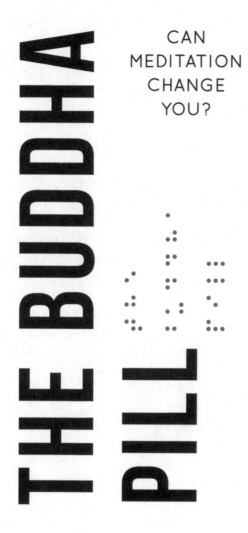

DR MIGUEL FARIAS & CATHERINE WIKHOLM

WATKINS
Sharing Wisdom Since
1893

This edition first published in the UK and USA 2015 by
Watkins, an imprint of Watkins Media Limited
19 Cecil Court, London WC2N 4EZ

enquiries@watkinspublishing.co.uk

1 3 5 7 9 10 8 6 4 2

Designed by Gail Jones
Cover designed by Jade Wheaton

Printed and bound in Europe

A CIP record for this book is available from the British Library

ISBN: 978-1-78028-718-8

www.watkinspublishing.com

CONTENTS

INTRODUCTION

My interest in meditation began at the age of six when my parents did a course on Transcendental Meditation. I didn't realize it then, but I was effectively being introduced to the idea that meditation can produce all manner of changes in who we are and in what we can achieve. Mind-over-matter stories are both inspiring and bewildering, hard to believe yet compelling. They have stirred me deeply enough to dedicate almost two decades of my life researching what attracts some people to techniques like meditation and yoga – and whether, like many claim, they can transform us in a fundamental way.

This book tells the story of the human ambition for personal change, with a primary focus on the techniques of meditation and yoga. Hundreds of millions of people around the world meditate daily. Mindfulness courses, directly inspired by Buddhist meditation, are offered in schools and universities, and mindfulness-based therapies are now available as psychological treatments in the UK's National Health Service. Many scientists and teachers claim that this spiritual practice is one of the most efficient and economic tools of personal change. Yoga is no less popular. According to a recent survey by the Yoga Health Foundation, more than 250 million people worldwide practise it regularly[1]. Through yoga we learn to notice thoughts, feelings and sensations while working with physical postures. Often, yoga practice includes a period of lying or sitting meditation.

Psychologists have developed an arsenal of theories and techniques to understand and motivate personal change. But it wasn't psychology that produced the greatest surge of interest of the twentieth century in this topic – it was meditation. By the 1970s millions of people worldwide were signing up to learn a technique that promised quick and dramatic personal change.

Transcendental Meditation was introduced to the West by Maharishi Mahesh Yogi, and quickly spread after the Beatles declared themselves to be followers of this Indian guru. To gain respectability Maharishi sponsored dozens of scientific studies about the effects of Transcendental Meditation, in academic fields ranging from psychophysiology to sociology, showing that its regular practice changed personality traits, improved mood and wellbeing and, not least, reduced criminality rates.

The publicity images for Transcendental Meditation included young people levitating in a cross-legged position and displaying blissful smiles. I recall, as a child, staring at the photographs of the levitating meditators used in the advertising brochures and thinking 'Can they really do that?' My parents' enthusiasm for meditation, though, was short-lived. When I recently asked my mum about it, she just said, 'It was a seventies thing; most of our friends were trying it out.'

Like my parents' interest research on meditation waned rapidly. Photos of levitating people didn't help to persuade the scientific community that this was something worth studying. We had to wait almost thirty years before a new generation of researchers re-ignited interest in the field, conducting the first neuroimaging studies of Tibetan monks meditating[2], and the first explorations of the use of mindfulness in the treatment of depression[3]. For yoga, too, there is increasing evidence that its practice can reduce depression[4].

Meditation and yoga are no longer taboo words in psychology, psychiatry and neuroscience departments. There now are dedicated conferences and journals on the topic and thousands of researchers worldwide using the most advanced scientific tools to study these techniques. Many of the studies are funded by national science agencies; just looking at the US federally funded projects, from 1998 to 2009 the number increased from seven to more than 120[5]. The idea of personal change is increasingly central to these studies. Recent articles show improvements in cognitive and affective skills after six to eight weeks of mindfulness, including an increase in empathy[6].

These are exciting findings. Meditation practices seem to have an impact on our thoughts, emotions and behaviours. Yet, these studies report only modest changes. But many who use and teach these techniques make astonishing claims about their powers. At the Patanjali Research Foundation in northern India, the world's largest yoga research centre, I hear miraculous claims about yoga from the mouth of its director-guru, Swami Ramdev: 'Yoga can heal anything, whether it's physical or mental illness.'

Teasing fact from fiction is a major aim of this book. The first part explores ideas about the effects of meditation and yoga, contrasting them with the current scientific evidence of personal change. The second part puts the theories to the test – we carry out new research and scrutinize both the upsides and downsides of these practices. We have dedicated a full chapter to the darker aspects of meditation, which teachers and researchers seldom or never mention. Although this isn't a self-help book, it attempts to answer crucial questions for anyone interested in contemplative techniques: can these practices help me to change? If yes, how much and how do they work? And, if they do change me, is it always for the better?

These questions have shaped a significant part of my own life. In my teenage years I believed that to seek personal growth and transformation was the central goal of human existence; this led me to study psychology. I wanted to learn how to promote change through psychological therapy, although it was only later, while undergoing therapy training, that I considered the subtlety and difficulties of this process. My undergraduate psychology degree turned out to not shed much light on our potential for transformation; it rarely touched on ideas about how to make us more whole, healed, enlightened, or just a better person. But rather than giving up, I read more about the areas of psychology I wasn't being taught – like consciousness studies – and started doing research on the effects of spiritual practices. When I decided it was probably a good idea to do a doctorate, I browsed through hundreds of psychology websites in search of potential supervisors; I found one at Oxford whom I thought was open minded enough to mentor my interests, and I moved to the city in 2000.

This is the pre-history of my motivation to write this book. Its history begins in the early summer of 2009, when Shirley du Boulay, a writer and former journalist with the BBC, invited a number of people to take part in the re-creation of a ceremony that blended Christian and Indian spirituality. Images, readings and songs from both traditions were woven together, following the instructions of Henry le Soux, a French Benedictine monk who went to live in India and founded a number of Christian ashrams that adopted the simplicity of Indian spirituality (think of vegetarian food and a thin orange habit)[7].

I met Catherine Wikholm, the co-author of this book, at this event. She had studied philosophy and theology at Oxford University before embarking on her psychology training, and was at the time doing research relating to young offenders. Catherine and I were both drawn to an elegant woman in her fifties called Sandy Chubb, who spoke in a gentle but authoritative manner. Sandy showed us a book she had recently published with cartoonish illustrations of yoga postures. I thought it was intended for children and asked her if kids enjoyed yoga. Sandy smiled and told us the book was meant for illiterate prisoners. That was the mission of the Prison Phoenix Trust, a small charity she directed: to teach yoga and meditation in prisons. Trying to escape my feeling of embarrassment, I praised the idea of bringing contemplative techniques to prisoners.
'It must help them to cope with the lack of freedom,' I suggested. Sandy frowned slightly.

'That's not the main purpose,' she said.

Although going to prison is a punishment, Sandy told us,

with the help of meditation and yoga, being locked in a small cell can help prisoners realize their true life mission.

'Which is?' Catherine and I both asked at the same time.

'To be saintly, enlightened beings,' Sandy answered.

Catherine and I kept silent. We were mildly sceptical. But also intrigued. Sandy seemed to claim that meditation and yoga techniques could radically transform criminals. I went back to my office that same evening to search for studies of meditation and yoga in prisons and found only a handful. The results weren't dramatic but pointed in the right direction – prisoners reported less aggression and higher self-esteem[6]. Reading closely, I noticed there were serious methodological flaws: most had small sample sizes and none included a control group – a standard research practice that ensures results are not owing to chance or some variable the researcher forgot to take into account. I wanted to know more. If Sandy's claims were true, if meditation and yoga could transform prisoners, this could have tremendous implications for how psychologists understand and promote personal change in all individuals, not just those who are incarcerated. Having no experience of prisons, I contacted Catherine to ask if she'd be interested in working with me on this topic.

'I'd love to!' she said, more enthusiastic than I imagine most would be at the prospect of interviewing numerous convicted criminals and in the process spending weeks behind bars. Having started working for the prison service in her early twenties, Catherine had a strong forensic interest, particularly in the treatment of young offenders. She was passionate about the rehabilitation of prisoners in general and was curious as to whether yoga and meditation might represent an alternative means of facilitating positive, meaningful change for those who were unable or unwilling to engage with traditional rehabilitative efforts, such as offending behaviour programs.

So Catherine and I arranged to meet with Sandy at the Prison Phoenix Trust. Walking through Oxford's trendy Summertown, where the Trust is based, we wondered what the meeting would bring. On arriving at the offices, we received a warm welcome. Sandy gave us the guided tour of their floor of the building, which comprised four rooms: the office, where she and her colleagues had their desks; a dining room for communal meals; a meditation room with cushions on the floor; and, along a corridor, a room that was wall-to-wall lined with metal filing cabinets. These, Sandy explained, were full of the letters the Prison Phoenix Trust had received from prisoners, estimated at numbering more than ten thousand.

If we were intrigued before, we were now completely hooked. Our minds filled with questions, we sat down with Sandy as she began to reveal the unusual story of how a small charity had persuaded prison governors to let them teach meditation and yoga to a broad range of prisoners, including thieves, murderers and rapists.

This story made quite an impression on us. So much so, in fact, that it inspired us to dedicate much of the following two years to designing and implementing a study of the measurable effects of yoga and meditation on prisoners. The findings of our research (which we'll reveal later on in the book) not only sparked a flurry of media interest, but inspired us to spend the two years after that writing this book.

Our initial focus on the potential of meditative techniques to transform the 'worst of the worst' broadened out, as we became increasingly interested in exploring its full potential. Might Eastern contemplative techniques have the power to change all of us? As we engaged with more and more research literature, the inspiring stories of change we uncovered compounded our broadened view of the potential of yoga and meditation. Our own personal experiences, such as those of my ongoing research and Catherine's clinical psychology doctoral training – and subsequent acquaintance with mindfulness-based therapies and their application within the NHS – in turn increased our curiosity.

What began as a perhaps unlikely marriage of my interest in spirituality and Catherine's in forensic and clinical psychology has evolved into a wider exploration of the science and delusions of personal change. Just as we worked on our research together, so we have written this book together. To reflect the dynamic process of our writing, with the combining of our ideas – and to avoid any messy jumping back and forth between us as narrators – we have chosen to write this book in first-person narrative, as a singular, joint 'I'. Although inevitably it may sometimes be apparent which one of us is narrating at a particular point, if simply by virtue of our gender difference, we have sought to write as a shared voice. The personal stories, interviews and accounts depicted in this book are all drawn from our real experiences. However, when discussing any examples relating to therapeutic work, we have anonymized all names and identifying details.

Over the course of the book, we will examine the scientific evidence that actually exists for the claims of change that meditation, mindfulness and yoga practitioners, teachers and enthusiasts propagate. We also bring together our own experiences as psychologists, one more research-oriented and one more practice-oriented, as well as the stories of some of the thought-provoking characters we've encountered along our journey. All that is to come. But for now let us begin by letting you in on the unique story that started it all.

CHAPTER 1

AN ASHRAM IN A PRISON CELL

'If we forget that in every criminal there is a potential saint, we are dishonouring all of the great spiritual traditions. Saul of Tarsus persecuted and killed Christians before becoming Saint Paul, author of much of the New Testament. Valmiki, the revealer of the Ramayana, was a highwayman, a robber, and a murderer. Milarepa, one of the greatest Tibetan Buddhist gurus, killed 37 people before he became a saint ... We must remember that even the worst of us can change.'[1] Bo Lozoff (American prison reform activist and founder of the Prison Ashram Project and the Human Kindness Foundation)

Knocking on the door of a house in a quiet street in Oxfordshire, notepad and pen in hand, I stood and waited on the front step. A minute later the door opened. A smartly dressed, elderly lady smiled at me from inside.

'Tigger?' I asked.

'Yes, do come in,' she replied.

    Still full of life at ninety years old, Tigger Ramsey-Brown was a

pleasure to interview. I was there to find out from her more about
the story of her late younger sister, who had founded the Prison
Phoenix Trust. Over cups of tea in her sunny conservatory, Tigger
began vividly to recount the story of her sister and how she had
started the Trust around thirty years previously.

In the beginning

Tigger pointed out that if we were going to go right to the
start, this story actually begins somewhat earlier, with the
marine biologist and committed Darwinist Sir Alister Hardy.
At one time a Professor of Zoology at Oxford University, Hardy
had happened to teach Richard Dawkins, an evolutionary biologist
and outspoken atheist. Knighted for his work in biology, Hardy had
a strong interest in the evolution of humankind, developing novel
theories such as the aquatic ape hypothesis (which proposes that
humans went through an aquatic or semi-aquatic stage in our
evolution). But he was also particularly interested in the evolution
of religion and religious experience. Hardy viewed humans as
spiritual animals, theorizing that spirituality was a natural part
of our human consciousness. He mooted that our awareness of
something 'other' or 'beyond' had arisen through exploration of
our environment and he wanted to explore this further.

However, aware that fellow scientists and academics
were likely to consider his interest in researching spirituality
unorthodox, he waited until he retired from Oxford University
before he delved deeper and founded the then-called Religious
Experience Research Unit (RERU) at Manchester College, Oxford.
(It is now the Alister Hardy Religious Experience Research Centre
and is based in Wales.) The goal of Hardy's research was to
discover if people today still had the same kind of mystical
experiences they seemed to have had in the past. He began his
study by placing adverts in newspapers, asking people to write
in with their mystical experiences, in response to what became
known as 'The Hardy Question': 'Have you ever been aware of or

influenced by a presence or power, whether you call it God or not, which is different from your everyday self?'[2]

'Thousands of people replied to the adverts, writing about their dreams and spiritual experiences. These responses were compiled into a database to enable researchers to analyze the different natures and functions of people's religious and spiritual experiences. This is where Ann came in,' Tigger told me. And so it was that in the mid-1980s in Oxfordshire, a woman named Ann Wetherall spent her days collecting and categorizing people's dreams, visions and other spiritual experiences.

Looking for a link

Over time, as she examined the letters, Ann began to wonder if there was a common denominator in the accounts. She noticed that it didn't seem to matter whether someone was religious or atheist, but, more often than not, it was people who were feeling hopeless or helpless who reported a direct experience of spirituality. Ann hypothesized that imprisonment might be a context that particularly inspired such despondent feelings and that it therefore might also trigger spiritual experiences. She got in touch with convicted murderer-turned-sculptor Jimmy Boyle, one of Scotland's most famous reformed criminals. Boyle helped her to get an advert published in prison newspapers, asking for prisoners to write in about their religious or spiritual episodes. She got quite a response – prisoners in their dozens wrote in to her describing their unusual experiences. Many of them had never mentioned these to anyone before and had wondered if they were going mad.

'Ann wanted to write back and reassure them that they weren't, and that these were valid spiritual experiences, which could be built on – but the Alister Hardy Foundation did not reply to letters,' Tigger explained. 'That's why Ann broke away from the research, so that she could start corresponding with the prisoners who were writing in, and offer support. Because of their confinement in cells and separation from the outside world, Ann thought that prisoners' experience was perhaps rather similar to that of monks. While for prisoners this withdrawal from society was not voluntary, she believed that they too could use their cell as a space for spiritual growth.'

'What was her interpretation of spiritual growth?' I asked.

'Not only becoming more in touch with a greater power, but also becoming more aware of inner feelings and thoughts, as well as more connected and sensitive to other people's needs,' Tigger explained.

'And the means of bringing about this kind of change?' I asked, already pre-empting the answer...

'Through meditation, of course.'

From spiritual experience to spiritual development

Tigger explained that she and Ann had spent their childhoods in India, growing up among Buddhist monasteries. Because of this upbringing, Ann had had a lifelong involvement with meditation, and believed that prisoners could benefit from learning it. In her letters back and forth to prisoners, she began sharing with them what she knew about meditation, in order to encourage and support their spiritual development.

Over the next couple of years, Ann's correspondence with convicts came to strengthen her belief that prisoners had real potential for spiritual development. 'She thought they had a terrific spirituality, a hunger that wasn't being met,' Tigger explained, as our conversation moved onto Ann's decision to set up a charitable trust, the Prison Ashram Project (now the Prison Phoenix Trust). Founded in 1988, the organization was at first very small, comprising just Ann and three other volunteers, who wrote to prisoners, encouraging them to use their spiritual experiences as a springboard for future spiritual development. 'You are more than you think you are' was the project's frequent message.

As the name suggests the Prison Ashram Project had the

central premise that a prison cell can be used as an ashram – a Hindi word that refers to a spiritual hermitage, a place to develop deeper spiritual understanding through quiet contemplation or ascetic devotion. Hermitage is not only an Eastern practice – in Western Christian tradition, a monastery is a place of hermitage, too, because it is partially removed from the world.

Furthermore, the word 'cell' is used in monasteries as well as in prisons, and there are a surprising number of similarities between the living conditions of monks and prisoners. Both live ascetic lives filled with restriction and limitation. Both monks and prisoners are able to meet their basic needs (but little more), both desist from sensual pleasures and the accumulation of wealth, and both follow a strict daily schedule. Despite these parallels, however, there is undeniably a big difference in how monks and prisoners come to live in their respective cells. For monks living communally in monasteries, as well as hermits who live alone, living ascetically is an intentional choice, aimed at enabling them to better focus on spiritual goals. But for prisoners withdrawing from the world is not their choice; rather, it is imposed upon them as punishment. Which leads to the question: can involuntary confinement really open a door to inner freedom and personal change?

Ann Wetherall believed so. Being confined to a cell for much of the day, even against free will, could be a catalyst for spiritual development. The conditions were conducive; all that anyone needed was a radical shift in thinking. Rather than punishment, incarceration could be reconceived of as an opportunity for positive transformative experience. Prisoners had lost their physical liberty, but they could nevertheless gain spiritual freedom. Ann thought that meditation was the ideal tool with which prisoners could build spiritual growth, requiring only body, mind and breath.

So far, so good. But as Tigger talked something seemed to me to be a distinct obstacle to peaceful meditation behind bars: the undeniable fact that prisons are busy, noisy places. Granted, there might be some similarities between prisons, monasteries and spiritual retreats, I thought, but surely finding peace and quiet in a prison would be a bit of a mission impossible. Wouldn't that render any attempt to meditate a bit futile?

'No.' Tigger smiled. 'Ann believed this actually increased the importance and worth of meditation practice; the practice would enable prisoners to find a sense of peace *despite* their surroundings.'

Crossing continents

As it turned out Ann was not the first to think of encouraging prisoners' spiritual development through in-cell meditation. A couple of years after setting up the Prison Ashram Project, she heard about Bo Lozoff, a spiritual leader and prison reform activist doing similar work in the USA. Curiously, his organization was also called the Prison Ashram Project. Bo first had the idea that a prison cell could be a kind of ashram when his brother-in-law was sentenced to prison for drug smuggling. At the time Bo and his wife Sita were living at an ashram in North Carolina. There, their daily routine involved waking early, wearing all white, working all day without getting paid, abstaining from sex and eating communally. Visiting his brother-in-law in prison, Bo realized there were remarkable parallels between their day-to-day lives. Around the same time he came across a book by renowned spiritual teacher Ram Dass, entitled *Be Here Now*[3]. The combination of these two events inspired Bo and Sita to set up their own Prison Ashram Project in 1973, in co-operation with Ram Dass. Just like Ann, they had begun corresponding with prisoners, offering encouragement and instruction in meditation and also in yoga. They also sent prisoners copies of Ram Dass's book, along with the book that Bo himself went on to write: *We're All Doing Time – A Guide for Getting Free*[4]. The central concept of this book is that it's not only prisoners who are imprisoned, but that we are *all* 'doing time' because we allow ourselves to be so restricted by hang-ups, blocks and tensions. The message is that through meditation and yoga we can all learn to become free.

The birth of the Prison Phoenix Trust

Not long after meeting Bo, Ann changed her charity's name to the Prison Phoenix Trust (PPT), in part because she was concerned that the word 'ashram' might prove an obstacle for the prison service. She was keen to step things up a notch from written correspondence and start setting up meditation and yoga workshops in prisons themselves. However, even with the new name, prison governors and officers were wary of the charity's efforts. The Trust tried to get into prisons through the chaplaincy; however, here too there was a surprising amount of resistance. It's worth remembering that in the late 1980s, prison chaplains were almost all Anglican. At that time the Anglican Church was still suspicious of practices such as meditation, which when compared with contemplation or silent prayer seemed 'unChristian'. Many ministers thought that meditation centred on a spirituality that might be Hindu, Buddhist or even evil (stemming from the notion that to silence the mind also means making it available for the devil). A 2011 article in the *Daily Telegraph* highlighted an extreme example of Christian opposition to yoga and meditation, reporting how a Catholic priest named Father Gabriele Amorth – appointed the Vatican's chief exorcist in 1986 – had publicly denounced yoga at a film festival where he had been invited to introduce *The Rite* (a film about exorcism, starring Anthony Hopkins): 'Practising yoga is Satanic, it leads to evil just like reading Harry Potter,' the priest is reported as stating, to an audience of bemused film fans[5].

Of course, not all devout Christians share such concerns that Christianity and Eastern spiritual practices are incompatible. Offering me another biscuit Tigger revealed the next chapter of her sister's tale, wherein Ann would join forces with 'a very forceful and very amazing character'.

A CATHOLIC ZEN MASTER

'*Spirituality is what you do with those fires that burn within you.*' –
Sister Elaine[6]

Thousands of miles away from Oxford and Ann's fledgling
charity lived a Catholic nun. As well as being a nun, Sister Elaine
was a Zen master. She grew up in Canada, where in her youth
she became a professional classical musician for the Calgary
Symphony Orchestra. At the age of thirty, however, she realized
her true calling and joined the convent of Our Lady's Missionaries
in Toronto. In 1961, after several years at the convent, she was
sent to Japan for her first assignment as a Catholic missionary.
Her mission was to set up a Conservatory and Cultural Centre
in Osaka, where she would teach English and music to Japanese
people, as well as to baptise as many of them as possible. In order
to get to know the Japanese people better, she began to practise
Zen Buddhism. She started *zazen* (sitting meditation) and *koan*
study, under the guidance of Yamada Koun Roshi, a well-known
Zen master from the Japanese *Sanbo Kyodan* order. Perhaps
surprisingly, it did not matter to him that Sister Elaine was a
Catholic nun with no intention of becoming a Buddhist. Yamada
Koun Roshi did not draw a division between different people or
religions, and similarly neither does Sister Elaine, who maintains,
'There is no separation. We make separation.[7]'

Devoted to her new discipline, Sister Elaine went on to spend
some time living with Buddhist nuns in Kyoto, where the daily
regime involved ten hours a day of sitting in silence. To call the
koan study lengthy would be an understatement; it took her nearly
two decades of studying with her Zen teacher before she was
made a *roshi*. This title, which translates literally as 'old teacher',
marks the top echelon of Zen teachers. There are an estimated
only 100 *roshis* worldwide. Very few of them are Westerners, but
in 1980 Sister Elaine finally became one of them – an accredited
Zen teacher of the Sanbo Kyodan order. Her achievement made

her the first Canadian, and certainly the first Catholic nun, to be recognized as one of the world's highest-ranking teachers of Zen.

In 1976, after 15 years in Japan, Our Lady's Missionaries back in Toronto transferred Sister Elaine to the Philippines. This was during the worst years of the Marcos regime, and Sister Elaine was to be involved with animal husbandry. However, she did more than merely raise livestock. Once in the Philippines she set up a *zendo* (Zen meditation centre), for the Catholic Church in Manila. Word spread about her work and a leading dissident, Horacio 'Boy' Morales, who had headed the New People's Army against the Marcos dictatorship, came to hear of her. Held as a political prisoner at the Bago Bantay detention centre, Morales asked Sister Elaine to come to prison to teach meditation to him and a group of fellow prisoners, each of whom had, like him, been tortured. His hope was that the practice could help them to cope with the stress of imprisonment and find inner peace.

Despite the hostility of the authorities and worrying reports of other prison visitors 'vanishing', Sister Elaine spent four-and-a-half years teaching meditation to those prisoners every week. During that time she witnessed a remarkable change: the prisoners transformed from being angry, tense men, trembling from torture, to being calm. This convinced her both of the therapeutic power of silent meditation and of the potential for prisoners to develop spiritually while incarcerated.

Sister Elaine's life makes for quite an unusual story, and her work in the Philippines caught the attention of the media – and subsequently of Ann Wetherall. Leaning forward in her seat, Ann's sister, Tigger, told me of the unexpected events that would subsequently unfold.

Ann's legacy

In 1992, four years after founding the Prison Phoenix Trust, Ann discovered she had terminal cancer. Coming to terms with this news, Ann felt fearful for the prisoners she was involved with; what would happen to her charity after she was gone? She had heard of Sister Elaine and wrote to her, asking if she would consider taking over as director after she died. Sister Elaine flew over from the Philippines to spend a week with Ann to try to come to a decision. Shortly after returning home, she phoned Ann to accept her offer, telling her 'don't die until I get there'.

Sadly, Ann passed away while Sister Elaine was on her way back to England. Over the six years Sister Elaine was director, the idea that yoga and meditation are beneficial for prisoners became increasingly accepted among prison governors and officers. They might not have been as interested in the potential spiritual development of prisoners, but many acknowledged the range of other, more down-to-earth benefits: prisoners doing yoga and meditation were reportedly calmer, slept better and felt less stressed – and so were easier to work with. While, like Ann, Sister Elaine believed that meditation was the key to stilling the mind, incorporating yoga into the classes was important: when the body can be still, the mind can be still. Aged 75, Sister Elaine left the Trust – not to retire, but to return to her native Canada to found a similar organization called Freeing the Human Spirit, based in Toronto.

In the years since Sister Elaine's departure, the Prison Phoenix Trust (PPT) has continued to develop its work, with classes now running in the majority of UK prisons. Reflecting on the Trust's progress, Sandy Chubb, the PPT's subsequent director, remarked to me with a smile, 'Yes, gone are the days when yoga teachers were branded yoghurt pots.'

Hearing the stories about Ann and Sister Elaine, so vividly recounted to me by Tigger and others, including the Trust's current director Sam Settle, it made sense to me that yoga and meditation could lead to personal change in prisoners. Certainly the PPT had a whole lot of anecdotal evidence attesting to its benefits. Over the course of 25 years, PPT letter-writers have received more than 10,000 replies from prisoners reporting the positive effects of these techniques. The benefits range from increased self-esteem, better sleep and reduced dependence on drugs, medication or cigarettes, to improved emotional management and reduced stress.

Anecdote or evidence

I was invited to come and have a look through the filing cabinets that contained these letters – the amount of correspondence astounded me. Yet despite all those positive responses, as a psychologist I couldn't help but be a little sceptical – testimonials are all very well, but what was the empirical evidence that yoga and meditation can help incarcerated criminals change for the better? Searching scientific databases I discovered there was very little rigorous research out there into the measurable psychological effects of these practices on prison populations. The majority of studies that did exist focused specifically on meditation – with some interesting results. Research into the effects of Transcendental Meditation (TM; see pp.47ff) on criminals had been taking place since the 1970s. For example, a study by US researchers Abrams and Siegel found that those prisoners who received a 14-week course of TM training showed a significant reduction in anxiety, neuroticism, hostility and insomnia compared with the control group[8]. This would seemingly constitute early evidence for the rehabilitative effects of TM. However, the study was criticized on the grounds that it had inadequate controls, limiting the conclusions we can draw from the findings and calling into question the authors' somewhat liberal interpretation of their statistical results[9].

More recent studies using other meditation techniques also yielded some promising evidence. In these studies, researchers concluded that meditation led to such positive results as improved psychosocial functioning[10], a reduction in substance abuse[11], and decreased recidivism rates[12]. However, while all that sounds really promising, most of this research also had serious shortcomings. For example, sample sizes were usually very small, there was not a control group, or the research drew evidence only from questionnaire measures.

I realized that if we were to draw any realistic conclusions about whether or not yoga and meditation are effective in bringing about measureable psychological changes in incarcerated criminals, we needed better research evidence. And so the seeds were sown for our Oxford Study, the journey and findings of which we reveal in Chapter 8. While this was in the planning, I wanted to gain a deeper understanding about the PPT's rationale for encouraging prisoners to practise yoga and meditation, and their conceptualizations of personal change.

PERFECT PRISONERS

While the PPT does believe that yoga and meditation can lead to beneficial psychological effects in prisoners, what they're really interested in is the possibility of a radical 'self-change'. This involves a significant shift in perspective. Sandy Chubb told me that in her experience (of teaching yoga in prisons), prisoners are lovely to work with. This didn't surprise me all that much – we all tend to be co-operative when we're getting to do something we want to do. What did surprise me was the comment that followed: Sandy told me that 'prisoners are all perfect'.

Perfect is certainly not the adjective most of us would choose to describe murderers, rapists and paedophiles; for many it's perhaps even the antonym of the word they would use. I needed Sandy to clarify. 'What's perfect about them?' I asked.

The answer appears to lie in Sandy's spiritual worldview. Like many others who believe in a universal spirituality, Sandy recognizes the divine nature of each of us – including criminals – and is convinced of the interconnectedness of all things. She smiles serenely when she tells me what to her is a simple, obvious truth: 'We are a whole creation that works dynamically.'

The concept of unity or non-duality is a central premise in some Eastern spiritual belief systems, and one that effectively eliminates the 'us' and 'them' mentality that most of us have in relation to convicted criminals. Early into my interview with Sam Settle, the current director of the PPT and a former Buddhist monk, I encountered the same belief: 'If prisoners realized that we are all connected,' Sam told me, 'then they would not commit crimes.'

So while reducing re-offending is not an asserted aim of the PPT, it is considered likely to occur as a side-effect of spiritual growth. The hypothesis is that it is criminals' mistaken idea of separateness that allows them to act in a harmful way towards others. From Sandy and Sam's perspective, there is no 'other', and there are no 'bad' people; we are all part of the same perfect whole – and meditation and yoga can help people to realize this. Later in the book I will discuss how many people share this perspective – people who believe that not just individual but worldwide change is possible, if only there are enough people meditating.

SILENT REHABILITATION

While we could dismiss some of these ideas about the transformative potential of meditation and yoga for prisoners as utopian, Romantic, or La-La-Land spirituality, we can also consider them in a purely secular sense, in terms of psychological and behavioural changes. But, even if we cast aside, for now, the spiritual dimension, the notion that yoga and meditation can produce meaningful change in prisoners might still be considered somewhat 'out there'. The very idea of the possibility of personal change is itself a loaded topic, especially in the context of prisons. Young repeat offenders are often labelled hopeless cases, written off by the time they have barely left their teens – undermining the ethos of rehabilitation that should be central to the prison system. However, for many offenders there are myriad factors that may obstruct attempts to rehabilitate – not only in terms of overcoming backgrounds of adversity, but also in terms of their perceived (lack of) prospects for the future.

The institution of home

For many who have lived in prisons from an early age, the prospect of going outside is daunting. I once worked with a prisoner, 'John', who was serving his tenth prison sentence at the age of only 21 years old. He attended every session of the offending behaviour program I was facilitating, only to – in the final session – suddenly become aggressive and disruptive to the point where he had to be removed from the group. Talking to him afterwards, trying to understand why he had sabotaged something that could have helped him towards securing an earlier release date, he admitted he was scared of being released. 'There is nothing for me outside,' he said, visibly upset.

When John was a young child, one of his parents murdered the other; he went on to spend the rest of his childhood in numerous short-term foster-care placements. Angry and distrusting of people, he would repeatedly run away from them. He committed his first offence aged ten and received his first custodial sentence aged 15. The frequency of his impulsive crimes meant that he had spent the majority of the past six years behind bars. There were no family or friends waiting for him on the outside. The uncertainty of how to build a meaningful life, alone, in the 'real world' was overwhelming. Prison was all he felt he knew.

Self-belief

All staff members working in prisons – from officers, to psychologists, to governors – are acutely aware that changing prisoners can be extraordinarily difficult – but it's not impossible. In my own work with young male offenders, I lost count of the number of times I heard 'he'll never change' from prison officers, who generally would have little idea of that individual's backstory and the factors that contributed to his offending behaviour. Often the prisoners in question were boys still in their teens, some of them coming from such difficult backgrounds that it would have been a miracle if they *hadn't* ended up in prison.

The desire to reform is often unsupported – sometimes owing to budget restrictions, but other times owing to a lack of belief. Changing is hard. And it's even harder without a helping hand. The support of others – whether friend, therapist or institution – can be fundamental in whether or not we succeed in bringing about a desired change. Feeling that others believe in us can significantly boost our sense of self-efficacy. Feeling that others don't believe in us at all undermines our self-belief so that we may start to feel a dramatic waning of our own confidence and motivation to try to change.

Changing attitudes

It was a Thursday afternoon and I was on my lunch break, in between research interviews at a West Midlands prison. I was accompanied by an officer in his late fifties, who had been assigned to facilitate the interviews; escorting prisoners from the wings to the interview room. As our break drew to a close, the officer suddenly deviated from his impromptu monologue on the joys of pigeon fancying, my knowledge of which had substantially increased over the hour, to ask whether I really thought that yoga and meditation would do anything at all for prisoners.

'Well,' I replied, 'we think it might. There's evidence that it works outside of prisons to reduce stress and increase positive emotions. So it may help prisoners to manage their emotions better and improve their self control, which might also reduce their aggression.'

'Ha!' said the officer. 'I doubt it.'

'Why?' I asked.

'I don't think any of these can change,' he told me. 'I'm a firm believer that leopards never change their spots.'

It wasn't just yoga and meditation the officer was dismissing as futile. He went on to say that he thought *nothing* could be done to change prisoners for the better; each and every one of them was a hopeless cause. 'No matter what,' he told me, 'they will always revert back to what they are. It's like a man who used to be a philanderer; he could get married to a woman and be faithful for, let's say, ten years, but in the end, he'll always cheat again.'

My attempts to debate failed miserably. When I maintained that I did think we could rehabilitate prisoners, he delivered his closing argument: 'Well I'm older than you and I've met quite a lot of different people, so I think I know.'

Fortunately, this old-style officer is not representative of the majority of prison staff I have encountered. Over the last twenty years, a number of accredited offending behaviour programs (psychological group interventions that aim to reduce re-offending) have been developed that have been shown to be effective in bringing about improvements in prisoner behaviour, such as reducing aggression[13]. Despite this positive progress, with the reduction-rate for recidivism being generally around 10 per cent for program-completers, there is still clearly room for new and additional approaches – particularly as many prisoners are reluctant or unable to engage with psychological treatment at all.

Arriving at a recent meeting at HMP Shrewsbury, I was escorted by a female officer who gave me a quick overview of the prison. She told me that the population was mostly sex offenders and that it was the most overcrowded prison in the country, adding, 'We're full of bed blockers.'

'Bed blockers?' I asked.

She explained that these are prisoners who had been through the sex offenders treatment program, but – for one reason or another – hadn't been moved on to a different prison. The result was that they were taking up spaces that other, as yet untreated, offenders could use.

However, the main problem at Shrewsbury was not the 'bed blockers', who had accepted their offences and received treatment, but the many sex offenders who were in denial, and so could not be treated. Owing to the nature of their offences, such prisoners may be limited in what activities they can undertake during their sentences. Typically, for their own protection, sex offenders are segregated from 'mainstream' prisoners and even with good behaviour are not deemed suitable for outside work.

HMP Shrewsbury was one of the prisons that participated in our own research study. This prison had by far the biggest number of prisoners keen to do yoga and meditation – many more than we could actually manage to interview during the time we had allocated there. As I interviewed prisoner after prisoner, all expressing a desire to do the yoga classes, it seemed to me that it could be possible that these techniques – if effective – could represent an alternative way to encourage positive personal change in prisoners whom the system might otherwise not be able to reach. Why? Because practising meditation and yoga doesn't involve asking probing questions about offences of which prisoners may be deeply ashamed, feel in denial of, or simply not yet ready to address. Sandy confirmed the particular utility of yoga and meditation for this demographic: 'Not only is silence therapeutic and inclusive, it's also safe for people with addiction and sex-offending histories.'

On the surface yoga is a physical activity, with desirable physiological benefits; it's unthreatening, non-blaming and doesn't require the admission of guilt. In this way it is possible that prisoners who would otherwise avoid explicit attempts to 'change' their behaviour, may nevertheless engage with a technique that could anyway bring about deep, personal transformation.

FROM MONSTER TO BUDDHA

The concept of a prison cell as an ashram is an idea that captures the imagination, and the paradox of finding spiritual freedom through the loss of physical freedom is intriguing. Might there actually be truth in this unusual idea – can daily yogic sun salutations and deep breathing really make convicted rapists and murderers less violent and impulsive? While it's unlikely that yoga and meditation could replace traditional rehabilitative approaches, it seems possible that they may have a unique ability to reach prisoners on a different level: to make them feel more at peace, and more valued and connected. Bo Lozoff summarizes the aim of organizations that teach contemplative techniques to prisoners worldwide when he says that we should 'allow for transformation, not merely rehabilitation'. In other words the change that charities such as his and the PPT seek to encourage goes far beyond the cessation of offending behaviour; we are talking about a radical change in worldview. The PPT's current director Sam Settle describes this transformation as 'the forgetting of one's self as one lives – the forgetting of *me*'. In essence moving from focusing on oneself as a separate individual to seeing oneself as part of a larger whole.

Whether or not we share these ideas about the possibility of the transformation of convicted criminals – from sinner to saint, from 'monster' to Buddha – on a theoretical and anecdotal level, there does seem to be reason to think that yoga and meditation can bring about positive personal change in prisoners. In Chapter 8 we reveal how we put that theory to the test, but first let's take a look at what science can tell us about the potential of Eastern techniques for bringing about meaningful change not just for prisoners, but for any of us.

CHAPTER 2

SET LIKE PLASTER

'Change is an odd process, almost contradictory: you want it, *but* don't want it,' said my clinical supervisor, playing with his curled beard and looking at me. *What was he talking about?* I had started my training in cognitive behavioural therapy (CBT) eight weeks earlier and was discussing my first client, 'Mary', a woman in her thirties, whose husband had died while on a family holiday. He had killed himself jumping off a cliff, right in front of his wife and their young child. Six months after the incident, Mary found herself depressed and sleepless.

'I felt shock and disbelief,' she told me, remembering. 'I felt like I had been disembowelled and bricks sewn inside. I had to register his death the next day and felt terrible anger at having to describe myself as a widow, 24 hours after I had been a wife. Bureaucracy shouldn't require that, you know?' I nodded but felt tense, eager to show empathy. For the past eight weeks, I'd spent most of my days reading manuals on the treatment of depression and grief, preparing detailed notes, attempting to write a script for the next therapy session. But the script was only good for the first few minutes; Mary would inevitably say something that I hadn't predicted and I'd glance nervously at my notes, feeling lost for long seconds.

I began fearing our sessions and unburdened my anxiety on my supervisor. 'I've helped her to challenge her negative thoughts, encouraged her to reconnect with friends and family, I've been very empathic with her grief, I...'

'OK, you're doing everything you can. Relax. Therapy takes time,' he said.

'But it's not making a difference. Every week I have to listen to her tell me the same story over and over and over again.'

'Life is repetitive. People don't like change; it's painful. That's how it is.' Noticing my unhappiness, he added, 'Listen, you can't work miracles. Just do your best.'

I was concerned that my best wouldn't be enough and I was dismayed to find that my supervisor wasn't too optimistic about people changing – at least not quickly; he wasn't alone in this view. Although many of us may hold positive views about a person's ability to change when it concerns ourselves, our faith in the ability of others to change is considerably dimmer.

This chapter explores the evidence for and against personality change. Many researchers favour the idea of a strong, unchangeable basis to personality, while others argue that life experiences play a crucial role in shaping personality, which is continually changing. Most of the ideas put forward on either side of the argument are old ones and stem from the classic maxim 'nature versus nurture'. But there is also surprising evidence showing a third, more controversial option: that we can induce personality change through extreme physical stimulation and psychotropic drugs. This is the focus of the last part of this chapter – first, let's cast ourselves back in time, to just over 100 years ago, when personality research was in its infancy.

A SHORT HISTORY OF PERSONALITY

The study of personality is heavily focused on what psychologists call 'traits'. These are patterns of behaviour, thoughts and feelings that we use to characterize people – think of one of your friends who is outgoing and adventurous (an extravert) and another who is often moody and over-sensitive (neurotic). Most of the time, psychologists argue, these key personality traits will be astonishingly consistent throughout our lives. The forefather of modern US psychology, William James, wrote in his *Principles of Psychology* (1890) that we are essentially creatures of habit: 'Already at the age of 25 you see the professional mannerism settling on the young commercial traveler, on the young doctor, on the young minister, on the young counselor-at-law. You see the little lines of cleavage running through the character, the tricks of thought, the prejudices, the ways of the "shop"... It is well for the world that in most of us, by the age of thirty, the character has *set like plaster*, and will never soften again."

William James wrote this before the turn of the twentieth century, but his concluding sentence still reverberates through modern textbooks on the science of personality. In his own time he was not alone in thinking that many of our behaviours are particularly resistant to change.

Bells, petals and electric shocks

On the other side of the Atlantic, in 1874, Francis Galton, a half-cousin of Charles Darwin, argued that both nature *and* nurture shape our personality, although nature played a major role. He was borrowing from Shakespeare, who in *The Tempest* first juxtaposed those two words. Referring to the beast Caliban, the magician Prospero calls him 'A devil, a born devil, on whose nature nurture can never stick.' Galton's own perspective was very similar to Prospero's: he believed that nature played a predominant role in the shaping of our personalities and intelligence. He based this view on his pioneering study of twins. By observing identical twins, who share all genetic makeup, and contrasting them with fraternal twins, who share only half, he noticed that identical twins were especially similar in temperament to each other. The implication was that nature, and not culture, education or the environment, played the predominant role in the making of our characters. Not all agreed with this view. Aristotle famously spoke of the human mind as an 'unscribed tablet'[2] – the infant's mind is like a blank slate on which experience etches a personality. Among psychologists the American John Watson was one of the strongest advocates of this perspective. He thought that none of our behaviours are instinctive, and that all we do is learn though our interaction with the environment. 'Give me a dozen healthy infants, well-formed, and my own specified world to bring them up in,' Watson wrote in 1924, 'and I'll guarantee to take any one at random and train him to become any type of specialist I might select – doctor, lawyer, artist, merchant-chief and, yes, even beggar-man and thief, regardless of his talents, penchants, tendencies, abilities, vocations, and race of his ancestors.[3]'

This perspective swung the pendulum of determinism in the other direction: we become not what nature or biology dictates, but what our environment provides and how our minds *associate* events with pleasant or unpleasant responses (such as relaxation or fear). For Watson's Behaviourism, not only is personal change possible, but it happens all the time. In effect we can learn one response, but also unlearn it and replace it with another.

Take a biologically pleasant stimulus, such as a flower, which you might expect to look upon with joy, breathing in its scent, marvelling in its colours. With the correct kind of conditioning, you can start dreading its sight and smell. English novelist Aldous Huxley vividly portrays this concept in his novel *Brave New World* (1932). In the story eight-month-old babies are conditioned to be afraid of books and rose petals. The babies are taken to the conditioning rooms, where petals, and books with brightly coloured pages are spread all over the floor. As soon as the babies are happily playing, the director of the conditioning centre gives an order to the head nurse. A lever is switched and suddenly:

'There was a violent explosion. Shriller and ever shriller, a siren shrieked. Alarm bells maddeningly sounded. The children started, screamed; their faces were distorted with terror. "And now," the Director shouted (for the noise was deafening), "now we proceed to rub in the lesson with a mild electric shock."

He waved his hand again, and the Head Nurse pressed a second lever. The screaming of the babies suddenly changed its tone. There was something desperate, almost insane, about the sharp spasmodic yelps to which they now gave utterance. Their little bodies twitched and stiffened; their limbs moved jerkily as if to the tug of unseen wires.[4]'

The electric shocks stop. But when the director instructs the nurse again to show flowers and books, the babies shrink away in horror. 'What man has joined,' Huxley writes, 'nature is powerless to put asunder.'

Of course, just as we are able to reassociate pleasant and beautiful things, such as flowers, with pain, so can we associate naturally unpleasant and dangerous stimuli, such as spiders and snakes, with positive feelings. Psychologists have used this technique countless times in the treatment of phobias. Imagine you are terrified of spiders, so terrified that you start hyperventilating and experience blurred vision just by seeing a picture of one. A behavioural therapist would attempt to change your panic response through counter-conditioning. Slowly and systematically, a therapist shows you a picture of the dreaded spider while giving you techniques that encourage you to relax. Eventually the fear subsides and you have learned a new conditioning – seeing a spider triggers a relaxation response – that replaces the old one. It's not necessarily a pleasant way to instigate change, but it is a potentially effective one.

Despite the possibilities that Behaviourism suggests for personal change, its premise that humans lack free will and rely upon conditioning to exhibit a certain behaviour has been severely criticized. Some psychologists believe that Behaviourism evades the complexity of mental life, denies the existence of unconscious motivations, and fails to explain how we develop a sense of identity, of who we are. At the method's heart there is a bleak determinism: the biological account of nature – how the encryption of proteins at the micro-level ultimately shapes our behaviour – is replaced by the mechanics of stimulus and response. It enables the possibility of personal change; but at what cost?

Extraverts, introverts and neurotics

At the same time as Watson was publishing his thoughts on behavioural change, other psychologists were developing new ideas about personality and ways to measure it. Researchers started using surveys that included lists of questions about an individual's behaviour: 'Are you outgoing? Do you enjoy parties? Does your mood often go up and down? Are you easily irritated?' Questions such as these are supposed to measure personality traits – that is, habitual ways to believe, think and feel.

The notion that we each have certain personality traits is not an entirely modern discovery. Around 2,500 years ago Hippocrates, the Ancient Greek physicist known as the father of Western medicine, conceived of four major temperaments – choleric, phlegmatic, melancholic and sanguine. In the twentieth century, British personality psychologist Hans Eysenck noted the similarities between Hippocrates' temperaments and the modern-day theory personality traits[5]. A *sanguine* individual, characterized as sociable, lively and carefree, combined the trait of extraversion with low neuroticism, a highly desirable pattern in Western societies. On the opposite side, a *melancholic* temperament, which describes someone as quiet, anxious and moody, and is characteristic of many artists, combines introversion with high neuroticism. A *choleric* individual is excitable, aggressive and optimistic, an explosive combination of high extraversion and neuroticism; and a *phlegmatic* person is controlled, reliable and calm, indicating an introvert with low neuroticism.

Looking through these personality characteristics and trying to attribute them to our own personality is not necessarily straightforward. I could say I have quite a lot of sanguine, but also some of choleric, and a small part of melancholic. Both Hippocrates' temperaments and Eysenck's traits are dimensions of our characters; our personalities are not black and white, and we all have elements of introversion–extraversion and neuroticism. What modern personality tests do is to quantify each and every character by positioning a person along a continuum – how much of an introvert or neurotic are you from 0 to 100?

Such questions may sound like the content of quizzes in women's magazines, rather than the measures of scientific instruments. However, the truth is they may have a place in both. Personality traits help us to make sense of other people's behaviours, but they also help us to choose our friends and, crucially, our partners. If at 18 many of us think that we can change the person we love to better fit with our needs, by our late twenties we're more inclined to try finding lovers and friends that match our personalities. People often say they want to 'be loved for who they are'. It seems then that while we recognize unchangeability in our romantic partners, we also may have a deep-rooted understanding that who we are fundamentally is set in stone – that nature ultimately wins out over nurture.

The idea that personality is rooted in our biology gained support with Eysenck. Like Francis Galton decades before him, Eysenck studied identical and fraternal twins. His conclusion was that our predisposition to be an extravert or a neurotic is mostly determined by the genes we inherit. Eysenck stirred the public mind when he extended the conclusions of his personality work to intelligence. He argued that it was not education or the environment that caused differences in intelligence scores between ethnic groups, but genetics. He gave the example of how Afro-Americans had lower IQ scores than white Americans, which implied that those genetically originating from northern Europe were intellectually more gifted than others. When giving public talks he was often confronted by angry protesters, and this hatred also extended to his old students and collaborators. Decades later Gordon Claridge, now a retired professor from Oxford University whom Eysenck had once supervised, told me that when in the 1970s he had applied to take up an academic position in Sweden, the student body were resistant to his appointment as a result of his (albeit past) association with 'a racist psychologist'.

During the 1980s and 1990s, personality research evolved in different directions. Throughout the world studies looked at different age groups and did further research with twins, some of whom had been raised separately. The conclusions reinforced the nature thesis, demonstrating that personality did change from childhood, through adolescence to early adulthood, but after early adulthood it seemed that personality changed little[6].

LET'S TRY RELAXATION

Returning to the story of Mary. After speaking to my supervisor, I felt disheartened with what I learned from personality research. If there were such a small possibility of changing our basic structure of behaviour after a relatively young age, then what kind of change could I promote working as a therapist? I pressed my supervisor for answers.

'Therapy isn't so much about personality change,' he told me. 'Personality traits are the skeleton, not the flesh. You can actually change people's way of thinking and acting, even if the underlying personality stays the same.' Given that my current therapeutic approach didn't seem to be working, I suggested that I try other methods and asked what I could use.

'I hope you're not thinking of joining the dark side of the force?' he asked with an anxious look. The 'dark side of the force' was my supervisor's metaphor for psychoanalysis, or psychodynamic psychotherapy, inspired by Sigmund Freud's concept of the unconscious mind. To my supervisor the therapy world was sharply divided between the 'good force' of CBT, which focuses on changing current problems using a goal-oriented approach, and the 'bad force' of psychodynamic therapy, which seeks to reveal and resolve unconscious conflicts. For a second I pictured him as Yoda and myself as Luke Skywalker in danger of turning into a Vader of the psychoanalytical world.

'Why don't you try relaxation?' he suggested. 'Didn't you say she was anxious and had trouble sleeping? Try relaxation; it can't hurt.'

I went to the psychology department's library and dug out an old manual, its pages slightly tattered, called *Progressive Relaxation* (1929) by American physician and psychiatrist Dr Edmund Jacobson[7]. On its back cover, someone had handwritten a citation presumably taken from within the book: 'There is no place for a tense mind in a relaxed body.'

The method was simple, if schematic. With your eyes closed, you were instructed to tense each group of muscles in turn, starting with the muscles of the feet and moving all the way up to your face muscles. For each group, you'd tense the muscles for 10 seconds, then rest for 20 more; then repeat. Once you'd tensed and released a group of muscles twice in this way, you moved on to the next group. The whole practice took about 30 minutes.

I tested it on a couple of willing friends. They both fell asleep within 15 minutes. I suddenly felt hopeful. Perhaps I could at least turn around Mary's sleeping problem, and then maybe the other issues would unravel easily after this. Perhaps change was possible, after all.

On the day of our next session, I tried out everything two, three times before Mary arrived: the blinds closed, the chair reclined to a completely horizontal position; I tested out the acoustics of the room like an actor before an invisible audience – 'use a soft but perceptible voice' the manual recommended. When Mary finally came I explained to her I would like us to try something different to help her sleep. For the first time since I started my therapy training I felt in control.

'It's a very simple technique where you contract and relax all the muscles of your body. Are you happy to try it?' She nodded agreement and slipped into a semi-passive role, not saying a word while I reclined her chair to a horizontal position and closed the blinds. I slowly instructed her to start contracting and relaxing her muscles, starting with her toes. She didn't say anything, which I took as a positive sign. Forty-five minutes later, I gently straightened the chair up to a sitting position. There was a soft smile on Mary's face; she looked like she'd woken up from a restful nap. Very slowly, Mary raised herself off the chair and put her shoes on. She then looked at me intently and said, 'Now, I believe in magic.'

LIFE-CHANGING EXPERIENCES

The following week Mary told me she was sleeping well for the first time in months. This filled me with hope. At the turn of the new millennium, a shift in the tone of literature about personality further encouraged me. Reviews of hundreds of studies found that we experience small to moderate changes in our personalities throughout middle and old age[8]. Other research showed that some life experiences, such as broken relationships in early adulthood, changed personality for the worse – those people who had suffered a break-up and then remained single became more neurotic later in life. However, the opposite was found for those who remarried: remarriage was associated with greater emotional stability. And when we look at the general evolution of personality traits throughout life, the news is good: as we age we tend to become warmer and more self-confident and self-controlled, and to gain emotional stability[9].

At about the same time, other approaches to understanding personality emerged. The study of personality using traits was criticized as 'the psychology of the stranger'[10]. US psychologist and professor at Northwestern University, Chicago, Dan McAdams argued that traits offer no context. His view is that traits don't tell us anything about who the person is, or that person's goals and motivations throughout life.

Leaving traits behind

Instead of using questionnaires, which McAdams believes provide only a rough skeleton image of who we are, he started asking people to write about their lives, to tell of moments during which they had experienced a sudden change in themselves. Most of us go through experiences that move us deeply, such as falling in love, getting married (and divorced), or the death of a loved one. For some women childbirth is a personality-changing experience, transforming their priorities and filling their lives with new meaning. At the other end of life, coming close to death has been reported as having a profound effect on attitudes and responses to life. People who go through near-death experiences often report feeling changed; not just spiritually, but in terms of finding themselves at greater peace, and experiencing more joy and vitality than before.

Experiences such as these can lead to a radical change in a person's life goals and priorities, which psychologists have termed 'quantum change'[11]. However, life events that shake a person to the core are not experiences that can be simulated in a lab.

That said there has been some experimental research – and with interesting findings. Like many scientific discoveries, one such finding was the result of an accident. The Russian scientist Ivan Pavlov, who won the Nobel Prize in Physiology and Medicine in 1904 for his studies on how the digestive system works, is best known for his work on animal conditioning. Animals naturally salivate when they are hungry and see or smell food. In one experiment Pavlov sounded a bell before food was presented to a dog. After repeated conditioning over some time, when the dog heard the bell it would salivate instinctively, regardless of whether or not there was food, demonstrating that it had been conditioned to expect food when hearing the bell.

Back in 1924 in St Petersburg, Pavlov kept a number of animals in his laboratory. He liked to be at work very early in the morning, but on 23 September his routine was disrupted. The river Neva had risen by 4 metres, flooding the city and causing the deaths of 600 people. Photographs taken immediately after the water had receded reveal the level of destruction: pavement stones overturned, the docks filled with debris, ships cast ashore, and dead animals in the streets. Pavlov's laboratory had also been partially flooded and, when he finally got there, Pavlov discovered that many of the dogs that were kept in cages were swimming at the very top, looking terrified and exhausted. They were rescued just in time, but some went into a state of apathy, not responding to any stimulus. Days after the incident Pavlov noticed something unexpected. The dogs that had come closest to dying no longer responded to the sound of the bell – the trauma had completely erased the dogs' conditioning. Reflecting upon this Pavlov considered that when animals or humans go through prolonged excitation, the body's natural response is to shut down, giving way to a state of extreme inhibition or passivity. This state can have such a deep effect that previously established conditioned responses are suddenly unlearned[12].

ALTERED STATES

Pavlov's accidental discovery of how it is possible rapidly to eliminate conditioning has strong implications for the idea of personality change. His findings after the flood of St Petersburg have intrigued psychologists ever since. The state of extreme inhibition followed by changes in behaviour that Pavlov described in his dogs is similar to that reported by people who undergo 'peak' and near-death experiences. Suddenly, the life led until the moment of the experience loses its meaning and new ideals and behaviours emerge. Did Pavlov's dogs have a kind of 'peak' experience? American psychologist Abraham Maslow popularized this phrase in the 1960s, describing a 'peak' experience loosely as an extraordinary sense of happiness, elation and connectedness. There is a long tradition in psychological science of trying to understand the effects of peak experiences. William James, the psychologist who argued that our characters were generally fixed by the age of thirty (see p.29), wrote a book about deep personal change following a peak or spiritual experience[13]. More than 100 years after its publication, it's still in print. In this book James gives a multitude of accounts of peak experiences, from West to East, and explains how, for many, these were preceded by a period of profound existential struggle and unhappiness, the supposed triggers for such experiences.

However, James also shows how it is possible to achieve a peak experience in a very different way – by inhaling nitrous oxide (commonly known as laughing gas), which at the time dentists would use as a form of pain relief. The English philosopher Bertrand Russell wrote about James's discovery in his *History of Western Philosophy* (1945):

'William James describes a man who got the experience from laughing-gas; whenever he was under its influence, he knew the secret of the universe, but when he came to, he had forgotten it. At last, with immense effort, he wrote down the secret before the vision had faded. When completely recovered, he rushed to see what he had written. It was: "A smell of petroleum prevails throughout".[14]'

By artificial means

More than sixty years after the publication of James's work on the varieties of religious experience and its effects, psychologists started looking at the possibilities for peak experiences as a vehicle for personal change and psychological healing. These were the days when drugs such as LSD were widely available and days when psychologists could use such drugs in their experiments.

In the 'Good Friday Experiment', theology students attending a religious service two days before Easter were either given LSD, or a placebo in the form of a sugar tablet. Just as would happen in a medical trial, the students were not aware which tablet they had taken. The researcher, William Pahnke, found that nine out of ten students taking LSD during the service reported having a mystical experience. In the other group only one out of ten reported having a mystical experience[15].

Pahnke's supervisor, Timothy Leary, encouraged by this and his own research at Harvard University, went on to become an LSD guru. His vision was that the drug so deeply transformed us that if enough people tried it, the world would inevitably change – and for the better. He believed that the deep spiritual experiences and 'journeying into new states of consciousness' that we could have as a result of taking LSD should be shared with all. In 1969, at the height of his popularity, he announced his candidacy for the post of Governor of California against Ronald Reagan. However, Leary didn't reach the end of the political race: he was sent to jail for possessing marijuana. Today, in London's Camden markets or in Paris's Marché au Puces, among old and new posters, it's possible to find prints of Leary from the 1960s inscribed with his philosophical motto: 'Turn on, tune in, drop out.'

As well as Leary and Pahnke, there was a growing number of psychologists studying the effects of LSD on a range of disorders, from anxiety and depression to sexual dysfunction. But the individual who made the decisive contribution arrived in the USA in 1967. Stanislav Grof had studied medicine, psychiatry and psychoanalysis in Prague, Czechoslovakia. In the USA he became assistant professor at Johns Hopkins University School of Medicine, where he developed LSD therapy for psychotic patients. The results of his work, entitled *Realms of the Human Unconscious: Observations from LSD Research* (1975), stands as one of the most ambitious contributions to the study of human psychology since Freud wrote about the unconscious. In its pages Grof compares the potential of LSD for psychology to the value of the microscope for biology, or the telescope for astronomy. He also writes about deep changes in the personality structure, worldview and hierarchy of value of those undergoing LSD therapy[16].

Research with LSD was outlawed in the early 1970s, following the United Nations' convention on psychotropic drugs, which declared these substances to be liable to abuse, the object of illicit traffic and to have limited therapeutic value[17]. But Grof's work on LSD survives in many bookshops and libraries. Today, if you walk through the psychology course books at the University of Oxford's Radcliffe Science Library, you will spot a dozen paperbacks of his first book on LSD with its unusual bright-orange cover. This means that at least one lecturer has considered its reading to be mandatory for a course within the Medical Sciences Division.

After he was forced to discontinue research into LSD at Johns Hopkins University, Grof moved to the Esalen Institute in California, where research into various types of body–mind therapies was happening at the time. He became a scholar in residence for almost ten years.

Grof had realized that LSD provided a fast way to reach the unconscious and to experience unusual states of consciousness. But drugs and heightened stress weren't the only catalysts for peak and life-changing experiences – as Grof was soon to find out. In the 1970s Esalen was a hub for counterculture and creative thinking, as well as for shamans and spiritual leaders, who gave workshops and lectured there. Coming into contact with shamanic and ancient spiritual techniques, Grof considered that he could generate strong altered states of consciousness by combining two very natural elements: music and breathing.

Breathing holotropically

During the 1980s and 1990s, Grof developed his ideas into something called Holotropic Breathwork Therapy and travelled widely, training people in this method. After my relaxation experience with Mary, I had decided I wanted to try out different techniques and enrolled in one of Grof's workshops. Physically, he was an imposing man, his shoulders about twice as broad as mine. When I shook hands with him, I noticed that my two hands would fit into one of his. Stan Grof (Stanislav, his first name, had been abbreviated to Stan after he moved to the USA) was wearing a colourful Hawaiian shirt and, despite the overpowering figure, he spoke with a deep but soft voice; so gentle, paced and certain that it was almost hypnotic. There were eighty of us in the audience, mostly women who looked half hypnotized by Grof's magnetic presence. He spoke for approximately one hour about the principles of Holotropic Breathwork and what would happen during the workshop. The underlying idea was both simple and incredible. Our deeper mind knows where it needs to go to heal itself – to promote wholeness between the various levels and forces within. To do this it just needs to be given a chance to bind the unconscious materials of our earlier life, when we lived in our mother's womb, with our conscious awareness. How to get there? Through altered states of consciousness.

Grof's words, I'd soon find out, were nothing more than a prelude to the unexpected, a lullaby before a jump into the darkness. I certainly wasn't prepared for what followed. Half of us were asked to lie down on yoga mats; each of us who was lying down then had someone else standing by our side. This person would assist us in the process and, on the following day, we would swap roles and the half who'd been lying down would become assistants. I had noticed large speakers set throughout the room and a sound-mixing table on top of the stage. Grof signalled to one of his assistants and the music started.

Loud drumming poured out of the speakers. It sounded like it had been recorded live in the African bush or in a South American rainforest – definitely not in a studio. Not because it lacked quality, but because it felt completely fresh and unrehearsed, part of a one-off ritual. The beating of drums increased in volume and Grof instructed us to breathe to its rhythm. After 20 minutes, it was difficult to keep up. My arms felt heavier and heavier. Then, the gravity push was so strong that when I thought I couldn't lift my arms at all, they gained a life of their own. With each fast breath they swung upwards and downwards, landing with a bang on the wooden floor. Without me telling them to do so, my arms kept jerking up and down, up and down as the music and my breathing got faster and faster. I'm sure this is how it must feel to have your arms electrocuted – a strong current flowing through them that precludes self-control. Up-down, up-down, the music growing louder and faster, the beatings of drums racing through the blood stream until they controlled both body and soul.

There was an explosion of sound within the loud music, a Babel of desynchronized languages. People screamed and sang in various keys and tongues. To my right a young blonde woman sat in a lotus position, with her back straight and upper body very still, and sang in a foreign language while doing what looked like yogic gestures with her hands (*mudras*); on my left a woman spread her legs wide and yelled painfully while trying to deliver an invisible child; at the back of the room, I heard a man howling like an animal, a wolf perhaps; a few people rolled on the floor as if possessed, their movements contained by those assisting. Grof's own assistants, trained in holotropic breathwork, moved around the room, quick and efficient, lightly touching, holding or massaging people.

Stan Grof, looking like a giant from where I lay, moved with the elegance of a ballerina and the discipline of a maestro keeping everyone in place: he'd point to his assistants to help someone, look approvingly or suggest a different physical movement; he would himself assist those breathing, his enormous hands softly comforting and his eye gaze reassuring that everything would be fine. I started longing for something else to happen to me other than the frantic up-and-down arm movement, but my mind didn't venture anywhere but the present place; the electrical-like current that moved my arms also moved through my body and, at one point, I felt as though I was going to be sick, but nothing happened. No visions, chanting, theatrical monologue or choreography emerged, only a body electric.

After two hours the music started winding down, the rhythm less frantic. Within the next 30 minutes, we quietly floated back to ground, some looking like they had come back from a trip around the universe.

'I was teleported to a different galaxy where I became a four-armed alien; I could actually feel how four arms worked together; then I came back to Earth but as a wolf – smells had an intensity I'd never felt before,' said a man speaking of his experience after the breathing session. I asked the young woman who had been chanting in an exotic tongue what language she had been singing in, but she told me she had no recollection whatsoever of what had happened. 'I was sort of floating in a warm liquid, feeling really, really peaceful,' she reported.

Grof explained how many people tend to relive part of their intrauterine lives through the hyperventilation. He believed that reconnection with our earliest life experience, when still in our mother's womb, has a deep, healing effect. This reminded me of Freud when he wrote about religious experiences as an 'oceanic feeling' that regressed an individual into the womb, when there was no separation between the self and the mother – and the whole cosmos, Grof added, speaking of a mystical sense of union.

At the end of the workshop, I spoke to him in private about my own experience. I was surprised when he asked if I'd had a difficult birth. Indeed. Both my mother and I had a near escape from death. He told me that it was very common for people who had gone through traumatic births to initially have a very bodily experience with hyperventilation, with some nausea or vomiting; it was part of the purging, the healing of the trauma before moving into other type of unconscious psychological structures. Then he advised me to eat some meat. 'You're tired and dazed from the experience,' he said. 'Eating meat will ground you.'

His gaze was empathic and calming. I remembered overhearing some of the women at the workshop commenting that Grof's presence was that of an archetypical father figure. 'Can I hug you?' he asked me. I nodded. When he gently placed his arms around my shoulders and upper torso, I felt like a child being enveloped by a friendly giant; I was completely safe.

There is little research on the efficacy of Grof's holotropic therapy. A search of the 'Web of Knowledge', a major database of scientific writing, found only six relevant articles. But Grof's intuition on the transformative power of altered states of consciousness has recently gained new support. More than thirty years after his work on the therapeutic effects of LSD at Johns Hopkins University School of Medicine, Roland Griffiths, a professor at the very same school, conducted a series of new studies on the effects of psilocybin. Like LSD, this is a hallucinogenic drug that causes deep alterations in the way we perceive reality, think and feel.

In a series of articles published between 2006 and 2011, Griffiths and his colleagues showed that when taking the drug a single time within a supportive and controlled environment, most people had mystical experiences that led to positive changes in behaviours, attitudes and values more than a year later. Spouses confirmed these positive changes in participants[18]. In the last published article, Griffiths wrote that the drug also led to long-term changes in how open a person is to experience, a trait characterized by creativity, imaginativeness and intellectual curiosity[19]. The study showed that that drug's ability to cause change is staggering – such differences in personality would usually unfold only after decades of life experience. Although these findings are promising, we need further research to understand their robustness.

Mary had given me a precious clue about the process of personal change when she described the physical relaxation session as 'magical'. It had had an impact on her; it very quickly changed her way of experiencing herself. Her experience led me to seek out other ways to stimulate altered states of consciousness. If Mary's relaxation experience and the experiences of those who had taken LSD or other altered-state drugs could have had profound and long-lasting effects in terms of the way people responded to the world, then why not techniques that have been available for millennia, such as meditation and yoga? Could they have similar effects?

CHAPTER 3

THE YEAR OF PLANETARY CHANGE

On 12 January 1975 the world welcomed the dawn of the Age of Enlightenment. It was a Sunday and none of the major European or US newspapers reported it: the headlines of the *Washington Post* focused on the booming of the 'Satellite Business'; *The Times* had a picture of a newly discovered furry 'marsupial' animal in Australia. But in Switzerland, at the headquarters of Transcendental Meditation (TM), this was an ominous day: Maharishi Mahesh Yogi, TM's spiritual leader, declared this Day One of 'the year of fulfilment for the World Plan'. In that year almost 300,000 people in the USA alone were to be initiated into TM[1]; there were more than two million people across four continents practising the technique and, according to Maharishi and TM researchers, their collective meditating effort raised the planetary consciousness to a new level – crime rates fell, while peace and harmony increased.

I remember my parents trying out TM. At the age of six, I was rather taken by the idea of seeing them levitating (a claimed 'side-effect' of advanced practice). Twenty years later, in the gloomy basement of the Radcliffe Science Library at Oxford, I came across the hefty first volume of research on TM. It included more than a hundred studies from 1970 to 1977 attesting to the impressive effects of the practice: decreased hypertension, reduced asthma and insomnia, improved intelligence, and positive changes in certain personality traits, such as neuroticism[2]. A wave of nostalgia overcame me when I found the photos I had seen as a six-year-old: young men and women smartly dressed (the men with ties and well-ironed shirts), all levitating. Their faces beamed with smiles as they sat cross-legged some 15 centimetres above the ground. Underneath the flying meditators were Maharishi's words: 'They are all up in the air, inviting everyone who still has their feet on the ground to join them.'

While doing research for this book, I spent weeks reading the scientific literature on TM. Its sheer quantity and variety overwhelmed me, although I soon realized that its ideals and aims were as simple as its practice: focus on a mantra for 20 minutes twice daily. TM not only promoted the practice of meditation more widely, bringing it out of a hippy niche, but produced the first large wave of scientific studies on the meditation's effects. Without it, it's unlikely that a second wave of interest in meditation, now focused on mindfulness, would have emerged thirty years later. But, can meditation really have such deep influence on the individual and society as a whole, as TM claimed? In this chapter I'll look at the major scientific findings and attempt to tease out facts from fiction about the effects of TM.

THE SNAKE IN THE ROPE

TM could have been just one more Hindu movement coming to the West. Other spiritual leaders from India, such as Vivekananda in the late 1800s or Yogananda in the 1930s, had started societies that stressed the importance of meditation for spiritual development. However, it was Maharashi's movement that changed for ever our understanding of meditation and triggered a boom of scientific research on its effects.

Embracing TM

Maharashi defined TM as: 'Turning the attention inwards towards the subtler levels of a thought until the mind transcends the experience of the subtlest state of the thought and arrives at the source of the thought. This expands the conscious mind and at the same time brings it in contact with the creative intelligence that gives rise to every thought[3].' (p.470)

What does this mean? And how does it work? After finishing an undergraduate degree in physics at the University of Allahabad, Maharishi became the follower of an Indian spiritual teacher, Swami Brahmananda, who for the subsequent 13 years taught him Advaita Vedanta. This is a non-dualistic philosophical system that proposes that the whole universe is made of the same spiritual essence and there is no division between its parts. In other words there is no real distinction between each of us and the creator of all things, or between you and me. According to the principles of Advaita Vedanta, seeing ourselves as autonomous individuals is just an illusion that we can overcome.

However, the various schools of Advaita Vedanta provide no absolute consensus on how to vanquish this illusion. Advaita Vedanta's main figure, Sankara, an eighth-century Brahmin who lived in Kerala, India, claimed that only true knowledge can spiritually enlighten, and that this knowledge is passed on by someone who possesses it and through the study of the Upanishads (sacred Vedic texts). He claimed that worldly experience, including meditation, cannot result in spiritual enlightenment. In contrast, most schools of Advaita Vedanta today, including TM, highlight the importance of meditation to access the true, undivided self.

Some years ago I spent part of a summer at Oxford's Hindu Studies Library browsing through yellowed and wrinkled pages of Sankara's works. There was a metaphor he came to time and time again – that of the popular Indian rope trick. You may have seen pictures of it: a rope rises out of a basket and behaves very much like a snake charmed by the sound of a flute. It's a centuries-old magic trick. Sankara's argument is that the reality we are used to perceiving as separate parts is very much like the snake we see in the rope: it looks so much like a snake dancing out of a basket, and we become so entranced by its movements and the accompanying music, that we end up not realizing the existence of the rope. In other words we see the snake – the illusion – rather than the reality of the rope; in life we become so caught up with separateness that we lose sight of the essential unity of all things.

Advaita Vedanta's ideas arrived in the West through the Theosophical Society, founded by the Russian Helen Blavatsky (1831–1891) and then directed by Annie Besant (1847–1933), an English feminist and socialist. The English writer G.K. Chesterton (1874–1936), well known for his detective series *Father Brown*, wrote of this Westernized version of Advaita Vedanta in the early 1900s:

'A short time ago Mrs. Besant, in an interesting essay, announced that there was only one religion in the world, that all faiths were only versions or perversions of it, and that she was quite prepared to say what it was. According to Mrs. Besant this universal Church is simply the universal self. It is the doctrine that we are really all one person; that there are no real walls of individuality between man and man. If I may put it so, she does not tell us to love our neighbours; she tells us to be our neighbours. That is Mrs. Besant's thoughtful and suggestive description of the religion in which all men must find themselves in agreement. And I never heard of any suggestion in my life with which I more violently disagree. I want to love my neighbour not because he is I, but precisely because he is not I.[4]'

Whether we agree or not with Chesterton's remarks, they remind us that the Advaita Vedanta concept of what reality is, and who we are in relation to it, is not intuitive. Western philosophy and theology don't tell us that God and the individual – or my friend and I – are one and the same. This actually goes against our cherished ideas of autonomy, freedom and self-fulfilment.

So, when Maharishi brought TM, his own version of Advaita Vedanta, to the West, he had to package it carefully. How was he able to succeed? Like Buddhist-based mindfulness did thirty years into the future, he did it by stripping down much of its religious garb and seeking scientific endorsement for the practice of TM.

A unique state of consciousness

If looking at Advaita Vedanta helps us to explain what TM is, let's now turn to the question of how TM works. The answer couldn't be simpler and that is the magic of contemplative practices: they're typically plain and repetitive. With TM, you are given a mantra (which would be a word in Sanskrit), you sit down in a comfortable position with your eyes closed and keep repeating this mantra in your head for 20 minutes. The process is supposed to be effortless, as if the mantra has a life of its own and repeats itself, like a catchy tune. You do this twice a day and, if you persist, the practice becomes easier and easier and you'll begin to notice positive changes within.

That's what got the US film director David Lynch hooked. When he first heard of meditation, he wasn't interested in it at all. However, one day Lynch was considering the idea that 'true happiness lies within' and, at the very moment he was entertaining this thought, his sister called to say she'd been doing TM for six months. 'There was something in her voice,' he writes, 'a change. A quality of happiness. And I thought, *That's what I want.*' Lynch tried out TM in July 1973 – his first session was a peak moment in his life: 'She took me into a little room to have my first meditation. I sat down, closed my eyes, started this mantra, and it was as if I were in an elevator and the cable had been cut. Boom! I fell into bliss – pure bliss[5].' (pp.3–4)

Not all experience such bliss, particularly at their initiation, but the claim that meditation improved personal satisfaction and created happiness formed part of TM's feature adverts during the mid-1960s. And there was more: the TM movement began a varied, scientific research program to validate its meditation technique and prove its effects.

LOOKING FOR THE EFFECTS OF TM

In 1970 two of the most prestigious science journals featured publications on the effects of TM. *The Lancet* reported that TM led to deep respiratory changes – a decrease of about half the rate of breathing expected in a resting state[6]. Then, *Science* published an article by US psychologist Robert Wallace entitled 'Physiological Effects of Transcendental Meditation', which showed that when practising TM there was a decrease in both oxygen consumption and heart rate, while it increased slow alpha and theta brain activity. The article concluded with the extraordinary suggestion that 'Physiologically, the state produced by Transcendental Meditation seems to be distinct from commonly encountered states of consciousness, such as wakefulness, sleep and dreaming, and from altered states of consciousness, such as hypnosis and autosuggestion.[7]'

If this were true, through TM we could experience an altogether *unique* state of mind, a fourth state of consciousness (after wakefulness, sleep and hypnosis). This supported the spiritual idea that a person is able to reach a 'higher state of mind' or 'cosmic consciousness', which, in the words of Maharishi, 'brings [our mind] in contact with the creative intelligence that gives rise to every thought'. In other words you could experience an undivided or non-dual sense of self just as described by Advaita Vedanta philosophy.

Other articles followed that substantiated TM's potential to generate unique and profound effects on consciousness[8]. In 1972 claims for TM were brought to a wider public when *Scientific American* published an article co-authored by Herbert Benson[9], a Harvard psychiatrist.

The TM organization used Benson's article and the emerging studies on the effects of TM in public lectures to attract new members, particularly university students. Between 1970 and the end of 1972, the number of people learning TM rose by 286 per cent. In 1966 there were only about 1,000 people initiated into the practice, but by the end of 1972 there were more than 180,000. Such scientific endorsement of meditation attracted a young and educated audience who were open to experimenting with mind-altering techniques.

Of science and spirituality

Whereas Western religious ideas sometimes clash with our scientific understanding of the world, Maharishi, a graduate in physics, didn't see a conflict between science and spirituality. He considered science itself a technique for the expansion of consciousness: it extends the mind through its discoveries of the atomic and astronomical worlds. Maharishi took the relationship between science and spirituality one step further with his vision of expanding the mind into pure consciousness. In the foreword to the first collected volume of scientific articles on TM, he writes: 'The fulfilment of science and man lies in the expansion of consciousness not merely to the stars but beyond; to the direct experience of that infinite, unbounded, eternal reality which alone can fulfill the natural direction of man's growth... Thus, the Age of Science, which has sometimes seemed to take man far away from nature has found as its ultimate achievement Transcendental Meditation, a method for establishing man's mind, heart and behavior deep in the source of nature's impulses within himself.'

If meditation and spiritual fulfilment are actually rooted in nature, it makes sense that we would be able to observe the *unique* effects of TM through scientific methods. The problem that the Indian guru may not have foreseen is that, unlike physics, the research fields of psychology and physiology very, very rarely yield clear, black-and-white results[10].

In 1976, only one year after Maharishi announced the dawn of the Age of Enlightenment, *Science* published two new studies showing that TM didn't produce effects any different from those of relaxation. The first study compared the concentration of stress hormones in the blood of meditators and those who had never practised meditation, before, during and after a 20-minute period of meditation or rest[11]. The results showed no differences in stress levels between the groups, or for the TM group before and after the meditation. The second study published in 1976 examined the physiology of five experienced transcendental meditators. There was an unexpected result: the measures of brain activity suggested that the meditators spent a substantial part of their meditation time sleeping[12]. The authors wondered if, although fully awake, meditation put the group in a brain state similar to that of sleep. It didn't. The meditators themselves declared that they had fallen asleep in most of the sessions. The article concludes that meditation gives rise to different mental states, but there is nothing physiologically extraordinary about it. Other researchers came to the same conclusion[13]. Even the Harvard psychiatrist Herbert Benson, who had co-authored some of the first studies claiming TM's uniqueness, changed his mind and wrote in his best-selling book *The Relaxation Response* (1975) that TM produces a response no different from relaxation techniques[14].

A critical gaze was cast over the existing evidence for the psychological and medical benefits of TM, which ranged from greater happiness and superior psychological health, to decreases in smoking, drug abuse, tension and anxiety, and in improved alleviation of asthma. One methodological limitation – which is the crux of almost all meditation research, not only TM, is that the effects were probably less driven by TM's ability to produce a 'fourth state of consciousness', than by the strong motivation of meditators to believe in its effects. A related problem was what scientists call a 'sampling bias' – basically, transcendental meditators were not the average American John Doe. They were generally individuals with a balanced personality, somewhat more anxious than the usual. But those with more serious mental health problems dropped out because they didn't find TM useful[15]. In other words those attracted to TM and taking part in the science research were quite similar regarding psychological characteristics, rather than being representative of the general population.

However, researchers in the TM organization disputed these biases. A number of studies that Maharishi had sponsored argued that TM could lead to personality change, particularly a decrease in anxiety and neuroticism, and motivation or personality traits shouldn't constrain these effects[16]. Independent research confirmed that, after only six months of TM, there could be a dramatic and positive shift in self-esteem; however, this sudden change was partly explained by a greater dissatisfaction with the self and a readiness to change before starting to meditate[17].

A placebo for meditation

So, how could scientists overcome the likelihood of TM initiates having a certain personality profile or being too eager to show the benefits of the technique? After all, to learn TM you had to invest time and money. There is an easy solution, which is the standard in clinical interventions: you pick up a group of individuals from a wide population and randomly allocate them to either a meditation or a control group. Even if some of these individuals are particularly interested in TM, the random allocation would distribute them evenly between the groups.

That's all well and good, but there is a much thornier problem with meditation research: finding the right kind of activity for the control group. If you're testing a new drug, you simply give a placebo, a tablet with no active chemical component, to the control group. But how can you find a placebo for meditation? Most scientists would say that you can't, which is why the active control groups in meditation research usually consist of people undertaking relaxation, hypnosis or exercise. It's not an ideal solution – you inevitably know whether you are in the meditation group or the control group. The best studies try to overcome this problem by 'blinding' the researchers, that is, keeping the researchers ignorant which is the experimental or control group until the study has finished.

This is what Jonathan Smith, then a young doctoral student at Michigan State University and an enthusiast of meditation, decided to do. However, he also did something else which, at the time of writing, remains unique in the history of meditation research: he created a meditation placebo.

When Jonathan Smith began his research in 1973, he felt passionate about meditation. He'd carefully read the first papers on its physiological and psychological impact and was eager to take this work one step further by conducting an experiment using the gold standard of medical research: a randomized double-blind procedure with a placebo. This would ensure participants' random allocation into a meditation or control group, without either the participants or the researcher knowing which group was the true subject of the study. Smith also came up with a placebo for meditation that was both simple and ingenious: outwardly it mirrored TM, but it left out the meditative component (focusing on the mantra). He named his placebo Periodic Somatic Inactivity (PSI)[18].

To make PSI credible he prepared a 71-page manual, which detailed all aspects of its theory and practice, including a section on 'frequently asked questions'. He then gave it to a researcher, who was unaware of the intention of the study and whose role it was to instruct participants on the use of PSI. Only at the end of the experiment was the instructor told that PSI was actually a bogus treatment. The manual explained the rationale for its effectiveness:

'Built into life are factors that disrupt inner calm and generate and maintain anxiety. Research has shown that one of these factors is the desynchronization of circadian rhythms, daily rhythmic changes in physiological functioning. Periodic Somatic Inactivity (PSI) works to bring circadian rhythms into synchrony... Periodic inactivity is the single commonality among a variety of highly effective growth and therapy techniques including progressive relaxation, biofeedback training, autogenic therapy, self-hypnosis, meditation and yoga. However, as PSI incorporates only the essentials of these techniques and does away with all the unnecessary and cumbersome extras associated with them, it is in fact more effective and efficient.'

Just as for the TM group, participants allocated to the PSI group had to sit and listen to two introductory lectures on the merits of the technique. The practice itself consisted of sitting down comfortably in a chair twice a day for 15 to 20 minutes, eyes closed. However, instead of repeating a mantra as you would in TM, participants were instructed to:

'Let your mind do whatever it wants. Whatever you do mentally will have little or no impact on the effectiveness of the technique. The important thing is to remain physically inactive. Do not talk, walk around, or change chairs. You may engage in an occasional action such as shifting your position or making yourself more comfortable. And you may scratch. At the end of the session, open your eyes, breathe deeply a few times, and continue with your everyday activities.'

In addition to the TM and PSI groups, Jonathan Smith had a passive control group, where participants carried on with their usual lives without engaging in any new activity. Before and at the end of three months, all participants were assessed for anxiety, muscle tension and autonomic arousal. The results showed that, compared to the passive control, TM and PSI led to a significant reduction in anxiety and a more relaxed physiological functioning. However, there were no differences between the TM and PSI groups; they both showed the same level of improvement.

Smith, disappointed that the TM group didn't do better than his meditation placebo, reasoned that perhaps three months of TM wasn't enough, so he extended the experiment for another three months; in all six months of twice-daily meditation or PSI practice. But again, there were no differences between the two groups. In a later reflection on his ground-breaking research, he confides that 'my assumptions about meditation were a bit grandiose and egocentric'[19]. But he is far from pessimistic. He believes that TM and other forms of meditation contain real potential for self-discovery and personal change, although not everyone benefits from it and those who do often benefit in different ways.

Levitation

Despite the findings that TM was not a panacea and had its limitations, the wave of optimism about its possibilities did not abate. On the contrary – the TM organization raised the claims to a level beyond the physiological and psychological. In 1977 the organization announced a new breakthrough in human potential. By attending the 'Age of Enlightenment Governor Training Course', a person would be trained in TM-Sidhi techniques that promised the development of supernormal powers. These included the 'knowledge of objects hidden from view, awareness of past and future, fully developed feelings of friendliness and compassion, enhancement of sensory thresholds to near the quantum mechanical level, invisibility, and levitation or "flying"[20]'. (p.701)

All of these benefits or powers were meant literally. Maharishi's inspiration for the development of these supernatural abilities was not state-of-the-art quantum physics theory, but an ancient text written more than 2,000 years ago: the *Yoga Sutras* of Patanjali. In four short chapters this ancient Indian text describes how yoga – which includes the practice of meditation – can lead an individual towards spiritual liberation. Along the way the *Sutras* explains how to make the mind still and, in the third part, describes the development of *siddhis* or extraordinary abilities. In Verses III.39 and III.42, Patanjali describes levitation and 'moving through space at will': 'From the mastery of the movement of subtle breath rising in the body, one is freed from being caught by mud, thorns and water, and one can rise above them ... From *samyama* [total attention] on the connection between the body and space and by *samapatti* [fusion] with the lightness of cotton, one can move through space at will.[21]' (pp.192 and 196)

The first study on the development of such extraordinary abilities, completed in 1977, describes how the TM-Sidhi technique increased the coherence of electrical brain activity, measured through electroencephalogram (EEG), and how the experience of feeling 'lifted' was associated with an increase of heart rate from 69 to 96 beats per minute[22]. The technique of levitation, researchers claimed, led to a number of unusual subjective experiences, such as a physical sensation of suspension and 'hopping'. The article quotes an account of someone's experience of the technique:

'I was sitting on a couch meditating at the time. I felt a tremendous amount of energy go through me and simultaneously I had a vision of my spine and chest being just white light and ... then my body moved up and down on the couch two or three times. I thought, "Oh, what is this?" and the next experience I had was hearing my body touch the floor. I say "hearing" because I didn't feel it until after I heard it. It touched down, very, very softly. There was very little feeling of contact. I moved about a six-foot distance at that time.' (p.708)

It's hard not to feel incredulous. That meditation can relax you and make you less anxious are perfectly believable – but that it can teach you how to levitate or develop other supernormal capabilities is quite an astonishing suggestion. However, many people do believe in paranormal powers, and a number of scientists have dedicated their lives to studying whether or not such abilities are real. This field is known as parapsychology.

While researching for this chapter, I came across a recently published book by Dean Radin, probably the world's leading researcher on the paranormal[23]. In his book he describes a series of experiments, some conducted at his lab in the Institute of Noetic Sciences, California, where researchers test abilities such as telepathy and psychokinesis (influencing matter through the mind). Many academics consider the study of the paranormal a waste of time and of resources; I disagree. There is plenty of anecdotal evidence for all these abilities, as well as broad public interest in the paranormal, in my view making this a worthwhile topic for investigation.

I read Radin's book quickly, looking out for any evidence of the development of supernormal abilities through the practice of TM. Unfortunately, as often happens with parapsychology, there is a wide gap between Patanjali's descriptions of unusual powers and the meticulous but comparatively dull scientific experiments and evidence. Although Radin reports statistically significant results for various PSI abilities, these data remain miles away from actual evidence for levitation. He shared with TM a deep interest in the ancient descriptions of the *siddhis* and in modern quantum theory. While reading the book I found something that I shared with him, too: we had both received funding for our research from the BIAL Foundation, a Portugal-based organization that sponsors work in the areas of physiology and parapsychology. I was due to fly to their symposium in the riverside city of Porto to do a presentation and, as it happened, Dean Radin was going to be one of the speakers. I emailed him and we planned to meet in Porto.

Meetings of minds

Radin looked tired, probably jetlagged, when I met him after lunch. He was quiet and self-possessed, yet resolute and passionate about his work. When I asked what was the most extraordinary event he'd witnessed as a researcher of the paranormal, he replied, 'My career; having a full-time job doing parapsychological research.' Previously, he'd worked at the Bell laboratories, developing the next generation of phones. 'Interesting,' he said softly, 'but not very meaningful.'

When I queried Radin about TM, he was on the whole positive about TM research, but hesitated when it came to levitation: 'A few years ago I was invited to a demonstration of the best TM levitators at the Maharishi School of the Age of Enlightenment, in Fairfield, Iowa. There wasn't anyone who even hovered. These were the best TM levitators in the world – and they only hopped.' He suggested that it had probably been a mistake for TM to advertise that its practitioners were able to levitate.

So, why did the TM organization advertise it in the first place? In an analysis of the TM movement, US sociologists William Bainbridge and Daniel Jackson describe a public disrepute of TM shortly after the announcement of the TM-Sidhi program in April 1977. By mid-May 'lecture teams were giving public talks that disappointed many by failing to demonstrate levitation while asserting that it had been achieved. The national television network news programs derisively reported TM's astounding new claims, and suggested that gymnastic meditators might have learned to hop aloft for an instant using their knees or a sudden thrust of their backs...'

On 13 June 1977, *Newsweek* commented that Maharishi had forbidden public demonstrations of levitation. On 8 August, *Time* suggested a hypothesis to explain the new turn in TM's fortunes: 'What is a maharishi to do when sales start to grow sluggish. One answer: announce a shiny new product.[24]' (p.154)

This cynical suggestion doesn't make sense to me. It's true that in 1975 a record number of people joined TM (almost 300,000 in the USA alone) and after that the numbers of new adherents began to fall. Yet articles from that time are filled with optimism. The TM-Sidhi campaign, with its levitation slogan, was more likely the outcome of a sense of triumph – that the world was about to achieve planetary enlightenment, everything was possible. This is spelled out at the end of the first collected volume of research papers published shortly after the public announcement of the Sidhi program. The two articles looking at the effects of the improved TM technique reported increased visual and spatial creativity, intelligence, motor-cognitive flexibility, and hearing. The researchers were so ecstatic with the results that in one article they stitched together all the elements they believed in – quantum theory, psychology and Patanjali's *Yoga Sutras* – as if each of these complemented the others perfectly. The utopian achievement of a new age in humanity's history comes across clearly:

'... the magnitude and range of these abilities have proved that we no longer feel that any goal is out of the reach of mankind. Instead we can look forward to the achievement of states of perfect health, complete mind–body coordination and major reductions in the process of aging, resulting from this new technology ... The vision of human possibilities opened by this preliminary research transforms our conception of individual and national life into one in which no problem can long remain unsolved and in which suffering becomes a thing of the past.[25]'

With the astonishing surge in TM recruits in the mid-seventies, Maharishi may have very well believed that the world was about to enter an age of miracles and supernormal powers; a kind of spiritual–magnetic domino effect in which the collective force of hundreds of thousands people meditating would change the 'consciousness field' of the planet. My intuition about his feelings was confirmed months later when I interviewed Alex Hankey, a Cambridge-educated physicist. In the late 1960s, shortly after taking on a job as an Assistant Professor of Physics at the University of Santa Barbara, he found TM, fell in love with it, tuned in to the practice and dropped out of academia for twenty years[26].

Hankey wore an elegant grey jacket adorned with a University of Cambridge pin. Well into his sixties when I met him, he was affable and bubbly. I began by asking him what happened to the dawn of the age of enlightenment.

'Oh, that... There were so, so many people joining the movement by that time that we believed all of us meditating would change the world. Anything was possible, we thought. But it didn't happen, I mean, the world enlightenment. And shortly after 1975 Maharishi decided to raise the prices of the course astronomically in the West, and to invest more in countries like India.'

'And the levitation,' I asked, 'Did you ever see it happening?'

'Oh, that was a bad idea. Apparently, they found this man in Indonesia who could actually float, and not just hop, but once they attempted to fly him to Switzerland, the moment he set a foot outside of his village, he couldn't do it anymore.'

'So, you've never actually seen anyone levitating?'

'No, no.'

'What about Maharishi, what kind of a person was he?'

'Oh, Maharishi was a truly enlightened being, full, full, full of light,' Alex replied with enthusiasm, stretching out and waving his long thin arms. 'When he stayed in a room for a few days, two months afterwards you could still sense his presence there.'

According to Alex, amid Maharishi's close circle of friends were people such as John Gray, the author of *Men are from Mars, Women from Venus* (1992), and the best-selling guru of self-healing books Deepak Chopra. I was surprised about the extent TM changed not only the scientific landscape of meditation studies, but also how its influence trickled down into the world of self-help writing.

I thought of the hundreds of thousands of people doing TM in the hope of either finding inner peace, a better or true self, or even extraordinary powers and world enlightenment. I couldn't help asking, 'Has it changed you, Alex? Has TM made you a different person?'

'Oh yes. Very definitely. I used to be a very frantic and frenetic individual,' Alex replied waving his arms and resting his hands on top of his head. I couldn't help smiling.

'But you still come across as frantic and frenetic.'

'Oh, but you should have met me before I started doing TM. I was much, much more frantic.'

Deepak Chopra gets into a 'Herbal Jam'

After the interview I checked if Alex Hankey was getting his facts right. He was. John Gray had been the personal secretary to Maharishi and, in the late 1980s, Deepak Chopra was invested with the title 'Lord of Immortality of Heaven on Earth' by Maharashi himself. Although most scientists frowned upon his books, Chopra's association with TM earned him headlines in major scientific publications.

On 11 October 1991 *Science* published a news article entitled 'JAMA gets into an Indian Herbal Jam'[27]. *JAMA* is the acronym for one of the most prestigious medical journals in the world, the *Journal of the American Medical Association*, and the 'Indian Herbal Jam' they got into was the publication of an article that presented TM's Indian herbal as the true and only Ayurvedic medicine – India's ancient system of healthcare. Deepak Chopra was one of the authors of the controversial article[28].

It is standard practice in medical journals for authors to disclose any conflict of interest, particularly a financial one. Imagine you are a biologist working on cancer and a large pharmaceutical company employs you as a consultant. If you write an academic article claiming that a drug manufactured by this pharmaceutical company reduces cancer, you are expected to report your involvement with the company. In the *JAMA* article, Chopra wrote about the medical improvements associated with Maharishi Ayurveda herbal products, but did not disclose his involvement with the TM organization.

Within days of the article's publication, readers inundated

JAMA with critical letters. How did the anonymous reviewers of the article not notice that the authors were advertising TM's herbal products? Andrew Skolnick, one of *JAMA*'s associated editors, wrote a response. He uncovered various connections between Chopra and TM: Chopra was the medical director of the Maharishi Ayur-veda Health Centre for Stress Management and Behavioral Medicine, and a former consultant and board member for Maharishi Ayur-Veda Products International[29]. Furthermore, in his book *Perfect Health: The Complete Mind/ Body Guide* (1991), he claimed to have treated more than 10,000 patients with these herbal products, which according to him are 'pure knowledge pressed into material form'. In a subsequent article Skolnick writes as an endnote: 'In the summer of 1992, Deepak Chopra and two TM associations filed a $194-million libel suit against the AMA [American Medical Association], *JAMA*'s editor, and me. The suit was dismissed without prejudice in March 1993.[30]'

Chopra has since left TM, but the 'herbal jam' episode made me aware that TM's attempts to present themselves scientifically were not taken very seriously by the early nineties. The levitation episode had probably harmed TM's image, but that wasn't the only cause of its declining reputation in the science community.

Peace-pumping factories

Extraordinary as levitation may be, TM's most ambitious aim was not the development of paranormal powers, but the creation of a peaceful world that is free from criminality and war. Again, this aim was loosely based on Patanjali's *Yoga Sutras*. According to Verse III.23, when an individual has mastered meditation to its highest level another extraordinary ability can arise: the emanation of a sense of love and peacefulness that permeates others.

David Lynch (see p.51) conveyed this using an electric metaphor: 'We're like light bulbs,' he explains. 'If bliss starts growing inside you, it's like a light; it affects the environment... You enjoy that light inside, and if you ramp it up brighter and brighter, you enjoy more and more of it. And that light will extend farther and farther.[31]' (p.105) In an interview Lynch explained that if 'you build a facility like a factory, you house the people, you feed the people, they do their meditation and it's a beautiful, beautiful thing for the world ... at least 8,000 beautiful souls working like factory workers doing their program, pumping peace for the world.[32]'

Beautiful as it is, how does it work? Back in the 1960s Maharishi proposed that if just 1 per cent of the world's population practised TM, the ripple effect throughout collective consciousness would improve society as a whole. He believed that it is the accumulation of stress in collective consciousness that leads a society into war. One TM researcher explains that when we meditate, the 'conscious awareness of the individual becomes experientially connected back to pure consciousness', which leads to 'increasing coherence, reducing stress, and accelerating development in the larger society'[33] (p.785). To put it simply if a tiny percentage of the population is able to connect to the creative intelligence we call God or ultimate reality, the level of harmony in the collective consciousness of all human beings increases and stress levels fall.

Many of the world's spiritual belief systems have proposed similar, although less elaborate versions of the same idea. If only Buddhists, Christians, Jews and so on would sincerely and wholeheartedly follow the moral guidelines of their religions, the world would be a much better place. The unusual claim of TM is that it need be only 1 per cent of the population, or even less (the squared root of 1 per cent) if those meditating have learned the advanced TM-Sidhi technique, to create a worldwide effect. Most astonishing of all is that the TM organization has put the theory to the test, analyzed it, and published the results.

The 1993 Washington, D.C. experiment

'Hundreds of clean-cut practitioners of Transcendental Meditation – followers of the guru Maharishi Mahesh Yogi – moved into apartment buildings and university dormitories in Washington this week to participate in a two-month experiment that has some ambitious goals. They plan to reduce the crime rate in Washington by 20 per cent.'

This was how, on 9 June 1993, the *Washington Post* reported the beginning of one of the most expensive and improbable research projects in the history of modern psychological science[34]. Called 'The National Demonstration Project to Reduce Violent Crime and Improve Governmental Effectiveness', the study was on a phenomenal scale: 4,000 transcendental meditators assembled at the centre of Washington, D.C., for almost two months – 7 June to 30 July – and meditated twice daily, from 7.30am until noon, and again from 5pm until 7pm. That's more than seven hours a day. The cost of this two-month research project was $4.2 million.

As the newspaper had reported, the aim of the project was to reduce violent crimes (including homicides, rapes, assaults and robberies) in Washington, D.C. The researchers had no control group (say, an equal number of people doing relaxation at a different time period), but increased the number of meditators in three waves to try to compensate for this shortcoming. The experiment began with 1,000 participants, increased first to 2,500, and then again to 4,000. If TM produced a stress decrease in the collective consciousness field that affected crime, the effect would be the greatest when more people meditated. The study also controlled for other factors that scientists know affect crime levels, such as temperature, number of daylight hours, and police activities, and compared the crime rates of those eight weeks of TM practice with the past rates of criminal actions in Washington, D.C.

Published in 1999 (six years later), the results showed that during the meditation experiment violent crimes fell by 15.6 per cent. The apparent effect was strongest in the last week of the study, when 4,000 people meditated together: the decrease in crime during that period was said to be 23.3 per cent. I looked closely at the results – crime rates appeared to drop only when there were at least 2,500 meditators. This is what TM researchers predicted: the more meditators, the greater the effect. However, there was a glitch in the results: rapes decreased by 58.1 per cent and assaults by 19 per cent, but there was no decrease for homicides and robberies. Still, as far as TM was concerned, these were encouraging results. During the study only two factors had an impact on crime rates: an increase in temperature (leading to more crimes being committed) and the number of people doing TM (which, they said, led to fewer crimes)[35].

I read the article again and again. The theory of a collective consciousness field – a three-way fusion of Indian philosophy, quantum physics and New-Age psychology – affecting the stress levels of non-meditators was hardly credible, but I couldn't spot anything wrong with the statistical analysis. However, I thought there was something odd about finding a steep decrease for rapes and assaults, but not for homicides and robberies. The researchers had no convincing explanation for this anomaly – perhaps robberies are less related to social stress than other crimes, or perhaps they are associated with long-established drug use and therefore it takes longer for changes in collective consciousness to trickle down into the individual mind, they suggested. They didn't attempt to explain the lack of drop in the numbers for homicides at all.

Scrutinizing the crime reports of the time, I found something the article doesn't mention, but explains why the researchers didn't try to justify the homicide rates. The police records show that, in fact, there was a 50 per cent *increase* in homicides during the experiment period compared with the previous year. In part this increase was driven by a gunman who fired at children in a swimming pool two weeks after the TM experiment began. When John Hagelin, the leading TM researcher, was asked about this, he said that homicide was 'the toughest nut to crack... The people who open fire on a crowd to kill one person in a gang are the most stressed, the most desperate individuals and it will really take more time to penetrate that level of society.[36]'

Other sources confirmed the increase in homicides. Robert Park, a physics professor at the University of Maryland, has written about the TM experiment in his book *Voodoo Science* (2000): 'Participants in the project seemed serenely unaware of the mounting carnage around them as they sat cross-legged in groups throughout the city, eyes closed, peacefully repeating their mantras. The murder rate for those two months reached a level unmatched before or since. At the end of the period, Haegelin ... acknowledged that murders were indeed up "due to the unusually high temperatures" but "brutal crime" was down.[37]'

What had happened to the homicide number that didn't make it into the research article? One of the TM researchers, Maxwell Rainforth, explains in a critical review of Robert Park's book that the extraordinary rate of ten homicides in a 36-hour period was considered a 'statistical outlier', which was removed from the final analysis[38]. 'Outliers' occur when one or very few participants in a study score much higher or lower than others in a certain measure (a questionnaire or a physiological outcome like heart rate). Because these scores can bias the overall statistical analysis, it used to be common practice to remove them. However, to remove the data of how people score in a test is very different from wiping from the data set ten people who were murdered. As it happened the ninety homicides that occurred during the eight weeks of the TM experiment accounted for 19 per cent of the total murders of 1993[39].

So, if the homicides *increased* during the experiment, the overall 15.6 per cent decrease in rapes and assaults doesn't look as impressive. The TM organization went on to conduct other experiments all over the world, from the Middle East to Africa, although none was as ambitious in scope or rigour as that in Washington, D.C. – except for one.

Back in the UK

An article published in the *Journal of Psychology, Crime and*

Law reported how the increasing numbers of TM practitioners in 1988 in England's Merseyside area, incorporating Liverpool, led to a 13.4 per cent drop in crime when compared to the previous year[40]. In contrast with the other TM articles on the subject, this one was short, snappy and provocative. Rather than getting a few thousand meditators to congregate somewhere for a few weeks, the Merseyside study tracked the increasing number of people practising TM in the region over a period of several years from 1988 to 1991. According to the leading author, Guy Hatchard, numbers reached a critical mass in 1988 with the opening of 'The Maharishi Golden Dome' in Skelmersdale, Lancashire, where a community of 138 people practised the advanced TM-Sidhi technique on a daily basis.

Hatchard explained that the effect in the collective consciousness is observed very much in the same way that water boils when it reaches 100°C, but not before. He calculated a geographical radius of the TM influence based on the principle that an effect would be reached once the number of meditators was greater than 1 per cent squared root of the population. The centre of his circle was the Golden Dome in Skelmersdale. He tracked outward circles increasing the radius by 1.5 kilometres each time, until he had a final circle of radius 15.5 kilometres, the limit of the influence of 138 meditators from the Maharishi Golden Dome. From 1988 to 1992 researchers noted a significant drop in crime statistics for this region – and not for any other in England and Wales. In a provocative nudge to the UK's government and social policymakers, the article suggested that 'If Merseyside had continued to follow the national trend of rising crime from 1988 to 1992 there would have been 255,000 more crimes than actually occurred, [which translate to a financial] saving of £1,250 million [on crime-fighting]. Each individual attending the group sessions in Skelmersdale apparently saves Merseyside £3,000 in reduction of crime costs for each hour spent ... practising the TM-Sidhi program.'

The article was brief, with no fireworks display of quantum-

Vedanta-psychology, and only a suggestion of the fact that many physicists believe that consciousness plays a central role in the universe. I wasn't the only one intrigued by this piece of writing. Huw Dixon, a professor of Economics at Cardiff University, was quoted on a TM website saying that 'this research and its conclusions are so strong that it demands action from those responsible for government policy[41]'.

I emailed him. Within a couple of hours, he had written back confirming that, from an economist's point of view, TM was a potentially cost-effective intervention in the reduction of crime. He reminded me that back in the early 1970s the link between meditation and relaxation was an innovative one and, while the many studies looking at its various physiological and psychological effects followed the accepted methods of scientific enquiry, nothing like the collective consciousness field studies had ever been attempted before. In his email he also lamented that owing to both a fall in the number of people practising TM and a change in Maharishi's strategy, there had barely been any new studies on the collective consciousness effects of TM since 1996.

The combination of sociology, forensic psychology, and parapsychology make the research into the effects of TM on collective consciousness one of the most uncanny enterprises in the history of modern science. Its mindset is unique: the individual who had proclaimed 1975 as the year of world change was definitely behind these idealistic experiments. I found myself experiencing a mix of delight and irritation about its naivety. There is something troubling in the idea that a single factor, such as collective consciousness, can play a more important role in rates of aggressive behaviour and crime than factors such as an individual's level of education, wealth or emotional maturity. Furthermore, the TM theory presupposes that we have quite limited control over our own behaviour (to be fair other psychological and philosophical systems would agree with that premise). Finally, my unease also came from the fact that so much money has been spent without thinking through carefully the best way to test for TM's collective consciousness effects. In science small is beautiful: there is no need to test the effect of a certain factor in a large population – whether it's meditation or a vaccine – unless you can first show that your theory, or drug, or technique works on a small scale. Smaller and more controlled experiments would have been a much more efficient way of studying whether TM works 'at a distance'. But Maharishi thought big, really big.

THE TOWER OF INVINCIBILITY

In the mid-1990s Maharishi created a trans-national political party in more than seventy countries. In the USA John Hagelin, the lead author of the Washington, D.C., experiment, was the presidential candidate of the Natural Law Party in three elections. His counterpart in the UK was Dr Geoffrey Clements, a well-spoken, moustachioed man. In the election broadcast for the EU elections in June 1994, twenty years back from the day I'm writing, Clements quotes the Merseyside study and declares his intention to establish a group of 7,000 experts in TM and yogic flying in the UK to reduce the rates of stress and negativity throughout the country, 'making the nation strong, dynamic and integrated'[42]. The Natural Law Party took tenth place out of 18 parties in the EU elections with 96,554 votes.

The dream to bring an Age of Enlightenment and peace to the world via 'factories of meditators' is very much alive. David Lynch is the present torchbearer. In early November 2007, the director flew to Berlin to unveil plans for a new university shaped like a 'tower of invincibility'. In *David Wants to Fly*, a documentary that records Lynch's university announcement, we see Lynch smartly dressed in a dark suit walking onto the stage of an auditorium[43]. Standing next to him is the TM Raja (prince) of Germany, a large, overweight man, dressed in a white toga, with a golden crown hanging on his head. Lynch introduces the Raja and sits down, while the large man announces, in German, the construction of a

Tower of Invincibility not far from Berlin, where people will gather to practise TM. The Raja displays a large poster with the colourful drawing of a phallic edifice. There is timid clapping from the audience, probably consisting in its majority of Lynch fans. Amid the clapping a voice speaks out: 'But who's attacking us? Invincible against whom?'

'I'm a good German, I'm a German who wants to make Germany invincible,' the Raja answers, sweat trickling down his face. A nervous laughter echoes through the auditorium.

'But that's what Adolf Hitler wanted!' someone shouts.

'Yes,' the Raja answers, 'but unfortunately he didn't succeed because he didn't have the right technique.'

David Lynch looks down confused when people get up screaming and booing. Eventually, he calms everyone down by reassuring them of the Raja's good intentions.

Lynch is not the only celebrity figure endorsing TM. The British comedian and actor Russell Brand is similarly outspoken about his involvement and freely admits, 'I have become a better human being through this meditation.'

Not everyone who experiences the benefits of TM has publicly endorsed it. A few million people worldwide have learned the technique and practise it without any formal ties to the TM organization. I once met a Catholic priest and theologian who had been practising TM daily for more than twenty years: 'It's the best thing to quiet my mental clutter,' he confided.

WHAT CAN TM DO FOR ME?

More than forty years after the publication of the first TM studies in *Science*, and with more than 600 studies analyzing its physiological, psychological and sociological effects, what is the current verdict on this contemplative technique when it comes to personal transformation? Despite its failure, so far, in achieving world peace, TM has two enormous merits. First, it brought an ancient contemplative practice into the modern laboratory and by doing so dispelled social prejudice about meditation in the West. Without TM paving the way with its hundreds of studies and its ability to spread the practise of meditation throughout social groups, it is highly unlikely that we'd now be experiencing a new wave of interest that focuses on other forms of meditation, in particular, Buddhist-based mindfulness. Second, it showed how a very simple technique that involves no physical strain can have a positive effect on both physical and mental health.

Many have criticized or satirized TM's use of scientific evidence to advance its own idealistic or religious agenda. Its tactics, some would claim, are those of a cult. I don't think so. If anything, Maharishi's goals and the actions of the organization he created are disingenuous. But the use of science to validate its technique, has always been sincere, despite being clunky or unpersuasive at times, and an integral part of what TM is about.

So, what can TM do for me? This is a difficult question. TM, like other contemplative techniques, will work better or worse according to individual temperaments, the teacher and the reasons you have to meditate. The most recent evidence, which analyzes dozens of studies conducted over more than forty years, suggests that if you are generally anxious or emotionally unstable, TM will help you to a moderate extent, and will be more effective than simple relaxation[44]. If you have high blood pressure, the American Heart Association recommends TM (while mindfulness is not recommended), although physical exercise, such as swimming or running, would be better[45]. If you're interested in self-exploration and personal development, regular TM will almost certainly produce some alterations in consciousness. However, the extent or depth to which this experience will improve your self-understanding will vary considerably from person to person. I am often asked if I would recommend regular TM *instead* of seeing a therapist. This is a much harder question to answer, and requires us to look deeper into the particular merits of talking therapies – which we'll do in Chapter 4.

And, finally, what about the collective consciousness effect? Can your own TM practice help to reduce stress or aggression in others? The answer to that is simple: we don't know. Current research is unconvincing and we need more elegant and better-controlled studies in order to have greater certainty one way or the other. However, if you are considering moving house and there is the option of living close to a TM university, dome, centre or Tower of Invincibility, I suggest you give it a go – it's likely that transcendental meditators will make good neighbours and they may even occasionally invite you over to watch repeats of Lynch's *Twin Peaks*.

CHAPTER 4

TO SIT OR TO SPEAK?

'It's probably best if you lie down on the floor for this,' suggested the lecturer. I lay down on the rough blue carpet of the teaching room and tried to get comfortable, aware my head was mere inches away from someone's foot. As I shifted to move my position, my arm brushed against the person lying next to me.

'Sorry!' I whispered.

'No worries,' she giggled. 'We're a bit packed in like sardines, aren't we? Wake me up if I fall asleep!'

'Welcome to our day of mindfulness,' said our lecturer for the day, a clinical psychologist based at a NHS Mindfulness Centre, addressing the roomful of trainee clinical psychologists. 'Today is going to be a bit different to your normal teaching; it's going to be a day of experiential learning. Later on I'll be talking to you about the theories behind mindfulness-based interventions, and the body of research that currently exists as to their effectiveness, but first I want you to experience for yourselves the kind of practice that takes place in a mindfulness-based program.'

THE THERAPEUTIC RESPONSE

The session began with a body-scan meditation, which involves moving your focus of attention to different parts of the body. The lecturer explained that we could do it sitting up, but that it was generally practised lying down and we might find it more comfortable to do so. Perhaps influenced by the general weariness of a Monday morning, most of us were quite enthusiastic about the opportunity to lie on the floor. Over the next half an hour, we were guided through the practice and afterwards we shared our reflections on our experience. We then went on to do a 30-minute sitting mindfulness meditation, again followed by group reflections.

As you would expect the reflections from the individual members of the group varied, but many of us noticed feeling more relaxed. Although bringing about relaxation isn't the aim of mindfulness, it appears to be a common side-effect. In contrast, 'relaxing' is not a word people commonly use to describe their experience of psychological therapy. Opening up to a therapist in a one-to-one situation can certainly feel cathartic, but is often quite challenging.

Scientific evidence indicates that a key predictor of successful therapy is the development of a strong therapeutic alliance between client and therapist[1,2,3]. However, that essential feature of talking therapy – the need to relate effectively with another person – can itself provoke anxiety. In my own therapeutic work, I am often moved by the courage of my clients in being able to trust me (yes, a healthcare professional, but initially a stranger and ultimately a fallible human being) with their vulnerabilities and deepest fears. Because, whether it's reliving traumatic past events, admitting 'silly little worries' or disclosing behaviour about which we feel deeply ashamed, revealing the hidden parts of ourselves to another person is rarely a walk in the park.

In contrast practising meditation – and mindfulness – is not as much about relating to another person, as about relating to the self.

In Mindfulness-based Stress Reduction (MBSR) and Mindfulness-based Cognitive Therapy (MBCT) – two of the best-known mindfulness-based therapies (and the two that we focus on in this chapter) – there is still a relational component, but it is within the context of group intervention. The focus is more on the sharing of experiences of group members in relation to the techniques members are practising, than any individual deeply exploring his or her difficulties through a one-to-one with a therapist. In this sense mindfulness or a mindfulness-based therapy might for some represent a more comfortable form of self-exploration than traditional forms of therapy. However, are mindfulness techniques as effective in changing people's thoughts and behaviour as we know more established psychological therapies can be? Fundamentally, is it more effective to sit or to speak?

Later in this chapter we'll look at theories about how mindfulness works differently from traditional psychological therapies, but first let's start with the basics of the therapy process. The first step in which, for many of us, involves overcoming our resistance to change.

THE FEAR OF CHANGE

The fear of change is a well-documented part of the human condition. Even people who on the surface appear to be seeking personal change – for example, by undergoing therapy – may still be fearful, hesitant, or resistant to it. There is a skilful explanation for this: even if you're unhappy you know where you are. The prospect of change brings uncertainty – what will happen? Who will I become? For many people the unknown is unsettling; much more so than a familiar feeling of unhappiness. Perversely, there may be a sense of comfort within long-term, enduring discomfort. Even when people are suffering, and recognize on a rational level the need to change for the sake of their own wellbeing, there can still be fear or ambivalence about actually effecting it. A woman in her thirties – let's call her Kim – who was referred to me with chronic depression, explained this core conflict like this: 'I just feel that depression defines me... I don't know how to be happy.'

Although on a rational level Kim wanted to get better, she was also afraid of the unknown. People who have been depressed for a long time may not enjoy their lives, but they may find some solace in the predictability of their predicament. As she put it: 'At least I know what's going to happen.' If Kim were to stop thinking of herself as 'depressed', she would need to redefine her sense of identity. What would her life as a non-depressed person look like? Her uncertainty about the answer initially felt more unsettling than her pervasive sadness.

What also contributes to our reluctance to change is our fear that we may regret it. 'I miss the comfort in being sad,' sings Kurt Cobain, over and over, in the Nirvana song 'Frances Farmer Will Have Her Revenge on Seattle'. We often struggle to let go of anything in which we have invested time and effort, even if we know that it is not working for us and may be causing us stress or pain – this can be particularly true regarding intimate relationships. Buddhists say that attachment creates suffering. However, when we look at human behaviour, the instinct to attach ourselves, and to seek to avoid the loss of these attachments, is deeply embedded in our nature.

Loss aversion

The term 'loss aversion' refers to our human tendency to strongly prefer accruing gains to experiencing losses. First introduced in 1979 by psychologists Daniel Kahneman and Amos Tversky[4], loss aversion is now an integral part of economics and decision theory. The idea is that the prospect of losses has a larger impact on our preferences and decision-making than the prospect of gains. Some studies even indicate that losses can be psychologically twice as powerful as gains, suggesting that the pain of losing something is more acute than the pleasure of gaining something[5]. So, when deciding whether or not to make a change in our lives, the potential rewards we see for ourselves may not tip the balance as much as the losses we anticipate the change might bring.

Intentionally bringing about a particular desired change in ourselves, in terms of personal improvement, is easier said than done. But when the 'pros' of changing begin to outweigh the 'pros' of familiarity and predictability, to the point where we are motivated to try to shift the status quo, what's the process? How can we go about changing for the better?

Varieties of 'talking cure'

'They fuck you up, your mum and dad
They may not mean to, but they do.
They fill you with the faults they had
And add some extra, just for you.'
Phillip Larkin, 'This Be The Verse'[6]

What would you like to change about yourself? Are you looking to become more insightful, more integrated, less depressed, less anxious, more positive, more spiritual, less stressed, less angry, a better version of yourself? The list of ways we might hope to improve ourselves is almost endless – as are the different therapeutic approaches and techniques that we may use to help us do this. Psychoanalytic or psychodynamic psychotherapy, as originally developed by Freud, works on the assumption that psychological problems are rooted in the unconscious. The aim of psychodynamic therapy is therefore to make the unconscious conscious, in order to increase insight, enable resolution, and develop a more integrated sense of self. Cognitive behavioural therapy (CBT), on the other hand, is based on the premise that the way we think or behave right now impacts how we feel. A therapist using this approach will encourage cognitive restructuring by helping you to identify and challenge unhelpful or irrational thoughts and come up with more balanced alternatives. He or she may also use behavioural strategies to encourage you to try to do things differently, to increase your level of activity (in order to improve your mood), or as a way of gathering new evidence to challenge negative beliefs.

Change comes step by step

No matter which school of therapy you follow, one of the most widely accepted theories is that there are various stages to the change process[7]. When you're a therapist and someone walks into your room for the first time, you can't expect he or she will necessarily be instantly ready for change. Initially, a client may vent distress and justify to the therapist why change *can't* happen. A client may be unhappy with his or her life but have no clue about what to do to change it; or, he or she may see a way through, but be ambivalent about putting that change into action.

The difference between contemplating change (that is, having a sense of what you'd like to change) and being ready to act sounds like an intuitive one, but what exactly makes a person move from one position to the next? Research has shown that the strength of the alliance between client and therapist plays an important role in helping clients to engage (and stay engaged) in the therapeutic process[8]. Furthermore, evidence drawn from thirty-years-worth of studies suggests that the most important factor, in terms of what leads to a good therapeutic outcome, is not the particular model of therapy used, but the quality of the therapeutic relationship[9]. Somehow, relating positively to a therapist can increase your motivation to change, help fix what went wrong a long time ago, or allow you to explore and integrate previously inaccessible aspects of yourself.

The therapeutic relationship

The start of a therapeutic relationship can be daunting. All sorts of unknowns go with it: when you meet your therapist for the first time you – and your therapist – may have no idea if it's going to work. But over time, through the building of trust, a unique relationship develops. This is a relationship like no other; a therapist is an impartial, empathic professional to whom you may reveal the most hidden parts of yourself (while he or she will typically disclose very little, if anything, about him- or herself).

A core part of the therapist's role can be conceptualized as becoming a 'secure base' for clients, from which they can carry out self-exploration with a sense of safety and being emotionally 'held'. The term 'secure base' is drawn from attachment theory, developed by British psychologist, psychiatrist and psychoanalyst John Bowlby in 1958[10]. As children our secure base is typically our primary caregiver; as adults we form new attachment relationships with our partners, or our friends. But for those who may not have had a secure base during childhood (for example, if a child was subject to neglect or maltreatment by his or her caregivers, resulting in an insecure attachment), developing trusting relationships in adulthood is often far from easy.

Especially for those with histories of trauma and abuse, the therapeutic relationship may be the first deep connection some individuals have experienced with another human being, during which he or she expresses profound thoughts and feelings. Recently, I worked with an eighty-year-old man who, over the course of our sessions, was able to verbalize for the first time in his life the extraordinarily difficult experiences of his youth. He had never felt able to disclose these events to his wife or children, because he feared that they might interpret his emotional expression as a sign of weakness. Yet, in the setting of the therapeutic relationship, he felt safe enough to process the events that had weighed so heavily on him for decades. Subsequently, he felt a great sense of catharsis: 'I feel like I'm coming out of a hole,' he told me.

Engaging in therapy is far from a sign of weakness, and much more an act of courage. As you build trust with your therapist, the relationship deepens – yet this is not to say that it becomes more comfortable. The more you open up and the more vulnerable and defenceless you allow yourself to be, the more challenging therapy may feel – but also the more you're likely to gain from the experience.

The other side of the chair

To train as a clinical psychologist in the UK, it is not a requirement to undergo your own personal therapy. Nevertheless, many of us do choose to pay to do so, not least because it provides valuable experience of what it is like to be the client. When I took the decision to try out being on the other side of the chair, I spent time considering what approach of therapy to undergo. Because the majority of my own clinical work involves CBT, I chose to experience a very different model (in order to heighten the leap into new territory) and began seeing a psychodynamic psychotherapist.

In contrast to some CBT interventions, which can be as brief as a handful of sessions, psychodynamic psychotherapy is typically longer term, often lasting months or even years. One of the most important lessons I learned first-hand during the sessions with my therapist is that the desire to change is not enough to manifest it. Sometimes I got exasperated; the same emotional patterns and the same thoughts repeated themselves – when were they going to change? My therapist couldn't give me an answer, of course, but as the connection between us developed, I felt like I was finding the end of a long and entangled thread. As I unwove it with her guidance, I experienced an elaboration in my understanding of present thoughts and past experiences in a way that I couldn't have foreseen when I started therapy.

While my therapist certainly used particular techniques to encourage me to explore thoughts and feelings differently, the personal change I experienced in therapy had really depended upon trusting a person I knew very little about. In part therapy is always a leap of faith – no matter how excellent the therapist, it requires you to journey into uncharted territory, without knowing for sure what you'll find and who will emerge at the end of it.

Many people are reluctant to enter a therapist's room because they can't face voicing their inner thoughts, trusting another human being with their vulnerabilities. Although we may rationally know that being non-judgmental and empathic is part of a therapist's requisite, we may still be hesitant to open up about our private experiences – the hidden parts of ourselves – afraid of what might be thought of us. It takes time to build trust, even with a professional. But it's not only deciding to trust another with our inner lives that involves overcoming fear; often, we are even uncomfortable with our own thoughts.

ARE WE AFRAID OF OUR THOUGHTS?

A recent research article[11] led by Timothy Wilson, a professor of psychology at the University of Virginia, yields interesting evidence attesting to the idea that many of us are afraid of or uncomfortable with our own thoughts. Wilson and colleagues describe a series of studies in which participants were invited to spend a set period of time (between 6 and 15 minutes) alone in a room, with nothing to do but think. Most participants reported that they had not enjoyed the experience and had found it hard to concentrate, and that their minds had wandered. Participants who spent time doing external activities, such as reading or listening to music, consistently reported much more enjoyment than those left alone with their thoughts. Age didn't seem to be a factor that made a difference, nor did personality – extraverts and introverts both appeared averse to quiet contemplation.

None of this is that surprising. Simply looking around any public space – train carriage, café and so on – provides evidence that people generally prefer to be doing something rather than simply sitting alone with their thoughts. We habitually distract ourselves with books, smartphones, people-watching. However, in one study Wilson found some quite dramatic evidence as to just *how* unwilling some of us are to be left alone with only our thoughts. Curious as to whether people would prefer doing something unpleasant rather than nothing at all, the researchers told their participants that, during the 15 minutes they were given to simply sit and think in an empty room, they also had the option of pressing a button that would deliver a painful electric shock – to themselves. Everyone taking part had previously stated that they would pay money not to receive an electric shock of this level owing to its unpleasantness. Yet, over the course of that short amount of time, many participants opted to administer themselves electric shocks rather than be left alone with their thoughts. To the researchers' surprise, 67 per cent of men and 25 per cent of women gave themselves at least one electric shock during the 15-minute contemplation period. Wilson and colleagues concluded that 'most people seem to prefer to be doing something than nothing, even if that something is negative'.

So, why are we so unwilling to just spend time with our own thoughts? The researchers suggested that it is very difficult for most of us to control our minds to allow us to dwell only on pleasant memories or experiences. Left to meander the halls of our inner sanctum, there may be a tendency to wander into the darker, more anxious corners where fear, discomfort or guilt may be easily triggered. This is probably a big part of the appeal of meditation and mindfulness – our perception of them is that they are techniques that help us to gain control over our wandering, untrained minds.

GOING BACKWARDS TO MOVE FORWARDS

A number of interventions have been developed that incorporate techniques adapted from Buddhist mindfulness; two of the most popular are Mindfulness-based Stress Reduction (MBSR) and Mindfulness-based Cognitive Therapy (MBCT). Both consist of structured group programmes that incorporate mindfulness techniques, including mindfulness meditation. This is different from other meditation techniques, such as TM (see p.47). Instead of focusing your mind on a mantra, you simply notice your thoughts coming and going, accept them, and let them go. The aim is to become aware, in a non-judgmental way, of what thoughts and sensations you have in the present moment.

MBSR was originally developed by molecular biologist Jon Kabat-Zinn, after he came up with the idea that training chronic pain patients in Buddhist meditative practices (without the Buddhism) could help them to manage their pain. Kabat-Zinn's program inspired psychologists and depression specialists Zindel Segal, Mark Williams and John Teasdale to develop MBCT, which is now commonly used in the UK's National Health Service as a treatment for recurrent depression.

In a recent book Williams describes a number of techniques that may be used within MBCT[12]. For example, if you're dealing with difficult feelings – say, after a disagreement with a friend or colleague, or if you need to make a difficult decision – you are advised to relax, bring to mind an image of the difficulty you're facing and explore the physical sensations associated with the thoughts, but not try to change them. You may also want to say to yourself that 'It's okay to feel this way.' The focus in mindfulness-based interventions is on developing an attitude of non-judgemental awareness and acceptance towards our thoughts, and our selves.

Mindfulness-based interventions, which marry modern psychology and Buddhist meditation, are known as 'third-wave' cognitive behavioural approaches – after the first (behavioural therapy) and second (cognitive behavioural therapy – CBT) waves. Both third-wave therapies and traditional CBT acknowledge the important role of our behaviour and cognitions in affecting how we feel.

However, third-wave therapies have called to question the utility of a key aim of traditional CBT: to identify, challenge and

change negative or unhelpful thoughts. Is trying to
control our thoughts and emotions really the solution to
resolving psychological distress – or is it part of the problem?
Third-wave therapies suggest a different approach, in which
the aim is not to modify unhelpful thoughts, but to develop an
increased awareness of how we think and feel in the present,
with a mindset of non-judgment and acceptance. For example,
while in traditional CBT, you would be encouraged to challenge
a negative thought such as 'I am a failure' by reminding
yourself of a time in your life when in fact you have not failed,
a mindfulness-based approach would encourage little more
than a mere acknowledgment of the negative thought –
something along the lines of 'Okay, I'm having that thought
again. It doesn't have to mean anything.' This is known as
'holding thoughts lightly'.

So with mindfulness-based interventions, the aim is not
to change your thoughts, but your global beliefs about
thoughts – essentially, you're expected to stop believing
that your thoughts are necessarily true or important. This is
where the Buddhist philosophy really kicks in: your thoughts
are mere 'mental events' – just thoughts, nothing more – and
they don't necessarily warrant any action. All you're aiming to
do is to be aware.

From its early psychoanalytical beginnings, the goal of
psychological therapy has also been about increasing awareness,
bringing into the light what was previously hidden, unobserved
or unacknowledged. But unlike in mindfulness practice, we don't
just stay with the awareness; we move onwards to explore what
we have observed. In this sense mindfulness as a therapeutic
technique seems somewhat limited in reach – but quite heavy
on time, as you have to practise the technique yourself if you
want to use it as a therapist. Still, I did practise it in case it might
prove useful – and it did.

USING MINDFULNESS TECHNIQUES IN THERAPY

'Even though we haven't spoken in years, I still have conversations with him,' my client, 'Sarah', said softly.

'How do you mean?' I asked.

'Well,' she replied, hesitantly. 'I sometimes ... I pretend that he's there in the room with me, like he's come back and he's just sitting in his chair. And then I have conversations with him. I say all the things I need to say to him.'

'What do you say?'

'I tell him how mad I am that he left me. How lost I feel without him. How angry and upset and alone I am.'

'And does it help?' I asked.

'At first... it feels good to get it out. But then it always ends with me talking to an empty chair, asking over and over, *why did you leave me?*' Sarah sighed, slumping back in her seat. She cradled her face in her hands. 'I just feel like until I get answers from him, I can never move on. I feel like I'm living in the past. Going round and round in circles.'

Sarah was a middle-aged woman suffering from chronic depression. Two years earlier Sarah's husband of twenty years had walked out on her with no explanation other than 'I am no longer in love with you.' She was shell-shocked; she felt there had been no indication that her husband was unhappy in their marriage. The sudden, painful loss of her life partner was quickly followed by the loss of their jointly owned home. Her circle of friends dwindled; many she had considered mutual turned out to be his. It was no great wonder that Sarah felt sad and angry, but the consequences of her husband's departure and their subsequent divorce ran deeper than that: her sense of identity and self-worth were badly shaken. For many years Sarah's poor physical health had prevented her from working, so her role as a wife and homemaker had defined her. She had loved her husband deeply and even after his departure, described him in very positive, quite idealistic terms: 'He was the perfect husband ... He was my world.'

With no partner, no children and a now-diminished social circle, Sarah found herself alone much of the time. The few friends that she did have were running out of sympathy, tiring of Sarah talking about her loss. She felt isolated and deeply unhappy – and confused. She also felt very stuck, unable to think of much else than her need to gain answers to the questions that went round in endless circles in her mind: 'Why did he leave? Why did he stop loving me?'

Unfortunately, Sarah's now ex-husband was not playing ball. Despite her concerted efforts to extract the answers she so wanted from him, he would give her nothing very concrete, merely 'we want different things' or 'I've changed.' Eventually, he stopped responding to her calls and emails altogether. This frustrated Sarah immensely – why wouldn't he tell her why he no longer loved her, so that she could change it and win him back?

Initially, I used traditional CBT techniques in our work together. We focused on identifying patterns of negative thinking, challenging unhelpful or distorted thoughts, and using strategies to try to reduce rumination. I asked her to complete activity-scheduling diaries as homework tasks, with the aim of introducing more mastery and pleasure into her life, which I hoped would in turn improve both her mood and her self-esteem. Yet, despite her willingness to engage with these techniques, Sarah remained stuck in the past. Rationally, she knew that she might never gain the answers she was looking for, but it didn't stop her looking for them, fictionalizing them in imaginary conversations with her ex-husband, and ruminating on the perceived failures that she now thought might have contributed to his leaving. She blamed herself, often harshly, listing numerous character flaws that she believed could have forced this 'perfect' husband to leave. She saw no joy in the present or future; she wished only for her rose-tinted past.

When I discussed Sarah's case with my supervisor, I explained that my current attempts to help Sarah move forwards with her life were not proving that fruitful. Traditional CBT didn't seem to be having enough of an impact on shifting her ingrained patterns of ruminative thinking about her loss. I needed something else, something perhaps more tangible, to help her to let go of the past. I wondered if it might be worth introducing Sarah to mindfulness techniques; my supervisor agreed.

In our next session I talked to Sarah about the concept of mindfulness. I encouraged her to try practising being mindful even when doing simple things, like the washing up. I suggested that she pay attention to the warmth of the water on her hands, the scent of the washing-up liquid, the smooth feeling of a plate, the look of the bubbles in the sink. I encouraged her to be accepting and non-judgmental of any thoughts that came into her mind; she was simply to notice them, and then to bring her focus back to what she was doing in the present. 'Focus on doing only one thing at a time,' I suggested. 'So if you are doing the washing up, just do the washing up. If you are watching a film, just watch the film. Try to immerse yourself in the experience of whatever you're doing. Notice the experience of all of your senses in the present moment.' Sarah agreed to give it a go.

The next time we met, she seemed a bit brighter. She told me that when thoughts about her ex-husband had entered her head, she had tried to simply notice the thought, without engaging with it, and then bring back her attention to the task at hand. I asked her how she found it. 'Different... Good, I think. Like I was giving myself permission to take a break from thinking about what went wrong. It was like a bit of breathing space.'

Over the course of the next few weeks, I introduced Sarah to other mindfulness techniques, including mindful breathing exercises. She found these deeply relaxing and began engaging in her own mindfulness meditation practice at home, usually for 10 or 20 minutes a day. Something started to shift: Sarah began to take more of an interest in her actual life, rather than the life she had lost. During our sessions she appeared less self-critical, less judgmental of herself (she stopped talking about being a 'failure' or a 'bad wife'), and began to make peace with the reality of her situation. As Sarah came to terms with the idea that she might never get the answers she sought from her ex-husband and stopped blaming and judging herself so harshly, she seemed to release herself from her torment a little. She began socializing again, and even began a new relationship; something that she had deemed 'unthinkable' at the start of the therapy.

Towards the end of our work together, Sarah mentioned that she had received an email from her ex-husband. I asked her about it – she hadn't opened it: 'I deleted it. I didn't feel the need to read it. I didn't want to be dragged back into the past. I feel like I'm finally living my life again.'

I can't be certain that the introduction of mindfulness was the turning point in Sarah's therapy. Certainly, Sarah's own feedback indicated that she liked mindfulness. She had had some prior experience of meditation as a teenager and considered herself quite a spiritual person. She also greatly preferred mindfulness practice as a homework task to filling out sheets about her thoughts. I believe that mindfulness helped her to feel more rooted in the present and encouraged her not to dwell so often on her loss. But was mindfulness really the unique key to Sarah's success? It's hard to say. It might be that a simple relaxation technique (such as that I used with Mary in Chapter 2) could have achieved a similar effect by encouraging her to focus on her body, rather than her thoughts. The passing of time might also play a role – a relationship break up is similar to the death of a loved one; we go through a mourning period, but eventually we naturally move on.

Another influencing factor – probably the crucial one – was the therapeutic alliance that we developed over the course of the sessions. As I've already discussed (see pp.84–5), the relationship between client and therapist is the most potent variable in therapy, widely indicated as the biggest predictor of successful outcome. As a matter of good practice, Sarah completed a brief session-rating scale[13] after each therapy appointment. Her rating of her experience of the therapeutic relationship increased over our initial sessions and remained high for the duration of her treatment. Arguably, then, it's possible that Sarah would have got better regardless of whether I had used mindfulness or not.

THERAPY OR THERAPIST?

We live in an age in which we could theoretically live our lives without the need to leave the house or see another person for days, weeks, months on end. (The Japanese have a name – *hikikomori* – for teenagers or young adults who live as modern-day hermits, refusing to leave their houses for months or even years.) We can do our shopping online, manage our bank accounts electronically, and run a business from a virtual office. If we want to learn a new skill – be it a craft, a language, or even meditation or yoga – DVDs, Apps and the Internet enable us to do so from our own homes. And if this isolation were to cause depression or anxiety, fear not! We can have a self-help book delivered to our door at the click of a button, and follow each step in its pages without anyone else intervening.

But sometimes we find ourselves unable to bring about the changes we desire even when we want to. It would be easy to think that when we fail, it's simply because we didn't try hard enough. Perhaps we lacked willpower or self-discipline, or simply felt half-hearted. We may locate the blame entirely in ourselves; we may think that we personally lack what it takes for success. However, perhaps what we are actually lacking is the relational component. It is a common experience that it is much easier to achieve change when we have a supportive relationship with another person (or a group) who understands, inspires and encourages us – this experience forms the bedrock of myriad group interventions, from Weight Watchers to Alcoholic Anonymous. Despite the strongly individualistic nature of Western society, there is only so much that we can achieve on our own. Perhaps this is also true of personal change.

There is considerable evidence that therapy works. In the UK the National Institute of Health and Care Excellence (NICE) provides specific guidelines as to which particular approaches a therapist should consider using according to a patient's psychiatric diagnosis. The treatments NICE recommends are 'evidence-based', which means that studies have indicated they are an effective intervention for a particular problem. For example, MBCT is a recommended relapse-prevention intervention for recurrent depression[14] – and is widely seen as the current treatment of choice. However, many psychologists argue that the evidence in support of 'one issue, one therapy' simply doesn't stack up. Psychologist Scott Miller states that there is a lack of evidence that the diagnosis a person receives is correlated with the outcome, much less that it informs us which particular treatment approach is best[15]. Along with many others, Miller believes that the field of psychology is so caught up in the notion of evidence-based practice, with its focus on technique, that we dismiss the most crucial influence – that of the therapists themselves. If the therapeutic alliance is a key predictor of successful outcome, finding the right therapist, rather than the right therapy, may be best for encouraging personal change.

Supershrinks

In 1974 US researcher David Ricks coined the term 'supershrinks' to describe a category of exceptional therapists[16]. Ricks's research investigated the long-term outcomes of 'highly disturbed' adolescent boys. When his participants were re-examined as adults, he discovered that a select group, who had been treated by one particular provider, had notably better outcomes. In contrast those who had been treated by the 'pseudoshrink' demonstrated very poor adjustment as adult men. His conclusion – that therapists differ in their ability to affect change in their clients – is not exactly revelatory, but what *is* surprising is how much this finding has been overlooked in favour of trying to determine what *therapies* are most effective.

More recent research has confirmed that some therapists achieve better outcomes with their patients than others. A 2005 study by psychologists Bruce Wampold and Jeb Brown[17] involved 581 licensed therapy providers (including psychologists, psychiatrists and masters-level therapists) who were treating a diverse sample of more than 6,000 people. The researchers found that the clients' age, gender and diagnosis had no impact on the success rate of the treatment, nor did the experience, theoretical orientation or training of the therapists. What they did find was that the clients treated by the best therapists in the sample improved at a rate at least 50 per cent faster than those treated by the worst. Miller and colleagues have pointed to this and other studies as 'incontrovertible' evidence for their position that '*who* provides the therapy is a much more important determinant of success than *what* treatment approach is provided.[18]'

It would be easy to assume a 'supershrink' would be someone very experienced – perhaps someone with 'consultant' in their title, or a full head of grey hair. But years in the job doesn't guarantee increased psychological knowledge, or therapeutic expertise and competence. In fact a recent study found that trainee clinical psychologists outperformed experienced therapists on psychological knowledge and skills[19]. So, simply accruing years of experience is probably not enough to turn an average therapist into a supershrink.

So what is the secret of supershrinks' success? What sets them apart from average therapists? This was the question that Miller, together with fellow psychologists Mark Hubble and Barry Duncan, set out to answer in the early 2000s. In an article detailing their quest[20], they reveal that finding that answer turned out to be harder than they anticipated: the best therapists in their studies varied considerably in terms of their personal characteristics, their approach and their technical prowess. Nothing tangible seemed to separate 'the best from the rest' – was it simply a matter of chance?

Then one day Miller came across an article written about the research of Swedish psychologist K. Anders Ericsson – widely considered to be the 'expert on experts' – entitled 'What it takes to be great.[21]' The subtitle was even more intriguing: 'Research now shows that the lack of natural talent is irrelevant to great success.' Having spent nearly twenty years studying the world's best musicians, chess players, teachers, athletes, and so on, Ericsson believed that greatness was not attributable to genetic endowment. 'Systematic laboratory research,' he writes, 'provides *no* evidence for giftedness or innate talent.[22]' Rather, the key to superior performance is very simple: those who are the best at something simply work harder at getting better at it than others do. This is rather intuitive – like the saying 'practise makes perfect' – but, importantly, what Ericsson is referring to is *deliberate practice.* So it isn't enough to just spend a lot of time doing something; it's about the amount of time specifically dedicated to striving for objectives, or performance targets, just beyond your current level of proficiency. According to Ericsson those who are the best at what they do are also *attentive to feedback* – which, he argues, is the crucial element that separates the best from the rest. Studies of physicians, for example, show that the most proficient at diagnosing medical problems tend to be the ones who follow up, who make the effort to find out whether they were right or wrong in their patient assessment. Ericsson claims that this extra step – seeking feedback – gives a significant advantage in that it enables us to better understand how and when we improve. Those who are the best at what they do maximize their opportunities to gain feedback – and aim to learn from it.

After reading Ericsson's article Miller and his colleagues were inspired to continue their efforts to understand how some therapists become better than others. What was the key to the superior performance of the supershrinks? Just as Ericsson had observed in champion chess players and Olympic athletes, Miller, Hubble and Duncan found that the best therapists work harder at improving their performance and, crucially, are consistently attentive to client feedback about how their clients feel about them and the work they are doing together.

So, we have some idea of what the best therapists do that helps them to improve and also of what we can do ourselves if we want to become better at something. It's not enough to just work hard; gaining constructive feedback from others – something outside our own subjective appraisal of ourselves – also appears to be crucial. And maybe that's something therapy does have over meditation; the feedback of the 'biased observer' might just be the very thing that gives us the edge in our quest to understand and improve ourselves.

TO SIT <u>AND</u> TO SPEAK?

Change is an unpredictable and difficult game. If we want to boost our chances of success, we need to find someone to support us through the process – someone whom we can trust and who can help us believe that change can actually happen. While the therapeutic alliance may be more important than the particular technique, the type of therapy that we undergo is still worth our consideration. What will be a good match for our own values, beliefs and goals?

Many people may prefer – or require – the in-depth self-exploration and development of a bond with a therapist that individual therapy can provide, in which case attending an MBCT or MBSR group program is unlikely to hit the spot. However, if you are someone with a spiritual worldview, it may well be that a mindfulness-based approach will particularly appeal to you – and this itself may increase your commitment to the change you're trying to make.

So, where are we in our quest to understand the concept of the 'Buddha pill'? Meditation and therapy might seem like an unlikely marriage, but integration of ancient techniques into modern interventions could be the way forwards. Can a shift in how we view our thoughts be a key to shifting our lives? The introduction of Buddhist meditation into modern therapy is arguably revolutionary. The principle is simple enough: you will start to change once you experience your daily flow of thoughts and feelings in a very different way. Recent research on the use of mindfulness meditation (for example, for recurrent depression) suggests this is a real possibility. Let's now take a closer look at the evidence for and against it.

CHAPTER 5

BLISS TECHNIQUES

Baroness Susan Greenfield was delighted. She sprang about the machine with a childlike excitement. It was tiny for a device supposed to measure brain activity, not larger than an average-sized handbag. Sitting on my right, Nick Shackel and Guy Kahane, the philosophers at the Oxford Centre for Science of the Mind, exchanged worried looks and kept quiet.

'We need a guinea pig to try out the consciousness machine,' Susan said. 'Who wants to volunteer?' Silence. She looked around impatiently. There were about 15 of us in the room, but I was the only psychologist; if no one else volunteered there was no way she wouldn't pick me.

'I'll do it,' I said. 'Let's see how much consciousness there is to measure.'

'Brilliant brilliant brilliant. Just sit down right here and do something like... like meditate! I'm sure you do that anyway, right?'

At the time I was actually weaning myself off meditation. For the past couple of years, it had been taking up quite a chunk of my time, often between two and three hours a day. More than relaxing or peaceful, it was deeply pleasurable, not unlike David Lynch's description of experiencing meditation as 'falling into bliss'. I'd get into a mental state where thoughts disappeared, like being in an empty room with all the blinds shut. Inexplicably, rather than being in a dull space where nothing happened, I would feel something I can only roughly describe as waves of blissful electricity moving through my body. There was a downside to it, though. Coming out of the meditation, I often felt I was hovering above reality and everyday concerns. Despite being able to control or even feel unattached from negative feelings – anger, sadness or frustration – I was shocked to find that, sometimes, this lack of attachment made me less sensitive and empathic to other people's feelings. It was only when a friend joked I was becoming a 'meditation junkie' that the penny dropped. He was right; meditation was turning into a way of bypassing real life, or at least of avoiding the parts of it that were difficult or bitter. I had decided then to drastically reduce my practice.

Back at the Centre I sat down and was plugged into the consciousness device. There was nothing to it, just a strip with three electrodes that were attached to my forehead. Susan Greenfield shifted around restlessly in her seat, eager for us to get started. Originally developed to use in surgeries so that doctors could be certain that sedated patients were no longer conscious, the machine had a digital monitor with red numbers that would indicate my level of conscious awareness. I closed my eyes and sought to enter that dark room of thoughtlessness. After no more than three minutes, Susan stopped me.

'Did you see that? The consciousness level dropped four, no, five points!'

I wasn't sure that was a good thing. I had always hoped meditation would make me more, not less conscious. There are many ways of training our minds to become more aware of what's going on outside or within us. In the previous chapter we looked at how psychological therapy can help us learn more about thoughts and emotions, and to eventually change them. Or, if we're doing mindfulness-based therapy, it can increase our level of self-awareness. The question we now need to address is whether or not contemplative techniques, such as yoga or mindfulness meditation, can lead to significant changes in the way we feel, think and behave.

MIND HYGIENE AND YOGA

'If you do yoga and meditation regularly, you will reach a state of cosmic consciousness; it washes out sadness and worries, everything. You become transformed.' Didi, my first yoga and meditation instructor, never tired of repeating this. A British Ananda Marga monk in his early forties, he was both prodigiously bendy and firmly dedicated to yoga. His daily routine included four hours of practice a day, one morning session at 5am and an evening one at 6pm.

'After two hours of yoga your body is soft, soft… just like butter,' he said, laughing. 'Then, your mind becomes so quiet that meditation arises by itself; no effort or need for instructions.' After six intense months of the hardest physical training I ever endured, I discovered that he wasn't exaggerating. The yoga was definitely not the 'don't-force-yourself' type. Didi helped me to extend my muscles and bend in extraordinary ways – the only time in my life I could ever do a full lotus cross-legged position and hold it for a while – but the stretching part was very, very painful. After two hours, though, it was as he said: the body softened and the mind silenced. I just had to cross my legs, focus on the breathing and, almost immediately, I'd fall into bliss.

Most yoga teachers wouldn't push students that hard, but nonetheless the millions of people in the West practising yoga do get something from it. The latest 'Yoga in America study' published by the Yoga Journal[1] indicates that 20.4 million Americans (82 per cent of them women) now practise yoga, an increase of 29 per cent from the previous study, in 2008. According to Sat Bir Khalsa, an assistant professor at Harvard Medical School and a leading researcher on the psychological effects of yoga, there are three main reasons that attract people to this ancient practice: seeking wellbeing, doing physical exercise and managing stress. A fourth, less common motive is the search for a blissful or spiritual experience[2].

Yoga as medicine

I first met Sat Bir Khalsa in July 2012. I learned he was coming to the UK to give a series of seminars and invited him to Oxford's psychiatry department, home to one of the world's leading centres for the study of mindfulness, to talk about his work. I'd seen pictures of him wearing a Sikh turban but, when we first shook hands, I quickly realized he wasn't Asian: born of Canadian parents, he was a pale-skinned and bright blue-eyed man. He was also thin with a long, untrimmed beard and he spoke softly, almost shyly, but had a generous, sharp sense of humour.

Sat Bir's approach to the study and uses of yoga was grounded and sensible. He talked about yoga as preventive medicine and was particularly interested in introducing the practice to children and schools.

'Think of it as kind of mental hygiene,' he said. 'One hundred years ago, dental hygiene was introduced in the school curricula and it completely changed our habits. Before then people didn't clean their teeth regularly. Now, we learn it at such an early age that we don't think about it. We can do the same with yoga and introduce mental hygiene early in children's lives.' Sat Bir believes that yoga can improve mental health, particularly through its deeply relaxing, stress-buffering effects – for which there is scientific evidence[3]. As I listened to him talk, I thought that it made sense that yoga would attract those living hectic lifestyles – it provides a way to de-stress after a busy day. In those cases, though, yoga isn't really promoting change, rather it's enabling stressed-out people to better cope with their fast-paced lives; if anything, in this scenario yoga reinforces that way of living.

Overcoming trauma

However, recent research has looked into yoga as a means

to treat a more specific kind of stress – post-traumatic stress disorder (PTSD)[4], the symptoms of which include flashbacks, nightmares, an exaggerated startle response, and a feeling of being constantly 'on guard'. Trauma, from the Greek word for 'wound', is one of the psychological words that made it into popular culture almost a century ago. According to Freud, the psychological difficulties many of us suffer as adults have their roots in trauma from our early lives. Research tells us that Freud's insight was right – but trauma, such as that experienced as a result of life-threatening accidents or violence, can of course also occur in adult life. Although not all people who experience a traumatic event will go on to develop PTSD, it is far from uncommon, with some studies suggesting a prevalence rate of around 20 per cent.

At the Trauma Center in Brookline, Massachusetts, therapists use yoga to help war veterans and victims of childhood abuse and neglect. The idea is as simple as it is innovative: if trauma leaves an imprint that makes you relive a horrific situation time and again, making you feel unsafe in your own body, yoga can create a new sense of safety and balance, helping counteract that imprint. Through its slow-moving postures and deep breathing, yoga enables you to find a calmer way of being in your body. The Trauma Center's director, Dr Bessel van der Kolk, acknowledges that doing yoga, focusing on body and breathing, can cause quite a reaction in traumatized people: 'the instructors should expect strong emotional material to emerge during the classes[5]'.

A forensic psychologist working with criminal psychopaths at a prison near Cambridge, England, has told me something similar. Many of these individuals have experienced severe childhood trauma, such as sexual or physical abuse, and don't have a positive experience of being in their own bodies. She is interested in introducing yoga classes for these prisoners to help them have a different – less threatening – embodied experience. It makes sense that the deeply embodied experience of trauma may emerge and perhaps be healed through yoga's simple but evocative postures; I can envisage how some of the *asanas* may work as a silent drama that creates a new relationship between the self and the body. But is this potential for healing through body exercises exclusive to yoga or could we see evidence of it in other, similar Eastern techniques, such Tai-Chi or Chi-Gong; or even in silent acting, or psychodrama? We need further and better-quality studies to be able to answer this question, although we know there are other mental health problems, such as depression, for which yoga seems to be effective, and it has been recommended as a complement to mainstream interventions[6]. On the other hand for conditions such as schizophrenia there is no evidence that practising yoga makes any difference[7].

I spoke to Sat Bir again at a conference and learned more about his interest in yoga. 'How did you get into the study of yoga?' I asked. 'I suspect there are not many people at Harvard doing it.'

'I had wanted to study it since the late 1970s. As soon as I finished my undergraduate degree at Harvard, I approached Herbert Benson; he was at the time doing studies on transcendental meditation and the relaxation response. "Are you a medical doctor?" he asked me. I wasn't; my degree was in psychology. He apologized and told me he could only take on people as researchers who already made enough from their practice to earn a living, because he had no funds to actually employ anyone.'

Sat Bir paused and looked straight at me; his eyes glittered. 'It took me over twenty years to do the research that I always dreamed of.' My jaw dropped – twenty years is half of a working lifetime! Sat Bir had to first gain an academic reputation in the treatment of sleep disorders before winning the funding to move into yoga research in 2000. I felt spoiled in comparison; the longest I'd had to endure to get a research idea off the ground was two to three years. I admired his perseverance and felt somewhat ashamed of my own hesitant position – although I enjoyed yoga and meditation, and *hoped* that they could lead to personal change, I needed to see the evidence to be convinced.

Buddhism for depression

While promising, the research into the psychological effects of yoga is far, far less than the whopping number of scientific publications that exist on the study of Buddhism-based meditation – many of them funded by government agencies. In the USA by 1998 there were seven agency-funded meditation studies – a number that grew to 89 in 2008 and 122 in 2009. Most of these studies focused on the effects of mindfulness[8].

Mindfulness has become something of a buzzword. Million-selling books, CDs and Apps tell you that mindfulness can make you happier, more compassionate, wiser, and less depressed. The UK's National Health Service (NHS) offers mindfulness-based therapy as a treatment for recurrent depression. Mindfulness has even made it into Parliament, where an all-party group practises it – on the Oxford Mindfulness Centre homepage, there is a recent photo of Mark Williams and Jon Kabat-Zinn, the two Western mindfulness gurus, standing together in front of 10 Downing Street, London, the official residence and office of the British Prime Minister. Some people even suggest that mindfulness should be mandatory practice in schools to fight mental health problems among the young[9].

Thirty years after Hindu-based transcendental meditation (TM) produced the first wave of meditation studies, which fell short of gaining wide recognition, the more publicized findings of the second wave of meditation research have made Buddhist mindfulness welcomed by health services, councils and schools. While TM is based on a technique of focused meditation that aims to achieve mystical unity with the universe, mindfulness practice originates from modern Theravada Buddhism and has the goal of creating a state of 'bare awareness', through non-judgment and acceptance of what you think and feel.

The attempt to shape mindfulness into a technique without Buddhist religion is probably why we're more readily open to accepting it in the West. Unlike TM, mindfulness requires no specific mantra, nor a single overarching organization to promote it. Its gurus are white-collar scientists, instead of ascetic Hindus. But within the realms of medicine and therapy, the scope and aims of mindfulness-based interventions are very similar to those of TM. We use mindfulness to help with an assortment of physical and psychological ailments – pain, depression, anxiety, eating disorders, neuroticism, negative emotions, heart disease, blood pressure – as well as to increase wellbeing and cognitive capacities. Both approaches also envision that meditation will reinforce peaceful, empathic and compassionate behaviours.

There is, at least, one major difference in the way these techniques were scientifically approached. While much of the original research efforts around TM focused on showing how it led to a unique state of consciousness, studies on mindfulness boomed after it started being used to treat depression. According to the World Health Organisation, 350 million people worldwide live with depression, and one million people commit suicide each year[10]. We also now know that depression has a very high rate of recurrence: if you have it once, there is a 50 per cent chance you will have another episode; if you have it twice the odds for recurrence increase to 70 per cent; and with three or more episodes you're almost certain (90 per cent likely) to go through depression again at some point in your life[11]. It seems that in some people, depression is like a dormant virus in the mind, and will come back to life again and again – unless, that is, you find an effective way of shutting it down and rebooting.

Defining depression

When something negative happens – a disappointment, a personal failure, or a relationship breakdown – it is perfectly healthy to feel sad. If you are depressed, however, even a relatively minor incident can trigger a shower of negative thoughts and feelings. Think of a time when you rang a friend a couple of times and she didn't return your call. Many of us would probably be mildly annoyed or reckon she must be really busy. If you're depressed, though, such an event could trigger off a spiral of negative thoughts: 'Perhaps I did something wrong', or 'She must be angry at me', which soon becomes 'Why am I so bad at relationships?' before the real hammering of self-esteem kicks in – 'Nobody loves me, I'm unlovable', finishing off with 'What's the point of being alive?' Negative thoughts and emotions, and feelings of worthlessness and hopelessness are draining and exhausting. Brain-imaging studies show that the neural mechanisms underlying the suffering of depression and the sensitivity to physical pain are very similar[12]: depression literally hurts.

When we talk about personal change, we think of it in a positive light – a change towards a better self. However, the most extreme instance of personal change you'll probably ever witness is the one in which a normally positive person enters a severe bout of depression. I was only nine years old when I first witnessed this dramatic level of personal change. Coming back from school one day, I noticed something odd with my grandmother. I knew her as an unusually energetic and cheerful person. She always had a song to help me go to sleep and another to make me rise in the morning. On that day, however, instead of hugging me and whizzing around the house, she sat on a chair in the bedroom with the blinds half shut, looking down and clasping her hands tightly. There was a sound of rubbing fingers and a gentle but pained muttering, like a mantra. I approached her thinking that perhaps she had hurt her hands. As I walked into the darkened room, I understood what she kept repeating in a low, tortured hum: '... at nothing, I'm good at nothing.'

I was very confused. When my mother arrived and saw what was happening, she simply turned to me and said, 'Grandma's

depressed, it's happened before.' Grandma stayed like that for
the next eight years – emerging from the cycle at about the same
time I became interested in psychology, spirituality and the idea
of personal transformation. No doubt her depression played a
major role in my growing interest. I wanted my loving, active
granny back, not that pale, tormented shadow. Antidepressants
didn't work and she refused psychotherapy. I'd begun reading
about relaxation and meditation and was seriously thinking
that they could help her when, one day, as suddenly as it had
appeared, her depression lifted. Some ten years later, when I
asked her about what had happened, she told me 'I can't explain
it; the will to live came back, but I don't know why.'

Mindfulness and transformation

In part because of my grandmother's experience, I'd been
interested in the idea that meditation might help with depression.
I realized that TM had been used as a treatment for more than
forty years, but what about mindfulness? It turned out to be the
trump card – using mindfulness to treat depression paved the way
for scientists, health organizations, politicians and the wider public
to welcome this practice with open arms.

It all happened rather quickly. The first major clinical trial
on mindfulness for the treatment of recurrent depression was
published in 2000, but the bulk of the research findings appeared
during the course of only six years, between 2004 and 2010. A first
review of the evidence published in 2007 wasn't very positive:
15 controlled studies of mindfulness meditation seemed to show
no reliable improvement in the symptoms of anxiety and negative
mood[13]. However, by 2011, an article that examined the combined
effect of six mindfulness trials on depression showed that among
those who had suffered three or more episodes of depression,
an eight-week course of mindfulness-based cognitive therapy
(MBCT) very significantly decreased the chances of becoming
depressed again. Overall, 58 per cent in the control group became

depressed again, but for those in the mindfulness treatment only 38 per cent had a relapse[14].

I remember first hearing about the early mindfulness research from Mark Williams himself. Shortly after being appointed as a Professor of Clinical Psychology at Oxford University, he gave a talk on his work at the Department of Experimental Psychology. My doctoral supervisor, Mansur Lalljee, suggested that I might find it interesting. Not long after his talk, my friend and colleague Catherine Crane joined Mark Williams' research team. Catherine and I had shared an open office in the department. She was doing research on irritable bowel syndrome patients, while I was hopping around spiritual talks and workshops trying to pin down the personality and cognitive profile of people interested in 'new age' activities such as reiki, past-life regression, shamanism – and also meditation. Back then she was my first port of call when I needed help with statistics; in exchange I kept her entertained with stories from my research. Neither of us dreamed that in the near future she would be working on major clinical trials using a Buddhist meditation technique very familiar to many of the spiritual people I was studying. Within a short time Catherine became a senior researcher heading the development of a number of studies on the effects of mindfulness in the treatment of depression and helping to set up the Oxford Mindfulness Centre. When she started I remember her telling me about meditating at work.

'That sounds rather nice,' I said.

'Well, yes,' she replied, 'except when it's really early and you have to make a huge effort to keep awake.'

I kept an eye on the growing literature on mindfulness. When, in 2008, I started lecturing at the same department where Catherine and I had done our doctorates, I chose one of the early articles on the use of mindfulness for depression for a master's level class I was teaching on research methods. The aim was to develop a critical look at published studies, point out frailties in theory and discuss problems with method and statistical analysis. By learning to critique other people's research, I hoped my students would learn to develop their own.

In one of these classes, an outspoken student pulled apart the first study from 2000, which showed that mindfulness helped prevent a relapse into depression[15]: 'To start with they don't have a proper control group. There are, like, people meditating for eight weeks, which is something they've never done before, so there is this whole build up of expectations and motivation to perform – did they check for these expectations? No. And, on the other hand, you have this control group or treatment as usual where they keep seeing their GP, what … once every six months, or seeing a counsellor once every couple of months? This is completely different from a medical trial with a proper placebo, right? No placebo at all. But what bugs me most is the very conceptual foundation: this is Buddhist meditation, right – so are these guys actually using science to validate Buddhist religion?'

THE 'RED BALLOON EFFECT'

Something of this student's remarks stayed with me. Pictures of the Dalai Lama with scientists involved in mindfulness research were popping up in the media and Catherine Crane told me he was a regular presence at conferences. Mindfulness research didn't seem to have the same kind of religious agenda as TM, but I couldn't see how it could possibly have cut the Buddhism from the technique. This was at the back of my mind when I taught a day course on the psychology of yoga and meditation with Catherine; she covered the mindfulness-based therapy on depression, while I focused on the psychological effects of yoga and TM.

It was a sunny day in early November and the course was fully booked. Most people had tried meditation before. Catherine and I had agreed to show a short video of Jon Kabat-Zinn leading a mindfulness workshop[16]. Despite not being a spiritual guru, he has the charisma of one: assertive, focused and empathic, he clearly knows how to engage with an audience. Early in the film he conveys that Buddhist-based meditation can be detached from its religious aura to help 'regular folk': '[People] are being sent by their doctors for all sorts of very real problems and they're not at all interested in yoga or swamis or gurus or Zen masters or enlightenment – they're suffering. And they're coming because they want some relief from their suffering.'

During her introduction to the use of mindfulness therapy for depression, Catherine explained that there were a number of important factors about how the technique works that scientists were still uncertain about. A crucial problem is how to pinpoint the active ingredient of mindfulness that helps with the depression. Is it the actual meditation or could it be the cognitive psychological education in recognizing one's symptoms and trying to detach from negative thoughts? Understanding this was one of the aims of the most rigorous study ever conducted on the effects of mindfulness therapy for depression. Catherine was on a team of researchers led by Mark Williams and they had been working on this project for the past three years[17]. Almost 300 people with at least three prior episodes of depression were randomly allocated to three different groups: an MBCT group, a group for cognitive psychological education (similar in all aspects to the first group, except that there was no meditation involved), and a regular control group in which people just kept visiting their GPs or counsellors as they normally did.

It was the first time that a mindfulness study used an active control group that so closely mirrored the intervention. Cognitive education participants met for the same amount of time in groups (two hours each week over the course of eight weeks) and learned to recognize the warning signs of depression and disengage from them, exactly as in the MBCT treatment group. They also did the same homework, which included worksheets on which they were asked to write down automatic thoughts, and pleasant and unpleasant events. Participants were assessed three,

6, 9 and 12 months after the treatment. I was impressed to learn that the researchers themselves did not know who received MBCT and who received cognitive education up to the moment the major results had been analyzed.

The Oxford Mindfulness Centre scientists expected MBCT to reduce depression relapse when compared with the groups undergoing cognitive pschological education and their usual treatment. Such a finding would prove that mindfulness meditation is the magical ingredient in the MBCT treatment of recurrent depression. However, the results did not support the hypothesis: the relapse rates were close to 50 per cent for all three groups.

I was focusing carefully on the graphs of the results Catherine was presenting of this yet-unpublished study. She caught my eye for a moment and paused to ask if everyone was still following her. Then she continued: 'But we did find something else. Mindfulness worked better for participants with a history of childhood trauma and abuse. If you had a high score on trauma and abuse as a child and were in the mindfulness therapy group, the rate for relapse was only 41 per cent compared to 55 per cent if you were in the cognitive education group and 65 per cent if you were on the control group.'

She showed a slide with the questionnaire they had used to assess childhood trauma. It had statements like 'I had to wear dirty clothes', 'I got hit so badly that it was noticed by someone like a neighbour, teacher or doctor', 'People in my family called me things like stupid, ugly or lazy' or 'Someone tried to touch me in a sexual way or made me touch them.' The study clearly implied that if you'd suffered events such as these as a child, MBCT may help prevent recurrent depression during adulthood. On the other hand if you'd had a fairly decent childhood, mindfulness seemed to have no greater or lesser effect for recurrent depression than a regular visit to your GP.

Students in the course looked mildly disappointed by these results. I was stunned. Only four years previously the British

National Institute for Health and Care Excellence (NICE)[18] had given MBCT a 'key priority status'. In other words MBCT had been recommended as one of the best psychological interventions to prevent recurrent depression, when drugs have failed – a recommendation that now seemed premature.

The study appeared online shortly after the day course, on 2 December 2013, in the *Journal of Consulting and Clinical Psychology*, the top journal for psychotherapy techniques. As well as confirming everything Catherine had told us during the course, the article ventured an explanation for *why* MBCT works better with people who suffered childhood trauma and abuse:

'Certain elements of the approach (e.g. acceptance, self-compassion, and decentering) are well matched for addressing the factors that increase risk in these patients [...] Indeed, MBCT may facilitate emotional processing by encouraging participants to remain in contact with painful material rather than avoiding it or becoming entangled in rumination about it. However, further research [...] would be necessary to test these specific hypotheses.' (pp.284–85).

I think the article's authors are right that mindfulness helps patients to avoid getting bogged down in ruminating, repetitive thoughts – after all, mindfulness meditation is about being fully present in the moment, noticing that a thought is there and letting it go before becoming carried away with it. But I'm not as convinced that mindfulness encourages patients to be in touch with trauma-related emotions.

Perhaps the study really showed that rather than putting the patients in contact with their underlying trauma, mindfulness meditation allowed them to bypass or flee the emotional pain – a kind of 'red balloon effect'.

The Red Balloon (1956) is a French film shot in the not-so-trendy streets of Paris. It features a young child who finds a large, bright red balloon. He keeps it and quickly realizes that the balloon follows him everywhere. As the boy–balloon friendship develops, we notice that this child has no human friends, is bullied by his peers and mistreated by adults. The other children covet his friend-balloon and find a way to steal it, but as they fight for it, the balloon bursts and 'dies'. The little boy finds what remains of his friend-balloon and as he holds it, alone and sad, all over Paris large balloons flee their owners and rush to comfort the boy. In the last scene of the film, we see the child floating into the sky holding dozens of balloons, moving away from all the people who mistreated him.

The image is as enticing as it is dangerous. Our natural reaction is to avoid pain, whether physical or emotional. Your mind will do all it can to keep away from where it hurts the most. Indeed, avoidance behaviours are characteristic of PTSD; sufferers seek to stay away from things or people that remind them of the traumatic event. The child flying away across the Paris sky provides a perfect metaphor for human desire to bypass reality, especially when the world has hurt us badly.

Of course, we'd need further research to know for sure that the participants in the study were succumbing to the red balloon effect. However, it's possible that people with a higher incidence of childhood trauma and abuse, who reacted better to the mindfulness intervention, were using the meditation as a way to avoid the pain rather than to acknowledge it and deal with it. Although meditation might have helped them in the short term, avoidance can't last for ever.

A soon as the article was published, I began to look forward to an open discussion of its results, including the possibility of a red balloon effect. I imagined dramatic headlines in the media: 'Mindfulness helps only the traumatized' or even simply 'Mindfulness study for depression fails.' But there was nothing. Days and weeks went by and there was no mention of the new article, either in the media or in science forums. I just checked it again, seven months after its online publication, and zip. Silence.

Sexy science

I kept an eye on mindfulness news. There was nothing on the depression study, but one journalist had been busy writing long pieces for the BBC and the *Guardian* on how mindfulness could help to prevent the effects of ageing; the subheading of the BBC news article read 'One Nobel Prize-winner is finding the scientific in the spiritual.[19]' The tone of the story reminded me of the early days of meditation research when top scientists were teaming up with TM meditators to show how meditation was able to produce a unique physiological state. In the BBC piece a psychiatrist influenced by Deepak Chopra joins forces with Elizabeth Blackburn, a Nobel Prize winner for her work on telomerase, an enzyme that plays a role in delaying the ageing process of cells. After working together on a project that investigated levels of stress and telomerase in mothers who looked after chronically ill children, they moved on to study the effects of mindfulness on this enzyme that facilitates the replacement of parts of the DNA, thereby 'rejuvenating' cells. In one study, the article reports, researchers had found that taking a three-month meditation retreat increased telomerase activity by 30 per cent when compared to a control group. This means that meditation may have the potential to slow down the ageing process.

I was intrigued and read the science papers on mindfulness and this enzyme. The most ambitious was the three-month meditation retreat study in which researchers flew sixty participants to a mountain resort in northern Colorado and randomly assigned them to one of two groups. One group would stay at the retreat meditating for at least six hours a day, while the other would return home to their everyday lives, flying back to the Colorado mountain twice more to fill in some questionnaires and once again to give a blood sample. It was a hugely expensive project – the BBC article mentions a $4 million figure, a figure in meditation research surpassed only by the transcendental meditation 'reduction crime study' in Washington, D.C., in 1993, which involved 4,000 meditators and cost $4.2 million.

Because the telomerase enzyme is sensitive to stress, Blackburn and her colleagues threw in a number of related psychological measures, including perceived control and emotional stability (neuroticism). They also assessed mindfulness through a questionnaire that included statements such as 'I watch my feelings without getting lost in them', 'When I have distressing thoughts or images, I am able just to notice them without reacting', or 'I pay attention to how my emotions affect my thoughts and behaviour.' If most questionnaires have a certain level of subjectivity, one that asks people actively interested in meditation about their level of mindfulness is really far from ideal. To control for what psychologists have called 'social desirability effects' – in this case the interest in showing off how mindful you are – researchers can use other questionnaires to ask about expectations of meditation practice or the tendency to project a favourable image of ourselves, neither of which were reported in this ambitious and expensive study[20].

Analyzing the results
After three months of meditation, the study found that neuroticism decreased while sense of control and mindfulness improved. The reduction in neuroticism was not that surprising – many TM studies have already shown it. What was interesting, however, was that telomerase activity improved in the retreat group compared to the control participants. But what was the cause? Was it as a result of the meditation itself, or simply because one group was away from the hustle and bustle of everyday life for three months? To answer this question, the researchers did a 'mediation analysis'. This allows us to understand if the relationship between two factors (imagine intelligence and body weight) can be explained by a third factor (for example, years of formal education).

The researchers found that perceived control and neuroticism mediated the level of telomerase activity, but mindfulness didn't. That is, the enzyme activity changes not because of how much more mindful you've become, but because of other psychological factors tied in to being away from your everyday busy life. The researchers tried a different way to find an association between the amount of time spent doing various types of meditation (mindfulness of breathing, observing mental events or observing the nature of consciousness) and the other factors, but failed to find any. The time their participants spent in any of the meditation practices was not associated with either the psychological or telomerase measures.

Moving forwards or moving in circles

I was mulling over these results and the BBC article as if they were pieces of a jigsaw that didn't fit when my phone rang. Ute, a postdoctoral researcher working with me, wanted to discuss a study we were planning that involved transcranial direct current stimulation, a relatively new and painless technique of brain stimulation. I went to her office to talk it over.

'First,' she said, 'I've got something that may interest you for your book. This paper on stress and meditation is hot from the press; it's really good, I think.' She handed it over; it had come out in *Psychoneuroendocrinology*, the same journal that published the three-month-meditation retreat study I'd just read. Despite its longwinded title – 'Brief mindfulness meditation training alters psychological and neuroendocrine responses to social evaluative stress' – the writing was clear and succinct and the study's method a lot more rigorous than we often find in meditation research[21]. To start with, the research team led by J. David Creswell, an associate professor at Carnegie Mellon University, never mentioned in the adverts calling for participants that the study would involve meditation. This alone reduces the potential for bias – there was less chance of recruiting volunteers with a particular interest in meditation. Then, instead of contrasting the mindfulness group with a group that did nothing, participants in the control group were engaged with analytical training, which carefully mirrored the mindfulness intervention by increasing the complexity of the tasks over three days.

To know for certain that the mindfulness and analytical training weren't perceived as more or less positive, all participants filled in a questionnaire about their expectations of both types of training. The answers showed clear leaning, however: those in the mindfulness group were more confident of the benefits of this intervention than those in the analytical training group. I suspect that this is the case with all meditation studies, but researchers rarely control for levels of expectation.

After three days of mindfulness or analytical training, participants were subjected to a nervewracking task known as the Trier Stress Protocol (it gets its name from the German city of Trier, where it was created). The article gives a good description of the task:

'Participants were seated in front of two evaluators trained to be cold and non-accepting. They first gave a five-minute speech addressing why they would be a good administrative assistant for a hypothetical job in the department, and then completed five minutes of difficult mental arithmetic (specifically, counting backwards from 2083 in units of 17). The evaluators interrupted participants during the speech task to ask critical questions and during the arithmetic task to point out mistakes and ask them to restart counting from 2083. The evaluators also instructed participants on several occasions to sit as still as possible in the chair and to maintain eye contact throughout the speech and arithmetic tasks.' (pp.4–5)

I have used this procedure before and it never fails to arouse high stress. In fact merely telling participants to prepare for the speech task is enough to raise heart rate and stress levels. Creswell's study was no exception: he found that the Trier task increased both the questionnaire reports of stress and the participants' levels of cortisol, the steroid hormone associated with stress. But did the mindfulness group react better to the stressful task? Yes, on the questionnaire measure; the mindfulness group participants had lower levels of perceived stress. But, surprisingly, the opposite was true for biological stress: cortisol was higher in the mindfulness group than in the analytical training group.

People in the mindfulness group had a higher expectation that the training would have positive effects, and this is likely to be why they scored lower on the stress questionnaire: they were more motivated, they wanted the training to have an impact. However, the biological cortisol analysis showed the opposite result. Creswell suggests that the short mindfulness training may have actually exhausted cognitive resources rather than improved them, especially among those with low mindfulness ability.

Sexing up the statistics

I thought the results of this study would be picked up by the media and searched various combinations of words such as 'mindfulness increases stress' or 'meditation fails to reduce stress hormone', but found media articles stating only the opposite. One of these was an article published on the US newspaper website, the *Huffington Post*, in March 2013, entitled; 'Mindfulness meditation could lower levels of cortisol, the stress hormone.' I scanned very quickly through it and stopped here: 'For the study, 57 people spent three months in a meditation retreat, where they were taught mindful breathing, observation skills, and cultivation of "positive" mental states like compassion.'

What's this? It looked like Blackburn's study, but using cortisol rather than telomerase activity (see p.115)[22]. I downloaded the scientific paper to find that it was, indeed, the very same. Blackburn wasn't one of the authors, but there were others who contributed to both articles; plus, the sources of funding and the details of the study were identical. This is an example of the old academic joke: 'If you have a rat in the lab and inject it with a substance, what comes out? Five science articles!' It's not only a bad joke; it's a sour one because it can make for bad science. By having a small number of participants and a large number of measures that you break into various analyses (and articles), you're increasing the chances of committing what scientists call a 'type-1 error'. This means you're much more likely to find a statistically significant effect where there is none.

The article reported in the *Huffington Post* looked like an example of 'sexing up data', an expression I learned years ago from a neuroscientist colleague. We were looking at some statistical results and, as it happens, they didn't completely fit our initial hypotheses.

'It's not too bad,' she said. 'We can sex it up.' She went on to explain that she meant selecting the best results and reporting only these or, if there were secondary results that were less sexy, framing them in a more appealing way and publishing them separately from the sexiest results.

'Isn't that Hollywood science?' I asked.

'Don't be stupid,' she answered. 'Everyone does it.'

How did the researchers in the three-month meditation retreat 'sex up' their results? First, they didn't clearly mention what other measures – many others! – had been taken; they reported only the mindfulness questionnaire, also used in the telomerase study, and cortisol. Second, they found no differences between cortisol levels before and after the retreat, which means that three months of meditating, far away from everyday hassles, didn't have an impact on stress. Instead of highlighting this as the most robust result, they swiftly moved on – because a negative result isn't that sexy. Third, not having found a difference in stress levels as a result of the meditation, the researchers reported a finding that was positive – a correlation between their questionnaire on mindfulness and stress, showing that the more mindful you are, the lower your cortisol. This was the result that I'd found in the *Huffington Post*. However, in reality, it's merely a weak secondary result based on a questionnaire.

A similar sexing up happened with the telomerase study: there was no mention of cortisol despite the fact that telomerase activity is particularly affected by stress. The end result: two articles published in good science journals (one of them including a scientist who's a Nobel Prize winner), which have gained widespread – but misleading – media coverage. Neither of them actually shows robust evidence that three months of meditation decreases either a stress hormone or a rejuvenating enzyme. Researchers selected and published the results separately when it would have been more honest to put them together, even if the conclusions would be less attractive.

But we can't blame the scientists; they're only following the rules of the game. Furthermore, they have expectations about what they'd like to find after spending months or years carefully designing and implementing studies. Psychology is particularly vulnerable to what have been called 'experimenter effects' – the way we may unwittingly direct participants towards the results we want to get. With the hype around mindfulness, experimenter effects are more likely to occur and, as the Creswell study on stress and mindfulness shows, it's not only experimenters but also participants who want the technique to work.

As I kept reading information about the science of mindfulness, I realized that not everyone was positive about it. There were a few critical voices – not of scientists, though, but of Buddhists.

FROM McMINDFULNESS TO MINDLESSNESS

I was so wrapped up with the writing that I barely noticed the arrival of summer; and it was a very good one. I needed to get away from Oxford. For all its beautiful colleges and gardens, there is something unreal about the place, a kind of Disneyland feel, which has only become more pronounced with the *Harry Potter* industry. When the second film was released I watched it in one of the city's cinemas, a stone's throw from the Ashmolean Museum. By the time the film had finished, it was dusk and the dark yellow street lamps showered the streets and buildings with a hazy glow. I paused for a moment outside the cinema: it all looked eerily similar to the setting of the *Harry Potter* film.

One day I drove into the countryside and stayed in a B&B that was run by an Italian couple. They were quiet but moderately affable – 'A bit too quiet for Italians,' I thought. Over breakfast I spotted a large number of Buddhist books on a nearby shelf. 'Are you interested in Buddhism?' I asked.

Carlo, my host, smiled timidly and nodded. He was holding a plate of scrambled eggs, mushrooms and toast, which he slowly lowered onto the table. I was beginning to think that the nod was the full answer, then he expanded.
'Yes, my partner and I trained in counselling and mindfulness at a Buddhist centre.'

'Ah, so you give mindfulness courses?'
'Yes,' he said.
'Do you follow Kabat-Zinn's model for stress reduction?
'No.'
'Mindfulness-based cognitive therapy?'
He sighed deeply before answering. 'No.' His face was flushed. 'We're interested in real personal change.'

'How's that different from what the mindfulness therapy models are looking for?'

'Well... it looks the same but it's not; they're not doing proper Buddhist meditation. The mindfulness clinical application is just the first step. I ... I'm not saying that it doesn't work; it can have a powerful effect – it makes you feel more in control, or excited about being more aware of what you're thinking and feeling. But if it stops there, the meditation will simply reinforce the ego, the egoistical self.' Carlo paused. 'I'm sorry, I'm not explaining it very well.'

'No, no, I think you are. What you're saying is that secular mindfulness models don't really lead to real personal change.'

'Not unless there is a call to go deeper. You can't inject some meditation into a person and hope that it will change her. To get to the heart of mindfulness, to the place where you find true compassion for all beings, you need to unwrap the self. And you can't do that without the other aspects of Buddhism – right thinking, right action ...'

'You mean ethical guidelines?'

'Huh, I suppose. Mindfulness is more than just awareness without judging; it's about developing the right mind, the right kind of awareness. Clinical or science mindfulness is a very, very narrow application of true mindfulness; it distorts its true goal.'

'Enlightenment?' I asked hesitantly. Carlo looked up, scratching his chin.

'The goal,' he said, looking straight into my eyes, 'is to end the illusion of the self; to end the cycle of birth and rebirth.'

Dilemma or dichotomy

I wasn't aware that any Buddhists were unhappy with the way scientists were using its meditation techniques – but I soon found that Carlo was not alone in his views. In fact some Buddhists were writing about the challenges of the secular approach. Wakoh Hickey, a scholar of religious studies and an ordained Zen priest is one of the discontented. In 2010 she published a critique of 'meditation as medicine'[23]. Her arguments were: first, the mindfulness-as-science movement erases the truth about Buddhist history. Buddhism isn't mostly about meditation, quite the opposite – its practices are centred on devotion and good deeds. Second, it neglects that the foundation of meditation is good moral conduct. Third, the mindfulness movement is highly individualistic, while Buddhist practice is centred on community. A fourth related problem is that it treats psychological suffering as an individual problem, and overlooks its social causes, like poverty and racism.

Hickey's fifth and last point is particularly revealing. Despite not being a scientist, she criticizes the lack of scientific rigour in mindfulness research and suggests there is a need for the scientific community to be honest about the limitations of this work. Surprisingly, she quotes some sharp comments by the Dalai Lama at a conference where scientists discussed the clinical applications of mindfulness. At the end of the meeting, the Dalai Lama remarked:

'For me, *analytical* meditation is more useful.' He explained that it is important to analyze the source of our pain, which is often rooted in an effort to grasp at impermanence, or in self-centeredness, or in an unrealistic view of our situation. Each of these problems requires a different kind of approach. (p.177) The Dalai Lama did not elaborate on what these suited approaches were, but at the end of his comments, he admitted that when he wants to use his intelligence more effectively, he prefers 'sound sleep better than meditation'.

All this is very sensible but, some could argue, it betrays Hickey and the Dalai Lama's interest in defending their own religious traditions from being distorted and commercialized – and prescribed – as a 'Buddha pill' for stress or depression. I guess it would be similar, from a Western Christian perspective, if one were to turn the Hail Mary prayer into a scientific technique to treat headaches. But if it works, why not use it? For Buddhists, though, that is distorting the purpose of meditation. Its original aim was to be a tool to go 'beyond the ego', but it has instead become a way of reinforcing our needs and desires. Some critics argue that this is not mindfulness but 'McMindfulness' – a contemplative technique that has moved from psychology laboratories and therapy rooms into large corporations, secular and sellable[24]. Why? To keep employees happy at work; after all, a happy employee is probably more productive. An article published in *The Economist* suggests that 'Western capitalism seems to be doing rather more to change Eastern religion than Eastern religion is doing to change Western capitalism.[25']

Thinking about Google's own mindfulness course for its employees – called 'Search Inside Yourself' – such a statement is not necessarily an exaggeration. Chade-Meng Tan, an exsoftware engineer who became a Jolly Good Fellow (his actual job title at Google), personally sponsors scientific research on mindfulness and believes it can bring peace to the world. Seeking to fulfil his job description at Google (which according to his website is simply to 'enlighten minds, open hearts, create world peace'), he started the course there in 2007 to change people's lives. According to website testimonials[26], Blaise, a sales engineer, is now much calmer in overcoming objections when doing product demonstrations and can speak compassionately about competitors. Another course completer now feels much more empathic and loves her 'new me'; another reversed her decision to leave Google after doing the course. Overall, Tan claims that all who took his course 'have become much better at what they do'. Or, in more cynical words, they have become more productive and reliable employees?

'McMindfulness' must present a double-edged sword for many Buddhist leaders. On the one hand scientists and the media all over the world are acknowledging the ancient tradition they teach, while on the other secular mindfulness is a watered-down or mutated version of what they believe and practise. Buddhists might not like this new way for their tradition, but feel they have to be careful about speaking against it.

I found one excellent example of this tension reading through the correspondence between Allan Wallace, a respected Western Buddhist monk and teacher, and the Venerable Bhikkhu Bodhi, a Tibetan Buddhist priest and scholar[27]. In the correspondence Wallace asks about the concept of *sati*, often translated as 'bare awareness' or 'bare attention'. Bodhi explains that while one of the aspects of *sati* can indeed be translated as bare attention, this is only the initial phase. In order to achieve right mindfulness, a practitioner also needs to develop *sampajanna*, which he translates as 'clear comprehension'. The Tibetan priest discusses the problem of leaving out this aspect of mindfulness and recounts an episode that happened to him when staying at the Insight

Meditation Society in Barre, not far from Boston, USA, a centre where many Americans come to experience meditation for the first time, or to develop their practice.

'At the end of the corridor where I did walking meditation, there was a sign that read, "Allow whatever arises." Whenever I walked toward the sign and it came into my field of vision, I would always think of the Buddha's saying, "Here, a monk does not tolerate an arisen thought of sensual desire ... ill-will ... cruelty ... or any other arisen unwholesome state, but abandons it, eliminates it, and completely dispels it." I was tempted to replace the sign there with one that had this saying, but fortunately I resisted the temptation. If I had been discovered, I might have been expelled.' (p.7)

There is some irony about a Buddhist priest and scholar having to repress his intention of removing a sign that portrays Buddha's teachings as 'value free'. However, the lack of ethical guidelines in Western mindfulness does not mean that its practice is belief-free. It certainly is individualistic, as Hickey argues, but its two root beliefs are: first, you believe that what is true and perfect lies *within*[28], and second that your inner experience is fundamentally true.

As far as the first belief goes, I had highlighted a couple of examples to write down here, but a better one popped up in my email. A friend of mine, currently doing a mindfulness-based stress reduction course in London, posted a picture of a short poem the instructor wrote in class as food for thought. This is what it said:

After all —
the world one carries
about oneself
is the important thing.
And the world outside
takes all its grace
and colour
and value.

The second belief means that what you experience through meditation is unarguably real. Put this together with the first and it makes perfect sense that you can and should allow any thoughts or feelings to arise. There is goodness and perfection within; you need only to experience it.

The experience fallacy

This is where I hoped psychology would come in and lend a hand to dispel an obvious fallacy. The 'experience fallacy' is the illusion that my subjective experience reflects true reality and is not affected by the thoughts or feelings I hold. In the context of meditation, the fallacy is this: what happens when I meditate, including the bliss or sadness I may feel, is not pure or unbiased. From the moment I recognize it as 'an experience', it means that I have thought of it and it is no longer 'it'. I am not implying that reality is a mere *Matrix*-like mental construction, I don't think it is; but especially when it comes to inner experience, we can never be too careful. It's not only psychologists who point this out – mystics from all traditions have warned against taking spiritual experiences for granted. St John of the Cross, for example, who was persecuted by the Inquisition for his unorthodox spiritual writings, noted that what one experiences in meditation as a voice coming from God is more often coming from one's unconscious mind[29].

Likewise, in Buddhism there is a long tradition of scrutinizing meditators' inner experiences. Robert Sharf, a professor of Buddhist studies at the University of California, Berkeley, has argued that the emphasis on unquestioned experience is a rather new development in the history of Buddhism[30]. In a recent talk he openly criticized psychologists and cognitive scientists for assuming that this unquestioned experience is the standard Buddhist position and suggests that the kind of mindfulness meditation they use in their studies 'emphasizes momentary states rather than long-term transformation and without a critical engagement it can lead to a kind of self-absorbing state which has been called a meditation sickness'[31].

Sharf mentions how even within Buddhist traditions such as Zen, which today we think of as strongly *experiential*, there used to be a suspicion of exalting 'inner experience'. Meditation without comprehension can be dangerous to our soul. An eighth-century spiritual teacher describes what happens to those who believe the purpose of meditation is to experience and stop thinking: they end up in a special realm – the hell of mindless beings.

LET'S THROW IN COMPASSION

Let me quickly recap on what appear to be the central implicit beliefs of the mindfulness-based therapy movement: you're more likely to find happiness within yourself than elsewhere, and what you experience through meditation is fundamentally true. A few paragraphs ago I wrote that I 'hoped psychology would come in and lend a hand to dispel an obvious fallacy'. Generally speaking, psychology has been doing exactly that for a very long time, at least since Freud. Psychologists have worked hard to determine and describe how we are biased not only in our thoughts, but our very visual perception of the world (for example, depending on which culture you come from, you tend to focus more on specific objects in front of you, or take a more holistic approach to what shows up in your visual field)[32].

Experience is very much like an autobiography – the story you tell of yourself is not what exactly happened. Furthermore, how you understand your own life's experiences actually changes with time. Over the course of your life, you'll retell the same childhood episode in different ways, according to the shifting perspective of your age, understanding and experience. Psychologists are acutely aware of all this; however, those studying mindfulness have, almost without exception, forgotten it.

Scientists introduced mindfulness as a method of experiencing reality without judgment: achieving 'bare attention' became not only an interesting concept, but a reality. Now the focus has moved on to a slightly different level. Mindfulness meditation seems to work for the individual – it alleviates pain and stress – but how does the mindful person act towards others? If some Buddhist moral precepts were added to the mindfulness technique, it wouldn't be a non-religious practice anymore. The solution: to add more experience to it. So, scientists have begun incorporating other Buddhist meditation techniques that focus on extremely positive feelings towards others – namely empathy and compassion.

This strand of research would not only show that meditation experience can change people, but that it can change them for the *better*. It would also silence the critics who looked down on secular mindfulness as self-absorbing or individualistic. And, apparently, the results show that it works: leading psychology journals have published a number of studies with titles such as 'Loving-kindness meditation increases social connectedness,[33]' 'Compassion meditation enhances empathic accuracy and related neural activity,[34]' or 'Loving-kindness meditation training decreases implicit intergroup bias.[35]'

Let me give a close-up of a study. In May 2013 one of the top experimental psychology journals, *Psychological Science*, published an article co-authored by Richard Davidson, one of the leading meditation scientists. Davidson and his colleagues studied the effects of compassion meditation on altruistic behaviour and brain activity[36]. The experimental design was elegant: participants were randomly allocated to either a compassion meditation condition or a control group of cognitive reappraisal. For 30 minutes a day for two weeks, they would either focus on feelings of compassion or reinterpret negative feelings associated with a personal stressful event.

If you were in the compassion meditation group, you began the training by thinking of a time when a friend or family member was suffering. After focusing on these difficult feelings, you wished their suffering to go away by repeating: 'May you be free from this suffering. May you have joy and happiness. May you be free from this suffering, May you have joy ...' As the days progress, you change the focus of the meditation. First, you try out being compassionate towards yourself, then towards a stranger, and finally towards a difficult person.

On the other hand if you were in the control group, you were asked to think of a stressful condition you had experienced from different perspectives: think how your friend, mum or dad would have reacted; then view the event with little emotion; finally, imagine you were looking back at it from a year's distance.

After two weeks of training, all participants were brought into the lab to undertake some tasks: the one reported in greater detail in the article involved playing an online economic game. These games usually work like this: you're given a certain amount of money and are then tricked to believe that you're actually going to play a game with people whom you can't see (often, you're told they're in the same building, but in a different room). Imagine you're given $5 to play. In this study participants were able to choose to use part of the money to help someone who was given only one dollar by a mean, dictator-like character. At the end of the game, each individual was paid the amount he or she kept. Basically, the more money you give to the unfortunate person, the less you keep for yourself; thus indicating your level of altruism.

The results showed that after doing the compassion meditation for two weeks, participants were more likely to give more money in the economic task. Those in the compassion group donated an average of $1.14, while those in the control group gave only $0.62.

The researchers had also brought participants into the lab before starting the training and put them inside a brain-imaging scanner. After two weeks they went into the scanner again – but this time with a difference. Compassion group participants were asked to spend their time in the scanner feeling compassion and repeating the mantra 'May you be free from suffering ...' while watching images of people suffering; the control group, on the other hand, were asked to reinterpret the 'emotional meaning of the images'.

Comparing the results of the economic test and the brain imaging, this is what the researchers found: participants in the compassion group showed a correlation between the amount of money they gave to the unfortunate fellow and greater activation of the inferior parietal cortex – a region of the brain that plays an important role in regulating how we think and feel about other people, including seeing others in pain. Researchers found this effect only for those in the compassion group, leading them to suggest that the activation of the inferior parietal cortex may be a 'unique neural marker for altruism' induced by compassion training.

If further research replicates and extends positive results such as these, the findings could become world changing. The TM movement had sought to change the world when practitioners attempted to prove that the concerted effort of meditators would eventually diminish aggression and increase peaceful and caring behaviours at the social level (see pp.65–9). However, where that attempt failed, the new wave of mindfulness studies seems to be succeeding, at least in gathering the hard data and spreading the message through media. Mindfulness-based interventions will always have critics – for example, atheists are likely to have a gut feeling against the whole procedure, finding such approaches as a compassion mantra far too like participating in prayer to make them comfortable.

Re-examining the evidence
For me, though, ensuring that each and every study – rather than each and every opinion – was methodologically rigorous and theoretically clear was most important of all. I took a step back to re-examine the evidence. By now, moving around my house and office was a hazardous activity – dog-eared piles of meditation papers were scattered precariously on tables, the floor; any bit of available space. I re-organized them and re-read the whole

batch of second-wave papers on mindfulness and compassion meditation. As I reacquainted myself with the body of research, the picture that emerged became ever-more clear to me. But I needed to make sure it wasn't just my way of looking at it.

Of all the articles I'd read, Jonathan Smith's accounts of TM (see pp.56–8) still scored most highly on the basis of rigour and ingenuity. No one but Smith had ever tried creating a meditation placebo to contrast against the Buddha pill. I looked him up and found that, although retired, he was still writing and lecturing on various topics, including mindfulness. A few days later we were talking over the phone. He was eager to discuss ideas. Since his early research on meditation, almost forty years earlier, he had written a number of books: a guide to relaxation, a critical book about parapsychological research and even a pseudo-religious epic entitled *God Speaks: The flying spaghetti monster in his own words*.

I told Jonathan I'd been carefully reviewing the second wave of meditation studies; the motivations and methodological problems I'd uncovered were very similar to those of the earlier TM research. 'No wonder,' he said. 'The corpus of mindfulness research is as sloppy as that of TM. No one ever bothered to come up with a credible placebo.'

'The motivations for the mindfulness research,' I told Jonathan, 'are quite similar to those of TM. There is an interest in showing that the experience of meditation can be a panacea: it not only makes people healthier and happier, but also less violent, and more caring and compassionate.'

'Listen, this new wave of studies on mindfulness is full of disingenuous scientists who are up to their necks in Buddhism.' I tried to protest, but he said, 'Look carefully. Check the control groups they're using.'

HUNDREDS OF STUDIES – BRINGING IT ALL TOGETHER

I wasn't sure Jonathan was necessarily right about mindfulness scientists being 'up their necks in Buddhism'. Most of them are probably just excited about a new technique with the power to help people. Among the hundreds of articles I had compiled, there were two recent meta-analyses on the effects of meditation. The first one, published in 2012, examined 163 studies conducted with non-clinical populations, and included such things as wellbeing, self-realization, negative emotions or intelligence[37]. The second article, published in 2014, analyzed 47 studies with clinical populations who were being treated for problems such as stress, depression or pain[38].

The first article showed that both mindfulness and TM had a moderately positive effect on most variables. These were the good news; the not-so-good news was that fewer than ten of the 163 studies had tried using an active control group (where people take part in an activity like muscular relaxation); most studies simply compared meditators with individuals who were put on a waiting list, during which time they kept on with their everyday lives. When you compared the active controls to the meditation condition, there were no differences; the meditation effect disappeared. Note that there is nothing scientifically wrong with using a waiting list as a control group; that's actually where you need to start if you're examining the effects of a new technique for the first time or testing it in a new population – in children, for example. When there is little or no evidence in the field, you need to show only that the activity you're evaluating is better than doing nothing at all. However, if someone else has already established that, you need to check that its effects are not owing to the fact that the participants are engaged in a new activity (and therefore feel positive about it, and expect it to have an effect).

The second article was more stringent; it included only studies in which the control group had also done some kind of task. Most of the time this was just a way to keep people occupied for the same amount of time as the daily practice of meditation. Some studies, though, had used more careful control conditions, such as physical exercise or relaxation. The results showed that, compared with a control group that was busy doing meaningless tasks, mindfulness had a moderate effect in reducing the effects of conditions such as anxiety, depression or pain. However, there was no evidence that mindfulness worked better than activities such as relaxation, exercise, or cognitive therapy. While you wouldn't necessarily expect mindfulness to work better than therapy, if the technique really makes a difference, surely it ought to have a deeper effect than simple relaxation or exercise.

There was no meta-analysis on the studies that focused on *how* people became better – that is, whether they became more altruistic or more empathic, for example – as a result of mindfulness or other Buddhist-adapted techniques, such as compassion meditation. To fill the gap I asked two postgraduate students to do a database search for articles related to meditation and various indicators of interpersonal behaviour and emotion, such as compassion, altruism, empathy, relationship quality, anger or forgiveness. They found more than 4,000 articles, but some of these were repeated. Furthermore, the vast majority either focused on the individual effects of meditation or were studies that did not have a random allocation to an experimental and control group. We excluded all of these from our assessments and ended up with thirty articles. I then asked Ute, the postdoctoral researcher I mentioned earlier (see p.117), to read those articles and categorize the main findings. Independently, I did the same.

Next time I saw Ute, I asked her about the meditation articles and she giggled. 'I'm almost done,' she said, giggling some more. 'I hope you won't be offended ... I know you're really interested in the topic but ... they're not very good.'

Ute had barely read any meditation studies before I asked her to do so. Her doctorate was on the neuroscience of emotions and she was working with me on a project unrelated to meditation. She had a vague interest in contemplative practices, but no clear ideas about whether they produced positive changes. Having read through the articles on how meditation can turn us into a better person, she and I reached the same conclusion – there are serious flaws with the research.

Generally, the studies lacked proper control groups; they also neglected to check people's expectations about the efficacy of meditation or the training in the active control condition, when there was one. The paper on compassion training by Davidson (see pp.129–30) turned out to be no exception: while the meditation group focused on extremely positive emotions to counteract suffering, the control group did a rather dull task of reinterpreting a stressful event – how do these exercises begin to compare when it comes to the emotional impact they have on the individual? They don't.

I felt dismayed. Despite the anecdotal evidence on the merits of mindfulness meditation, and despite the hundreds of studies produced in the last twenty years, there was no robust scientific evidence that mindfulness has any substantial effect on our minds and behaviours. It was strange to come to this conclusion. I'd grown up believing in mind-over-body effects and that meditation was the queen of techniques when it came to personal change. As an undergraduate I tenaciously defended meditation's therapeutic value at a behavioural psychology class. With hindsight I now acknowledge that old-fashioned behavioural strategies can do wonders. Basically, if you want to make people more empathic and compassionate, having them engage in behaviours where they actively help others may be better than meditating and saying goodwill mantras. Furthermore, there are other psychological strategies, such as rewarding co-operative rather than competitive behaviour, that work, too. Something along these lines may actually be a good control group in a study of compassionate meditation.

It also works the other way around: it may be more effective in terms of increasing our compassion and lovingness to others to discover ourselves how it feels to be on the receiving end of cruel or uncompassionate behaviour, rather than simply meditate on it. There is a Buddhist fable about this in the South Korean film *Spring, Summer, Fall, Winter ... and Spring*[39]. The movie is set on a lake, in a floating Buddhist monastery. A Buddhist monk is raising a child who one day, for fun, ties small stones onto a fish, a frog and a snake. From a distance, the monk watches the child, but does not interfere. During the night, though, while the child sleeps, the monk ties a large rock onto the child's back. In the morning, the monk tells him that he will take it off only after the child unties all the creatures he has tormented. The message, of course, is that real-life experiences are crucial in the development of our moral compass – perhaps even more than meditation.

Within spiritual communities, behaviour itself is part of the arsenal of techniques to promote personal change. All monks and nuns living in a community have to do manual labour and, perhaps, this is not simply borne out of the necessity of having food, shelter and clean clothes, but is instead a strategy to make the individual learn to help, be empathic, and realize interconnectedness – simply, if the washing up isn't done or lunch isn't cooked, everyone is affected.

But monastic life is not the answer to the millions of people who are looking at meditation as a simple and effective means to feel calmer, more positive, happier, and even more compassionate. Can mindfulness-based programs help any of us to achieve any of these goals? I think it may work with some individuals to a certain degree, but the scientific evidence is simply not robust enough to convince me that mindfulness is as good as other methods of promoting change. For example, we can't yet tell that mindfulness is better than cognitive education when it comes to dealing with persistent depressive thoughts; or better than exercise to cope with stress.

Testing the water

Having come to these conclusions, I wanted to see how mindfulness scientists would react. I met with Harald Walach,

Professor for Research Methodology in Complementary Medicine at Viadrina European University Frankfurt, Germany. Walach has conducted original studies on the effects of mindfulness, as well as doing systematic reviews about its efficacy[40]. I was aware that he also publishes articles on the less mainstream areas of complementary medicine and parapsychology, which I thought would make him more open to speak about his beliefs on meditation. When we met he was smartly dressed in a light grey suit with a striped green tie.

'I think meditation works a bit like a hygiene of the mind, a hygiene of consciousness,' he said. 'We live in a highly individualized society but, if you meditate, you realize how important it is to be in good relations with others.'

Sat Bir's similar words about meditation as 'mental hygiene' echoed in my ears (see p.102). 'How does that happen?' I asked.

'In different ways, I suppose; it may help you see better the glitches in yourself or understand better other people's behaviours; and it gives you a sense of connection to other people.'

'Meditation isn't only about non-judgmental perception,' I said. 'Buddhists are criticizing the science mindfulness movement because, without the community and moral teachings, you don't really get a deep change in behaviour.'

'That's rubbish! Meditation in itself is enough to make people change.' Walach paused and looked upwards, thoughtfully. 'Actually, having just said this, I must admit that there are other factors to consider.'

'Like...?'

'Motivation, for example. You can meditate as a way of relaxing or zoning out; but you can also do it with the purpose of self-transcendence and growth. One thing may actually lead to the other!' he laughed.

'Right. I think the idea behind the science of mindfulness is that if you go within, you reach some kind of unbiased experience of yourself. If this is true, then it's arguably much better to meditate than to find a therapist because a therapist is a person and a person is inevitably biased – would you agree with this?' Walach's deep grey eyes seemed to scrutinize me, but he didn't become less affable or open.

'No, no, I don't think that's right. A therapist would not be more biased than you, even if you were in a state of meditation. There are, how shall I call it, blind spots that no amount of meditation can take away. Actually, to be perfectly honest, advanced meditators who may even have had a glimpse of nirvana can still be assholes!'

Walach laughed again and I laughed with him. A memory sprang into my mind of a female friend telling me about a recent first date she had been on, with a man who was a psychotherapist and an experienced meditation teacher. It had started promisingly, but over the course of dinner she became somewhat put off, not only by his unabashed arrogance, but by the fact that every ten minutes or so, the conversation would abruptly halt as he ignored her and stared off blankly into the middle distance. Out of politeness, she refrained from commenting, remaining quietly perplexed. Eventually, he drew attention to his odd behaviour himself. 'So, have you noticed that every now and again I just slip into meditation for a few seconds?' he declared, as if she should be impressed. Although pretentious micro-meditation during a dinner date does sound pretty ass-holey, I imagined that Walach might be referring to something else, although I wasn't certain what.

'But how do you explain that a highly advanced meditator can still be an asshole – isn't this a contradiction?'

'Well, we know that it's difficult to grow up. The kind of attachment you develop in your relationship with your parents is very important. All psychologists know this. And if you haven't had a secure attachment as a child, you *can't meditate away* the emotional problems that come with an avoidant or insecure attachment style.[41]'

'No? I've met a number of people who believe they can,' I said. 'You can't. I'm a clinical psychologist too and I've never seen it happening. You can understand better your wounds through meditation, even become more sensitive to them, but meditation won't change your emotional vulnerability.'

'Many therapists would say that it's only through a consistent positive relationship that insecure attachment can be fixed.'

'Yes,' Walach said, 'I think that's right. Mindfulness can at most make you more aware of your emotional patterns. And sometimes you also need to make decisions; if you're in an abusive relationship, meditation won't help you. You need to decide whether to stay or to leave.'

I'm inclined to agree; through my doctoral training and my own therapeutic work, I can appreciate that mindfulness may for some clients (say, those who are stressed, depressed or anxious) be a useful technique to use with those who are interested in it and *may* help to bring about therapeutic change, But there is no guarantee that practising meditation will bring about anything more than mere relaxation. If so, while a nice experience for them, this is unlikely to have any impact on shifting the cognitive, behavioural, or interpersonal patterns that are maintaining their difficulties. So if you're a therapist and your client asks you about using meditation – of any kind – what should you do? Personally, I would want to know what they believe they would get from it. Are they simply looking to feel less stressed – in which case, go ahead and try it – or are their aspirations for what meditation can do for them somewhat higher? A fast-track route to increased compassion, better relationships with others? I'd be inclined to think that where interpersonal issues are concerned, these might be best worked on interpersonally – with a therapist. If they are keen to combine the two and you yourself aren't trained in how to incorporate mindfulness techniques into therapy, then perhaps they're a suitable candidate for the NHS-supported MBCT and MBSR interventions.

Later that day, as I typed up the interview, I thought back to the study where no effects were found on depression relapse, except if you had undergone abuse and trauma as a child (see p.103). Walach had suggested that mindfulness couldn't make that go away when he said that meditation couldn't touch underlying emotional attachment patterns. The idea of a red balloon effect (see pp.113-114) was appearing increasingly likely to be true.

Something else Walach said - the possibility of advanced meditators with deep spiritual experience acting like assholes - stayed with me. I had found out how most sexy positive findings of the science of mindfulness did not stand up to close scrutiny, but could there also be a dark side to meditation itself?

CHAPTER 6

THE DARK SIDE OF MEDITATION

Aaron Alexis was in search of something. He started attending a Buddhist temple and learned to meditate; he hoped it would bring him wisdom and peace. 'I want to be a Buddhist monk,' he once told a friend from the temple. His friend advised him to keep studying. Aaron did. He learned Thai and kept going to the temple – chanting, meditating. But other things got in the way.

On 16 September 2013 Aaron drove into Washington's Navy Yard. It was eight o'clock in the morning. He'd been working there not long before, and security let him in. He walked out of the car with a large bag and briefly disappeared into a toilet. Minutes later the security cameras caught him holding a shotgun. Aaron walked briskly and hid behind a wall for a few seconds before advancing through the building. Within 30 minutes 12 people were dead. He killed randomly, first using his shotgun and then, after running out of ammunition, using the handgun belonging to a guard he'd just killed. He died after an exchange of gunfire with the police[1].

It took only 24 hours for a journalist to notice that Aaron had been a Buddhist, prompting her to write an article[2] that asked, 'Can there be a less positive side to meditation?' Western Buddhists immediately reacted: 'This man represented the Dharma teachings no more than 9/11 terrorists represented the teachings of Islam,' wrote one. Others explained that he had a history of mental health problems. However, some noted that Buddhism, as other religions, has a history that links it to violence[3]. And meditation, for all its de-stressing and self-development potential, can take you deeper into the darkest recesses of your own mind than you may have wished for.

This chapter asks difficult questions that are seldom given a voice. They are questions I have wrestled with, both as a psychologist and in my own spiritual practice. Do I have unrealistic positive expectations about what meditation can do? Can it also have adverse effects, finding its way to non-spiritual, even non-peaceful ends?

When something goes wrong, the way it did with Aaron Alexis, we can't look the other way – rationalizing that he wasn't a true Buddhist or meditator isn't enough. We need relentlessly to examine the less familiar, hidden facets of meditation – a technique that for centuries has been used to cultivate wisdom, clarity of mind, and selflessness. We need to ask ourselves if meditation has a dark side.

ADVERSE EFFECTS

I'd come across the idea that without the guidance of an expert teacher meditation can have adverse effects, but I'd thought that this was a metaphor for the difficulties we might encounter as we venture deep into ourselves. I hadn't considered that the adverse effects might be literal ones. Then, one day I heard a first-hand account that opened my eyes to my naïvety. At the time I was teaching an open course on the psychology of spirituality. There were a few twenty-year-olds, but the majority of students were in their late fifties and early sixties and represented a combination of retired lawyers, Anglican priests, psychiatrists, and three or four yoga and meditation teachers. Louise was one of them.

In her late fifties and lean with dark, short hair, Louise was a quiet member of the group, who in general spoke up only when she felt she had something important to say. She had taught yoga for more than twenty years, stopping only when something unexpected happened that changed her life for ever. During one meditation retreat (she'd been on many), her sense of self changed dramatically. 'Good,' she thought initially, 'it must be part of the dissolving experience.' But she couldn't help feeling anxious and frightened.

'Don't worry, just keep meditating and it will go away,' the meditation teacher told her.

It didn't. She couldn't get back to her usual self. It felt like something was messing with her sense of identity, how she felt in her body, the very way she looked at the world and at other people. The last day of the retreat was excruciating: her body shook, she cried and panicked. The following day, back at home, she was in pieces – her body was numb, she didn't want to get out of bed. Louise's husband took her to the GP and, within hours, she was being seen by a psychiatrist. She spent the next 15 years being treated for psychotic depression; for part of this time, she had to be hospitalized.

Louise had chosen to give a presentation on the psychology of spiritual experience, as part of her assessment on the course. She talked lucidly about her illness and its possible origins, including a genetic predisposition to mental health problems. She explained that she had gradually taken up yoga practice again, but had never returned to meditation retreats. 'I had to have electro-convulsive therapy,' she told the class. That means strong electric shocks going through your skull, a treatment that is not only painful, but leads to memory loss in the short term.

I was stunned. I couldn't know for sure; perhaps her mental illness could have developed in some other way but, as it happened, those three days of intense meditation are likely to have triggered it. I mentioned this to a friend who, in the 1970s, had taught meditation to 13- to 14-year-olds.

'Oh yes,' he said, 'I once had two boys who were becoming quite emotionally disturbed; the meditation practice was unleashing emotional material that they couldn't deal with.'

'So what happened?'

'I told them to stop doing it,' my friend told me. 'I had twenty other children to look after. And as soon as they did, they were fine.'

Two in twenty – that's a 10 per cent probability that meditation could have an adverse effect on young adolescents. But this was anecdotal evidence taken from a single meditation class that happened forty years earlier – indeed, if the hundreds of scientific articles I'd read on the effects of meditation were to go by, there seemed to be only good news. So, are cases like Louise's and the boys in my friend's class the exception? I looked through the medical and psychological databases in search of articles on the possible adverse effects of meditation. There were some, most of them case studies. One of the most striking, written in 2001 by a British psychiatrist, told the story of a 25-year-old woman who, like Louise, had a serious mental health problem following meditation retreats. The first time she was admitted to hospital her symptoms included: 'thought disorder with flight of ideas, her mood was elevated and there were grandiose delusions including the belief that she had some special mission for the world: she had to offer "undying, unconditional love" to everyone. She had no [critical] insight.'[4] (p.210)

This woman, referred to as Miss X, was diagnosed with mania. After six weeks of medication her symptoms were controlled. A psychiatrist saw her regularly for two years and she started twice-weekly psychotherapy. Then, she took part in a Zen Buddhist retreat and was hospitalized again. She couldn't sleep for five days and, according to a psychiatrist who saw her, displayed a number of unrestrained behaviours: she was irritable, sexually disinhibited, restless, made repeated praying gestures, and attacked a member of staff. Miss X had to be transferred to an intensive psychiatric care unit for three days.

Interesting, I thought, but I was still unconvinced. All these examples could be individuals with a strong predisposition to mental illness. As I looked further into the scientific literature, though, I found other kinds of evidence. In 1992 David Shapiro, a professor in psychiatry and human behaviour at the University of California, Irvine, published an article about the effects of meditation retreats. Shapiro examined 27 people with different levels of meditation experience. He found that 63 per cent of them had at least one negative effect and 7 per cent suffered profoundly adverse effects. The negative effects included anxiety, panic, depression, increased negativity, pain, feeling spaced out, confusion and disorientation[5].

Perhaps only the least experienced felt these negative experiences. Several days of meditation might overwhelm those who were relatively new to the practice. Was that the case? The answer was no. When Shapiro divided the larger group into those with lesser and greater experience, there were no differences: all the meditators had an equal number of adverse experiences. An earlier study had arrived at a similar, but even more surprising conclusion. Not only did those with more experience of meditating find themselves with negative symptoms – particularly anxiety, confusion and restlessness – they also had considerably *more* adverse effects than the beginners[6].

Amid the small pile of articles on the adverse effects of meditation, I was surprised to find two by Arnold Lazarus and Albert Ellis, co-founders of CBT (see p.81). In a 1976 article Lazarus reported that a few of his own patients had had serious disturbances after meditating; these included depression, ongoing tension and a serious suicide attempt. Lazarus strongly criticized the idea that 'meditation is for everyone'. Instead, he argued that 'one man's meat is another man's poison', and that researchers and therapists need to know both the benefits and the risks of meditation for *different* kinds of people[7].

Albert Ellis shared Lazarus' misgivings about meditation. He believed it could be used as a therapeutic tool, but not with everyone. 'A few of my own clients,' he writes, 'have gone into dissociative semi-trance states and upset themselves considerably by meditating.' Overall, he believed meditation could be used only in moderation as a 'thought-distracting' or 'relaxing' technique[8]:

'Like tranquilizers, it may have both good and bad effects – especially, the harmful result of encouraging people to look away from some of their central problems, and to refrain from actually disputing and surrendering their disturbance-creating beliefs. It may also be perniciously used to enhance self-rating or "ego-strength", so that people end up by believing "I am a great meditator and *therefore* am a good and noble person!" I therefore recommend meditation... as a palliative, a distraction method, and advise most of my clients to use it with discretion and not to take it too seriously or view it as a generally therapeutic method.' (p.672)

A SPIRITUAL EMERGENCY?

I felt like an archaeologist digging up long-forgotten artefacts. How could this literature on the adverse effects of meditation, including short – but sharp – comments from founding cognitive psychotherapists be completely absent in the recent research on meditation? It was conceivable that clinicians and researchers simply did not report the negative consequences of meditation in their articles, but it was more likely that the *meditators* themselves did not talk about it. Many who encounter difficulties during or after their practice may feel they're doing something wrong, or even that their distress is part of the process and will eventually pass. That was the case of Miss X, who had two manic episodes following meditation retreats, but eventually refused continuous treatment, explaining that her mania was nothing more than a release of blocked energy from years of not dealing with her emotions adequately. Many meditators thinking like Miss X could, to a certain extent, explain why negative reports didn't make it into scientific journals – adverse effects could be regarded as mere stones on the road to peace or spiritual attainment.

I was thinking about this when Jo Lal, our publisher, emailed to ask how the book was going. I told her what I had found.

'Have you heard of Dr Russell Razzaque?' Jo asked. I hadn't.

'We're about to publish his book *Breaking Down is Waking Up*[9]. You may find it helpful.'

Razzaque is a London-based psychiatrist whose own Buddhist meditation practice has led him to re-evaluate the meaning of mental illness. He argues that many of the psychotic experiences his patients describe resemble mystical experiences of ego-dissolution that are known to occur after years of meditation practice. Razzaque suggests that mental breakdowns are part of a spiritual-growth process, in which we learn to see the self for what it is: an illusion. He describes his own mystical experience in the book:

'I found myself descending into a deeply meditative state; I somehow travelled through the sensations of my body and the thoughts in my mind to a space of sheer nothingness that felt, at the same time, like it was somehow the womb of everything. I felt a sense of pure power and profound energy as I came upon a sudden brilliant light and a profound feeling of all-pervading joy ... I was everything and nothing at the same time.' (p.40)

In the days that followed, however, life wasn't so blissful. Razzaque found that he couldn't contain his joyful experience and there was something deep within pulling him in the opposite direction. 'I could sense the powerful currents in my whirling mind – the self-doubts and the dents in self-esteem sucking me towards a ball of depression, the anxieties and fears threatening to balloon into full-blown panic, obsessions or defensive compulsions, and the speed of it all that risked pushing me into a manic state.' (p.44)

Razzaque managed to keep grounded and, as a result of his difficult experience, felt greater sympathy towards his psychotic patients. Wait a minute, I thought; here we have a trained psychiatrist who can identify his symptoms and fight them off – but the majority of people meditating know next to nothing about psychiatric diagnosis; nor are they familiar with seeing patients experiencing unusual states of mind. Can these difficult emotional experiences arising from meditation really be a sign of spiritual awakening?

Others before Razzaque have trodden a similar path and pointed out similarities between the symptoms of psychotic people and spiritual experiences. In the late 1980s Stan Grof (see p.40) edited with his wife a book on spiritual emergencies[10]. They caution clinical psychologists and psychiatrists to be aware of and respect what on the surface may look like mental illness, but is, in fact, the expression of spiritual experiences that are having a profound, though momentarily stressful, effect. The Grofs mention shamanism and near-death experiences, as well as meditation and other spiritual practices, in association with spiritual emergencies.

Their pioneering work came to fruition when a new category was added to the fourth edition of the *Diagnostic and Statistical Manual of Mental Disorders* (DSM-IV), used by psychiatrists worldwide – that of Religious and Spiritual Problems[11]. This category acknowledges that some mental health problems, such as depersonalization, may arise as a temporary result of spiritual practices. If you have ever felt a strong state of depersonalization, you wouldn't forget it easily! The Cambridge Depersonalisation Scale, a questionnaire that measures symptoms, includes unusual experiences, such as: 'Part of my body feels as if it didn't belong to me' or 'I have the feeling of not having any thoughts at all, so that when I speak it feels as if my words were being uttered by an automaton.[12]' But other statements, such as 'I feel so detached from my thoughts that they seem to have a life of their own' might be quite familiar to mindfulness meditators.

With a category of religious and spiritual problems, clinicians are potentially able to recognize what are genuine manic, depressive or psychotic episodes and what are the non-pathological, although sometimes difficult effects of meditation. But it's far from a straightforward distinction. David Lukoff, the clinical psychologist who co-authored this new category[13], admits that his interest in the topic arose in 1971 when he spent two months experiencing his own spiritual crisis – fully convinced that he was the reincarnation of Buddha and Christ with a mission to save the world[14].

But how many clinicians worldwide, I wonder, even those with a spiritual faith, would not deem someone whose life was dominated by delusion for two entire months to be seriously mentally ill. The problem centres around how we define mental illness as distinct from a spiritual emergency – clearly, not all spirituality-related experiences are benign. The late Michael Thalbourne, an Australian psychological scientist, suffered from bipolar disorder, wherein periods of mania would trigger messianic delusions that had a spiritual element:

'I sometimes get into this very focused state of mind that I can't shake, where I believe I am Christ,' he told me once, opening wide his eyes and gazing intensely 'I don't just believe I am in communion with Christ, but that I actually am *the* Christ.'

Michael Thalbourne had a deep personal interest in spirituality, but didn't look at his mental suffering as a benign stone on the winding road to spiritual growth. It affected both his personal life and his academic career. 'My university has never given me a proper academic post; they see me as unreliable and potentially dangerous,' he explained.

The Grofs cautioned that not all difficult experiences associated with spiritual practices are necessarily 'spiritual'. A psychotherapist or an expert spiritual teacher may have the power to help to turn a difficult experience into a meaningful one, but not always. With the growing number of people interested in meditation in the West, many will walk away from their weekend meditation retreat or eight-week mindfulness course without expert guidance. How many of them in their search for a moment of peace and quiet, I thought, can end up having a bumpy ride, not to mention the real danger of a journey into the hell of mental illness.

CONVULSIONS, TWITCHING AND NUMBNESS

A number of Western Buddhists are aware that not all is plain sailing with meditation – they have even named the emotional difficulties that arise from their meditative practice, calling them the 'dark night'. The concept of a spiritual dark night isn't originally Buddhist. Coined by the 16th-century Christian mystic St John of the Cross, the phrase originally described an advanced stage of prayer and contemplation characterized by an emotional dryness, in which the subject feels abandoned by God[15]. Buddhists, in principle, ought not to feel abandoned by God, but their accounts of the dark night associated with meditation are riddled with emotional and physical turmoil. A Buddhist blog sharing experiences of the dark night features a number of testimonies[16]: 'Nine years on and off of periods of deep depression, angst, anxiety and misery'; 'there was a nausea that kept coming up, terrible sadness, aches and pain'; 'I've had one pretty intense dark night, it lasted for nine months, included misery, despair, panic attacks... loneliness, auditory hallucinations, mild paranoia, treating my friends and family badly, long episodes of nostalgia and regret, obsessive thoughts (usually about death).'

Willoughby Britton, a neuroscientist and psychiatrist at Brown University who has conducted studies on the positive effects of mindfulness, is now trying to map these more difficult experiences, which she calls 'The Dark Side of Dharma'. Her interest arose from witnessing two people being hospitalized after intense meditation practice, together with her own experience after a retreat in which she felt an unimaginable terror. Reading through the classical Buddhist literature to try to understand what was happening to her, she realized that these negative experiences are mentioned as common stages of meditation.

'I was woefully uninformed,' she admits in an interview[17].

Meditation retreats easily led people to sense the world differently: the hearing gets sharper; time moves slower. But the most radical change that can occur is in what Britton calls 'the narrative of the self'. Try this out: focus on the present moment, nothing else than the present moment. You may be able to do it easily for a very short time. However, if you try extending this 'presentness' for one, two hours and keep trying for some days, your usual sense of self – that which has one foot in the past and the other in the future – collapses. The practice may feel great for some, but for others it is like being continuously tossed around in a roller coaster. Vertigo, rather than blissful realization of the emptiness of the self, may be the end result. Other unpleasant things happen, too, as Britton discovered through interviews with numerous individuals: arms flap, people twitch and have convulsions; others go through euphoria or depression, or report not feeling anything at all – their physical senses go numb.

Unpleasant as they are, if these symptoms were confined to a retreat there wouldn't be much to worry about – but they're not. Sometimes they linger, affecting work, childcare and relationships. They can become a clinical health problem, which, on average, lasts for more than three years. Some people 'seemed to go through these experiences fairly quickly, like under a year, and in other people can last a decade', Britton reveals[18].

Britton hasn't yet published her research, but it confirms the case studies, earlier findings with groups of meditators, and Lazarus's and Albert Ellis's comments on the adverse effects of meditation. These negative effects may very well turn out to be a stage in our spiritual journey, but if we don't address them properly they can be destructive and harmful. Meditation teachers know about it – Britton says – but meditation researchers are usually sceptical; they ask about the prior psychiatric history of meditators who develop mental health problems, as if meditation itself had little or nothing to do with it[19].

I thought the same before starting the research for this book. Its title was originally going to be *From Monster to Buddha*, intending to highlight the astonishing possibility of personal change arising from meditation. I haven't stopped believing in meditation's ability to fuel change, but I am concerned that the science of meditation is promoting a skewed view: meditation wasn't developed so we could lead less stressful lives or improve our wellbeing. Its primary purpose was much more radical – to rupture your idea of who you are; to shake to the core your sense of self so that you realize there is 'nothing there'. But that's not how we see meditation courses promoted in the West. Here, meditation has been revamped as a natural pill that will quieten your mind and make you happier.

I recently asked students in a class I was teaching on the psychology of contemplative techniques what they thought the similarities and differences were between meditation and psychotherapy. A student who was a regular meditator argued that doing psychotherapy was all about past wounds and relationships, while meditation, she said, was 'free from all that crap; it's all about being in the present'.

But it's not. Repressed and traumatic material can easily resurface during intense meditation.

From the moment I accepted this and started talking to regular meditators, I kept finding more and more evidence. I discovered even more online – and sometimes in the least expected places. Take Deepak Chopra's website, for example. There is a correspondence section where readers post their questions or experiences and Chopra answers. A number of these posts concern physical or emotional symptoms that arise from meditation. On 11 April 2014 an individual who had been meditating for one year – and finding in it 'true bliss' – describes having twice experienced a deep emotional sensation, 'like something is being ripped from me', that left her wanting to cry and yell. Chopra's reply is optimistic:

'It's both normal and okay. It just means there is some deep emotional trauma from your past that is now ready to come to the surface and be healed. After meditation I would recommend you take a few minutes and sing out loud. Find a song you love that resonates with the emotional tone of your pain. Listen to it at above normal volume so that you can really feel the sonic effect of the song and music. When you feel it has engaged your emotions, start to sing so that your voice translates your feelings into sound. If you do this every time you feel some unresolved residue of emotion after your meditation, it will facilitate the release and healing process.[20]'

What if someone like Aaron Alexis had emailed Deepak Chopra and received a reply like this – would singing along to his favourite song, turned up nice and loud, have healed his past emotional traumas and led into the wisdom he sought, rather than a killing spree? Unlikely. Furthermore, there is a real danger that what the person who wrote to Chopra asking for advice is feeling is not 'normal and okay', and that if she keeps meditating without an expert teacher, it may disturb rather than heal her.

WHAT IF HITLER HAD MEDITATED?

'If every eight-year-old in the world is taught meditation, the world will be without violence within one generation.'

The Dalai Lama

When best-selling spiritual author Marian Williams tweeted the above quote, it quickly went viral. It probably helped that her friend Oprah Winfrey re-tweeted it to her 24 million followers with the comment, 'This I believe is true. Have seen it in action.[21]'

The notion that religious or spiritual practice is something of a cure-all isn't unique to Eastern practices, though. Fundamentally, all religions moot that spirituality can make you a better person. The evidence for this is ambiguous. It is true that religions emphasize the caring part of our human nature – from the 'thou shall not kill' of the Hebrew scriptures, through the Hindu praise in the Bhagavad-Gita of the person who hurts nobody and is compassionate towards all beings, and the Quran's rule to be kind to orphans, the needy and travellers, to the Buddha's precept to 'avoid killing, or harming any living thing', and the Christian golden rule of treating others as you would want them to treat you. While there is psychological evidence that practising religious people are more charitable[22], our ability to differentiate between good and bad deeds is already in place before we acquire religious ideas.

Studies have shown that from as young as six months old, we have a preference for those we see helping another, and we'd rather be with someone neutral (who acts neither positively nor negatively) than with an uncooperative individual. And from eight months old, we are able to appreciate when a helpful individual acts against another that has behaved badly. This ingenious research was conducted with computer images and puppets, so the babies could effectively recognize positive and negative moral behaviour in strangers[23].

The idea that we seem to be biologically predisposed towards morality does not answer the question a 16-year-old once asked me at a public lecture in India: 'If we are born good and kind, how come there is so much violence and evil in the world?' Religions have dealt with such 'problem of evil' questions for a long time and have come up with various answers – the existence of free will, disobedience to God, the work of the devil, and the concepts of illusion, karma or greed. Psychologists rarely come up with such enticing explanations about the origins of violence and immorality. We simply know that while we are born with the ability to tell a helpful from an unhelpful gesture, a caring from a callous person, we are also rooted in our needs – our desire to want things, to achieve – and in trying to reach our goals we are able to hurt, and even kill. While some of us have more of a propensity towards doing this than others – for example, those with psychopathic traits – hurting someone else in order to meet our own needs is something we are all potentially capable of; and to at least some small degree, probably do.

While there is evidence that religion can make people act better towards others, there is also plenty of evidence to the contrary: religion can make you more prejudiced towards the non-religious or gay[24]. But we can detach meditation from groups and religions. You can use meditation to de-stress or explore the self just as easily whether you ascribe to a set of religious beliefs or a religious group or not. The beauty of meditation is just that – its separateness from the necessity of divine rules of morality and punishment. But, if we take this view, we return to the question that we asked in Chapter 5: meditation without religion might improve its attraction, but is its lack of attachment to spiritual moral guidelines also a weakness?

I asked an old friend who runs a sociological research centre specializing in equality and racism issues what he thought of the Dalai Lama's idea that meditation could eventually eradicate violence. He gave me a puzzled look before answering.

'There are various factors that explain violence, right? Some psychological, others societal. Put them all together in a statistical regression model: start with level of income, education, access to health, then consider psychological factors such as the presence of childhood abuse; see how much of these explain the likelihood of my neighbour being in a fight at the pub or hitting his partner. Then, add meditation to your statistical model – would it add anything in predicting violence compared to the other factors?'

'Well ...' I started, but he interrupted me.

'Would it have made a difference if Hitler had meditated?' he asked grinning.

I saw what he meant. You can't remove an individual from the larger context and one's psychological makeup. It would not have made much of a difference if Hitler had meditated – like Aaron Alexis did – unless he removed himself from the society that raised him to power and he radically changed his ambitions and ideas. On the other hand practices such as meditation and yoga are rooted in inner peacefulness, and the spiritual traditions upon which they're built believe that radical personal changes are possible, regardless of the environment we live in. All in all I felt I had a puzzle with quite a lot of missing or ill-fitting pieces. I couldn't quite see the larger picture. Very soon, though, I was challenged to look in a completely different way at the question of the extent to which contemplative techniques are associated with violence.

THE MISTY ROAD TO HARDIWAR

'KINDLY BE CALM', read a sign in large capital letters above the reception desk. On the other side of the lounge, there was a picture on the wall of a forty-something bearded man with a pristine smile, wearing the traditional orange robes of Indian yogis. I yawned and rubbed my eyes, trying hard to keep awake. It was past midnight and I'd been travelling for eight hours on a dimly lit motorway, thick with fog, clotted with buses and trucks without rear lights.

'Don't go, it's suicide,' a friend had told me in Delhi. 'Get the train in the morning.'

I didn't listen. I was in awe of the driver's night vision and his ability to notice the invisible buses and trucks just before crashing. 'No worry, no worry,' he said halfway through the trip. 'My name is Bobby and everyone in India knows that no Bobby has ever been in a car accident.'

Travelling with me in the same taxi was Bishal Sitaula, a friendly and talkative professor of environment and developmental studies from Norway who had arrived from

Nepal. He took out his video camera to show me footage of his Nepalese trip.

'Then I met with this really revered Buddhist monk. Here I'm asking him a question – do you want to hear?' I looked at the screen as he pressed play. The monk had a benevolent smile. Bishal was telling him about a personal moral dilemma. 'When my wife makes herself pretty, I look more at her. But, when I am walking up the road and see a woman with long beautiful hair and wearing nicer make up than my wife's, and I stare at her, then, I walk five more metres and stare back at her again – is this a sin or bad for my karma?'

The monk continued smiling. I imagined that if the whole world collapsed around him he would still smile.

'No, no, it's not a sin to look,' he replied. 'You may enjoy looking at a beautiful woman. That is fine. But if you crave and run after her, that is no good, no good; no good for your karma.'

Stopping the video, Bishal laughed loudly and put his arm around my shoulders.

When we arrived at the Patanjali Research Foundation, where I am taking part in a conference on the effects of yoga, I could make out only tiny fairy lights scattered around the complex. In the fog they looked like blurred dragonflies. Inside the accommodation block a sleepy lady handed me a key after I showed her my passport. The bedroom's floor was paved in black-and-white marble. It was the coldest January recorded in Indian history; in Delhi homeless people were dying because of the low temperatures. I took out all the blankets from the drawer and laid them on the bed. I had travelled to India on a few occasions, but had never come so far north, only a few miles away from the source of the Ganges and the river village of Rishikesh, home to a number of celebrated ashrams and yogis. It seemed the right place to build the Patanjali Research Foundation, which holds masters and PhD programs on the science of yoga and has the largest research centre in the world dedicated to the study of this millennia-old practice.

Lying under three heavy blankets, I gazed at the puffed steam coming out of my mouth and eventually fell asleep. A few hours later the radio switched on. I opened one eye and looked at my watch on the bedside table: it was 4am. 'Where's the damn switch?' I thought to myself. The music poured out of the speakers within the room and out in the corridor, a smooth stream of sitar and lulling voices. I walked to the reception, but saw no one. As I turned around I noticed a man by the door with a scarf wrapped around his head.

'The radio inside the bedroom, how do you turn it off?' I asked. He smiled.

'The radio,' I gestured, pointing at the speakers in the corridor. 'Off, off.'

He smiled again and tilted his head from left to right repeatedly. 'No sir, no sir. Wake up, wake up. Yoga,' he said, still smiling and pointing outside. It was pitch black.

The music continued. At 5.30am I ventured outside. There was daylight, but the thick fog from the previous night hadn't yet lifted. I followed some people who seemed to know where they were heading, and entered an enormous auditorium, where approximately 2,000 people were sitting on yoga mats. The spiritual guru of the Patanjali Research Foundation, Swami Ramdev, was on top of the stage, alone and wearing nothing but an orange loincloth.

A man sitting next to me whispered into my ear that he was a medical doctor at the foundation and offered to translate what Swami Ramdev was saying.

'It's *pranayama*. We start with breathing; right breathing can heal anything.'

Yoga with machine guns

For the next hour we breathed together and listened. First, how *not* to breathe. Then, how to breathe through alternating nostrils, and how to use your belly and diaphragm in a syncopated way.

'Like this!' and *'Don't* do this!' he said, hyperventilating with a contracted abdomen and eyes wide open, looking like he was having a fit. 'This breathing cures asthma; this one heals all types of arthritis; if you're depressed, this will cure it.'

There was clapping from the audience. Steam clouds came out of people's mouths. The list of diseases that yoga and *pranayama* can heal was almost endless – dementia and cancer among them.

The breathing exercises went on, but my feet and hands were getting colder. After an hour of breathing, the swami stood up and began a series of *asanas*. 'Finally,' I thought, 'we're going to gently warm up.' But it was far from gentle; more like a kind of yoga-on-speed mixed with aerobics. I looked around and noticed only one man among the audience who could keep up with the guru. For the last posture Swami Ramdev walked around the stage on his hands – for about 1 minute. There was more clapping.

We finally moved towards a peace chant, which was interrupted by a few minutes of yoga laughter – 'very good for depression' – and followed by singing from the swami alone. 'He has the personality of a rock star,' I overheard someone with an American accent whisper behind me.

When the solo chant ended, Swami Ramdev uttered a shrill cry, which was imitated by most of the audience as they repeatedly raised their fists upwards. It was a strange sight. The cry and fist waving were the kind you'd see in a political or military gathering. As the session ended the translator held my hand: 'Come, I'll take you to Swami Ji for a blessing.'

I followed him. There was a queue of people waiting. I looked around: there were numerous posters of the Patanjali Research Foundation and university, mostly in Hindi. My translator pushed me forwards; I was now very close to the Swami. The man in front of me was carrying a beautiful, handcrafted bag. On it, next to the foundation's name, was written 'Self and National Character Building by Yoga'. Finally, it was my turn. Swami Ramdev smiled;

I smiled back. I slowly tilted my head forwards to greet him as my translator introduced me, but halfway to the full nod, I froze.

'Bloody hell,' I caught myself saying. A man came from behind the Swami holding a machine gun about the length of an extended arm. He was pointing the gun at me. My translator guided me away while the Swami smiled and waved goodbye.

'What was that?', I thought, my eyes fixed on the gun. 'He's a very holy man, don't you think?' my translator said, still holding my arm and apparently unfazed by the bodyguard with the machine gun.

Outside I saw Bishal, the professor who had travelled with me the night before. I felt like hugging him. He was in his perennial chatty mood. 'Hello, my friend! Chilly, huh? Did you enjoy the session?'

I asked Bishal about the sort of war cry at the end of the session and the armed bodyguard. He told me about the political influence of the swami – that he's pressured the parliament to put an end to corruption and some politicians don't like him. 'Look, look,' I interrupted, pointing at the person holding a bag I'd noticed inside the yoga hall. 'Do you see what's written on that bag: Self and National Character Building by Yoga. What do they mean by *national*?'

'Oh, that. Well, it's all around the place. This is not only about yoga, but about social transformation.'

'But why national?'

'Yoga comes from India, right? It's India's trademark. Here, that's part of their message, that yoga is Indian.'

I stared back in silence. As we made our way back to the accommodation hall, I noticed a large banner with a picture of the guru holding up his fist with an angry face. The writing was in Hindi. 'And what's that about?'

Bishal reminded me of a horrendous gang rape that had recently happened in Delhi, inside a moving bus. The girl died shortly afterwards and there had been a public outcry. My friend in Delhi had told me that Indian culture, particularly in the north, was not only sexist, but violent towards women.

'So the banner literally asks,' Bishar translated, 'What shall we do with the rapists? And the red letters say: Death Penalty! Death Penalty!'

'Are you serious?'

'I find it strange, too,' Bishal replied. 'But they believe in harsh punishment.'

It was my fourth time in India, but the first that the contradictions of this country were pressing on me. Yoga, an instrument of serenity and enlightenment, was serving political purposes. The Patanjali Research Foundation is powerful: it has its own TV satellite channel, factories producing a variety of health products, a university and a leading yoga research centre. They also commission cartoons that portray Swami Ramdev as an enlightened yogi to educate children not just about the technique of yoga, but about its whole philosophy – even its nationalistic and punishment views, I suspect.

There were other odd things going on. The foundation's wireless Internet server was excellent, but it didn't allow you to access a number of webpages. The first banned site I noticed was Facebook. I checked with a German conference participant and he couldn't access it either. Most web searches related to drugs were forbidden, as I discovered while trying to read about the uses of morphine as a painkiller. When I asked Nandim, a Master's student at the university, why they had censored Facebook, he laughed.

'Very few people from the outside notice it.'

'Why can't you use it?'

'Oh, you know, students were spending too much time on it.'

'That's rubbish,' I said. 'Students can spend too much time just browsing the web. Why Facebook?'

Nandim looked around before answering. 'You know... many boys were using Facebook to talk to girls.'

'So?'

'Well, that's not allowed.'

'What do you mean?' I ask. 'The university is not sexually segregated; you have men and women.'

'Yes, yes, but Swamiji doesn't like us to be together,' Nandim said speaking in a hushed voice.

I looked at him puzzled.

'A couple of incidents happened last year,' he said. 'There were boys and girls spending time together, you know, like they were a couple.'

'Yes, it does happen.'

'Not here, sir, not here. They were expelled from the university.'

On my way back to Delhi, this time on a sunny though heavily congested road, I saw graffiti on the wall of a tunnel. No pictures, only wide letters written in black across the extension of the wall: 'I HATE MY LIFE.' I felt a sudden wave of empathy for whomever had doodled it; the land that had given birth to numerous sages and yoga, the soil of non-dualistic Advaita Vedanta was riddled with contradictions. At the Patanjali Research Foundation, ideals and techniques for inner-peace-making were fused together with nationalism, violence (guns and the endorsement of capital punishment), censorship and sexual repression. When I returned to my friend's house in Delhi, he teased me for my naïvety.

'Many of these yogis are millionaires. They live in fancy air-conditioned flats. And the nationalism and violence, give me a break: do you know how many wars we, the very spiritual Indian people, have been involved in during the last fifty years?'

My doubts about meditation and yoga having a role in solving the world's violence substantially increased after this trip. When I returned to England, I emailed Torkel Brekkel, an Oxford colleague who specializes in the study of Asian religions. I asked what he knew about violence in the Eastern spiritual traditions. My general understanding was that in a religion such as Buddhism, which has compassion and non-violence as central principles, you would find few, if any, displays of violence among its followers. 'That's not the case,' Torkel replied and added that he had lost count of the times his colleagues, students and journalists had tried telling him that Buddhism, unlike Christianity or Islam, is an essentially peaceful religion. 'It's not,' he asserted, referring me to some books on the topic, including one he'd recently edited[25].

COMPASSIONATE KILLING

During the first decade of the new millennium, while psychologists and neuroscientists were examining the positive psychological effects of Buddhist mindfulness meditation, scholars of religions were looking in the opposite direction; they were examining the violent history of Buddhism. The book edited by Torkel Brekkel is only the most recent in a number of publications looking at the use of violence by Buddhist monks and *bodhisattvas* (enlightened persons). The titles of the volumes are revealing: *Buddhism and Violence*, *Buddhism and Warfare*, *Zen at War*.

Apparently, the early Buddhist views on violence were astonishingly similar to those of the Christians who tried to follow Jesus's saying, 'if someone slaps you on one cheek, turn to them the other also'[26]. Like the early Christians, followers of Buddha prided themselves on being different from the fallen world. One early Buddhist text recognizes that violence should be avoided:

All
tremble at the rod,
all are fearful of death.
Drawing the parallel to
yourself,
neither kill nor get others to kill.
(*Dhammapada*, 129)[27]

In another early text, the *Yodhajivasutra*, the Buddha explains that warriors are to be reincarnated in hell or as an animal, rather than in the company of heavenly deities (*devas*). There is a particularly striking story of how the Buddha personally walked into the battlefield and avoided bloodshed. Four years after he attained enlightenment, two armies were facing each other because of a dispute about access to water. The Buddha came between the armies and asked their commanders:

'How much value do you think water has in comparison with the life of men?'

The commanders agreed that the value of water was infinitely less important than human life.

'Why do you then destroy lives that are valuable for valueless water?' the Buddha asked, thus preventing the oncoming bloodshed (p.194).[28]

Many have reiterated this view. Buddhism's precept of non-violence has inspired people in Asian countries living under its influence, so that 'throughout its peaceful march of 2,500 years, no drop of blood has been shed in the name of the Buddha' (p.195), writes Narada, a distinguished Sri Lankan monk and scholar.

But a cursory glance at the news broadcasts about Buddhist countries challenges this peaceful image. Let's start with Sri Lanka. In 2013 groups of monks were holding rallies against the Muslim minority; since 1983 many Buddhist monks have been directly involved in military campaigns against a separatist faction in northern Sri Lanka. In the first half of the twentieth century, monks joined and led the struggle for independence against the British. Two thousand years ago, King Duttagamani fought a war to re-establish Buddhism in the country 'where he used a Buddha's relic as his banner' (p.200). One thousand miles from Sri Lanka in Burma, in May 2013 Buddhist mobs were killing Muslims and burning mosques; one Burmese monk, jailed for inciting religious hatred, likes to call himself the 'Burmese Bin Laden'[29].

These events, I soon found out, aren't exceptions to the rule. Although preaching non-violence to his followers, the Buddha didn't try to persuade kings to adopt a pacifist stance. He clearly separated the waters by not allowing former soldiers to become monks and forbidding his followers to preach to soldiers – violence was understood as part of life and there was no attempt to eradicate it entirely from the world. The effort was in trying to contain it in Buddhist monks. But even that failed. Just as Christianity developed its 'just war' theory – wherein, according to St Augustine, an early Christian theologian, war could be an instrument of divine justice on wickedness – Buddhism came to develop its own theory of *compassionate killing*. A text written in the fourth century entitled 'Discourse on the stages of yogic practice' argues that under certain circumstances even an enlightened person is allowed to kill *out of compassion*.

'If a *bodhisattva* meets an evil person who is going to kill many people… he will think to himself: if by killing this bandit I fall in hell, what does it matter? I must not let him go to hell! Then the *boddhisatva* … will kill him, full of both the horror of the crime and compassion for that person. In doing so, he will not commit any transgression; rather, he will acquire much blessing.[30]' (p.9)

The Buddha himself told the story of how, in a previous life, he had killed out of compassion. As narrated in the *Mahaupaya-Kausalya sutra*, there was a time when 500 merchants went to sea in search of treasures, but one of them schemed to kill the others and keep all the treasures for himself. A deity discovered this and informed the Buddha who had the following dilemma: if the other merchants learn of the evil merchant's plot to kill them, the evil merchant will be killed and the 499 merchants will go to hell. However, if nothing is done, the merchants will be killed and their murderer will go to hell. So, the Buddha decided to kill the evil merchant and save the others. He explained to his followers that his action was the result of compassion for the sake of a greater number of living beings[31].

It's not difficult to follow the Buddha's logic – it's similar to the tram problem first posed by British philosopher Philippa Foot in 1967, and subsequently often used in psychology experiments on moral behaviour[32]. In this scenario there is a runway tram that is heading straight towards five workers. A large man is standing on a footbridge over the tracks. If you throw him off the bridge his body will block the tram and the five men will be saved. What would you do? Rationally, you ought to kill the single man on the footbridge to save the greater number of people. But this involves choice – a conscious decision to kill a man, at your will, rather than the tragic but accidental killing of the people on the track. As a result most people's gut reaction to this moral problem is not necessarily the most reasoned one: it may *rationally* be better to kill the man, but *intuitively* you feel it's wrong and opt against it, letting the five workers die in a tragic accident instead.

Through dilemmas such as these, psychologists have shown that many of our moral decisions are intuitive rather than rational. However, there is a problem with these findings. New studies have found that for people who display lack of empathy – such as psychopaths – the intuitive answer is to kill the large man, because to them the act of killing is not particularly aversive[33]. There is a kind of indifference or amorality about killing for people with a psychopathic personality. Although, on the surface, this seems the very opposite of what Buddhist practice is seeking to attain, something similar to this emotional indifference comes across in some Buddhist texts. One of the crucial teachings of Buddhism is that of emptiness: the self is ultimately unreal, so the *bodhisattva* who kills with full knowledge of the emptiness of the self, kills no one; both the self of the killer and the self of the killed are nothing more than an illusion.

In the *Nirvana sutra*, there is the story of a prince who murders his father, the king, so he can accede to the throne. Heavy with remorse he consults the Buddha for advice. The Buddha makes him see that he is not responsible for the killing for two reasons. First, the king was killed as the consequence of his karma – in a previous life he murdered a holy man. Second, and most important, the Buddha states the unreality of killing:

'Great King, it is like the echo of a voice in the mountain valleys. The ignorant think it is a real voice, but the wise know it is not. Killing is like this. The foolish think it is real, but the Buddha knows it is not.[34]' (p.196)

Another Buddhist text (*Jueguan lun*) echoes the idea of the *emptiness of killing*; if you do it as if it were a spontaneous act of nature, then you're not responsible for it[35].

'The fire in the bush burns the mountain; the hurricane breaks trees; the collapsing cliff crushes wild animals to death; the running mountain's stream drowns the insects. If a man can make his mind similar [to these forces], then, meeting a man, he may kill him all the same.' (p.226)

This idea is reinforced in various other texts. If you are in a selfless and detached state of mind, you can do anything, even 'enjoy the five sensuous pleasures with unrestricted freedom' (the *Upalipariprccha* explains), as your actions will have no negative karmic consequence[36]. In other words *bodhisattvas* are not morally responsible for their actions because they act without self-interest. The Fifth Dalai Lama used this argument to justify the violence of the Mongol king Gushri Khan, who in the 1630s and 1640s violently unified a large portion of Tibet and converted the people to Buddhism. The Fifth Dalai Lama glorifies this because the Mongol king was an emanation 'of Vajrapani, the *bodhisattva* representing perfect yogic power', who had realized emptiness and 'would radiate 100 rays of light in the ten directions[37]'. (p.94)

The idea that Buddhism, unlike other religions, did not force people to convert, but 'pacified' the new lands to which it spread, is also a myth. Just like Christianity and Islam made churches and mosques from pagan temples and fought animistic ideas as heretical, something similar happened with Buddhism. Shamanic practices were prohibited in Mongolia from the 1500s, spirit figurines were burned and replaced with Buddhist images of six-armed Mahakala. Those who continued to practise Shamanic rites were subjected to brutal punishments or executed. These acts were justified because of the spiritual status of rulers, who were recognized as living Buddhas, accomplished in virtue and wisdom, and endowed with unbiased compassion. Mongol laws regulated the privileges of the Buddhist clergy and the punishment of any attacks on monasteries depending on the social class of the offender: if a nobleman, the punishment was exile; if a commoner, the sentence was more likely to be death[38].

Bernard Faure, a professor at Columbia University, suggests that forced conversion is sometimes brutally visible in religious imagery. In the case of Tibet, there is the myth that its first Buddhist king subdued the demoness who ruled the land by nailing her down to the ground. The holiest of places in Tibetan Buddhism, the Jokhang Temple in Lhasa, is symbolically known as the nail that was driven into the vagina of the demoness. 'The rape imagery,' Faure writes, 'could hardly be more explicit[39].' (p.231)

The demonization, dehumanization and social discrimination of rivals seem to be as prevalent in Buddhism as in other faiths. In one sacred text often used by the current Dalai Lama (the *Kalachacra-tantra*), the final battle of the world will be between Buddhists and heretics – the heretics are identified as Muslims.

In Thailand, Buddhism needed to tackle other classes of enemies. In 1976 a leading monk declared in an interview that 'killing communists is not a sin'. These were his reasons:

'First, killing communists is not really killing; second, sacrifice the lesser good for the greater good; third, the intention is not to kill but to protect the country; fourth, the Buddha allowed killing.'

And he concludes: 'Our intention is not to kill human beings, but to kill monsters. This is the duty of all Thais.[40]' (p.179)

This extraordinary statement doesn't come out of the blue. In Thailand, as in other Asian countries, the state protects its Buddhist religion and Buddhist monks protect the Thai state. Thai temples are used as military bases and some soldiers are ordained as monks – they are known as 'military monks' and one of their primary duties is to protect, using violence if need be, Buddhist temples.

All of this was new to me. As a reader of books on Ea spirituality and meditation since my teens, I had never co across any remote suggestion that Buddhism was similar to other religions when it came to justifying and using violent means. If Buddhist monks and enlightened teachers can be violent towards others, why would Western meditators be any different? I was coming to the conclusion that meditation is only a process: it can sharpen attention, quiet thoughts and angst, increase positive emotions towards ourselves and others and, in the extreme, it can lead to a deep alteration of our identity – a kind of ecstatic annihilation of the ego. But with the wrong kind of motivation and without clear ethical rules, that very spiritual selflessness can serve all kinds of ill purposes. That happened with Japanese Buddhism not long ago.

Zen soldiers

'Why didn't we have the religion of the Japanese, who regard sacrifice for the Fatherland as the highest good?'

Adolf Hitler[41]

In the late-1950s journalist and author Arthur Koestler travelled to the East and met with a number of leading spiritual teachers. The narrative of his travels was published as *The Lotus and the Robot*[42]. In the last chapter, entitled 'The Stink of Zen', Koestler takes issue with Zen's amorality and goes as far as criticizing Suzuki, the Zen scholar who made Zen known to a wide Western audience. He quotes from Suzuki's book *Zen and Japanese Culture*:

'Zen is ... extremely flexible in adapting itself to almost any philosophy and moral doctrine as long as its intuitive teaching is not interfered with. It may be found wedded to anarchism or fascism, communism or democracy, atheism or idealism.[43]' (p.63)

Koestler commented that this passage 'could have come from a philosophical-minded Nazi journalist, or from one of the Zen monks who became suicide pilots' (p.271). His meetings with

Zen teachers only reinforced the idea that Zen has no interest in morality or social ethics. When he asked about the persecution of religion in totalitarian countries or Hitler's gas chambers, the answers generally showed a lack of interest in differentiating between good and ill deeds. He regarded this as a 'tolerance devoid of charity' and was skeptical about the contribution Zen Buddhism had to offer post-World War II to the moral recovery of Japan, or any other country.

In this short chapter Koestler pointed his finger at a phenomenon of unimagined proportions. Forty years later it became public knowledge that the 'stink of Zen' dominated Japan during World War II; Koestler was right.

It was Brian Victoria, a Zen priest and historian of religions, who brought the evidence to light. He has shown how, during World War II, the Japanese military used Zen Buddhist ideas and meditation techniques and how Zen Buddhist leaders showed explicit support of the war[44]. Victoria's verdict is as sharp as a samurai's sword. He reveils that nearly all of Japan's Buddhist leaders were fervent supporters of Japanese militarism. As a result, he argues, Zen Buddhism so deeply violated Buddhism's fundamental principles that it should no longer be recognized as an expression of the Boddidharma[45]. Within a Western religious context, this would be the equivalent of saying that during a certain period (such as the Inquisition), the Catholic Church was not an authentic expression of Christ's teachings.

Victoria methodically reveals how warfare and killing were regarded as manifestations of Buddhist compassion, selflessness and dedication to the Japanese emperor. The soldier's code, which all soldiers had to learn by heart in 1941, had a section entitled 'View of Life and Death' which read:

'That which penetrates life and death is the lofty spirit of self-sacrifice for the public good. Transcending life and death, earnestly rush forward to accomplish your duty. Exhausting the power of your body and mind, calmly find joy in living in eternal duty.[46]' (p.110)

This is eerily familiar to us living in a post-9/11 world. The violent rhetoric of religious extremism is probably universal, but, in the case of Zen Buddhism, its very spiritual pinnacle – the attainment of enlightened selflessness – was used to train soldiers during World War II, who would sacrifice themselves as if their lives were of no consequence. Thus, an army major advised his soldiers:

'[The soldier] must become one with his superior. He must actually become his superior. Similarly, he must become the order he receives. That is to say, *his self must disappear*.' (p.103)

Islam or Christianity's promise of eternal life is here exchanged for the Buddhist idea that, by becoming selfless, life and death become undifferentiated; there is nothing to lose by dying on the battlefield once you realize the emptiness of the self. This spirit is deeply entrenched in Japanese Buddhism, going back at least to the samurai age. Takuan, a famous Zen master from the 1600s, wrote:

'The uplifted sword has no will of its own, it is all emptiness. It is like a flash of lightning. The man who is about to be struck down is also of emptiness, and so is the one who wields the sword. None of them are possessed of a mind that has any substantiality. As each of them is of emptiness and has no mind, the striking man is not a man, the sword in his hands is not a sword, and the "I" who is about to be struck down is like the splitting of the spring breeze in a flash of lightning.[47]' (p.131)

D.T. Suzuki expressed the same view in the twentieth century. He eloquently compared the Zen master's use of the sword to the production of an artistic masterpiece. Although it is not the intention of the Zen master to harm anybody, the enemy appears and makes himself a victim of the enlightened swordsman, Suzuki suggests; it is as if the sword acts without an agent – or through a robot, if we want to use a less poetic image. It is then no great wonder that Hitler and the Nazis were fond of the Zen. Heinrich Himmler, leader of the SS (*Schutzstaffel*), who was obsessed with esoteric ideas and sent expeditions to Tibet and India, believed tary had to act with 'decency'. By decency he meant that they had to remain untouched by human weakness when staring at the thousands of corpses, lying side by side, as they tumbled into the pit at concentration camps. When he was caught and questioned after the war, he didn't have a shred of insight about the villainy of his actions[48]; like a Zen master, he seemed indifferent.

When Brian Victoria's book, *Zen at War*, was translated into Japanese, it had an unforeseen impact. Instead of trying to deny Japanese Buddhism's ties to militarism, a number of Zen masters admitted this had happened and formally apologized. It was a long journey for Victoria, who had been ordained as a Zen priest in 1964 because he believed Zen Buddhism was free from the violence that had marked Western religions[49]. But he hasn't lost his faith. He upholds Buddhism's non-violent principles and denies the possibility of compassionate killing, arguing that under no circumstances can a *bodhisattva* legitimately employ violence to the point of actually taking the life of another human being.

However, this leaves us with another, no less difficult question to answer: what do we make of a *bodhisattva* or, in the Zen tradition, someone who has reached *satori* (the realization of selflessness) and still commits violence – is this person truly enlightened? Paradoxically, yes. After the war Suzuki, although not retracting any of his former works, argued that enlightenment alone is not enough to make you a responsible Zen priest. A Zen priest also needs to use intellectual discrimination, because enlightenment in itself is just a state of being that cannot tell right from wrong.

This is not what we're used to hearing. Enlightenment in the East is regarded very much like saintliness in the West – whomever reaches such a state of being is expected to be the pinnacle of selflessness and love. Followers revere their spiritual teachers, often treating them like the living embodiment of nirvana or God. The idea that the highest attainment of spiritual development may not be enough to tell right from wrong is disturbing. Two hypotheses come to mind: either enlightenment does not necessarily make you act in an unselfish or a peaceful way; or perhaps those whom we think of as enlightened aren't as holy as they seem. Mystics of all times have warned against the dangers of spiritual infatuation. The Spanish Christian mystic Theresa of Avila went as far as suggesting that we should never trust the goodness of the holy people who are still living[50]. In the Christian tradition it is a sin of vanity to believe you are holy. In the Buddhist tradition it would probably be proof that the egoless master still has some ego to shed. But in the East it's widely accepted that some people are real embodiments of compassion or God, and it's not unusual for the masters themselves to proclaim that. Recently, in India, one man was revered by millions and looked upon as the living God.

The most selfish man on Earth

I first heard of Sai Baba through a friend who was doing a Master's degree in the sociology of religion. Having been raised by Marxist parents, Joana was curious about religion and went off to southern Italy to do fieldwork with a community of Sai Baba followers. It was very much like any other Hindu devotional community, she told me, with lots of chanting, praying and some meditation – but there were a couple of unusual things. First, there were various gifts – bracelets, watches – that, apparently, the guru had produced from thin air and offered to his followers. Second, the guru often showed up in people's dreams – an event that had been the catalyst for conversion to Sai Baba's doctrine for many of the people Joana interviewed during her fieldwork. Joana herself, despite being an atheist, had dreams about Sai Baba while staying with the community. This frightened her, but it didn't turn her into a believer[51].

The first time I considered the idea that an enlightened person could be flawed was in relation to Sai Baba. I was talking to Carlos do Carmo Silva, a philosopher of religion based at the

Catholic University of Lisbon. A tall, thin and unassuming man in his late fifties, he has produced work on the parallels and tensions between Buddhist and Christian mystical attainment that is the most insightful I've ever encountered[52]. I was asking what he thought of Sai Baba's claim to being an 'avatar', the very embodiment of God on earth.

'Perhaps he is,' he said gazing upwardly. 'But other times he can be the most selfish man on Earth.'

I looked at him, puzzled. He didn't offer an explanation for this contradiction and I wasn't expecting him to – he often challenged me to think out of the box. His words popped into my mind when a few months later a BBC documentary on Sai Baba accused the guru of sexually abusing some male teenage American devotees. Shocking as the revelations were, the way an Indian minister treated the BBC journalist who confronted him with the allegations was no less brutal[53]. The auras of devotion and power surrounding the guru were astounding.

The sexual abuse allegations probably did not harm Indian devotion to Sai Baba, but they did have an effect on Western devotees. Many centres in Europe and the USA closed down. I didn't think about it any further, though, until one evening in Oxford I was invited to comment on a lecture by the Icelandic psychologist Erlendur Haraldsson. He was speaking about some work he had done on children who claimed to remember past lives, but I knew that Haraldsson had written a book about Sai Baba's miracles[54]. At the end of the event, I asked him if he had personally met the Indian holy man.

'Oh, yes, on quite a number of occasions. I spent some time at his ashram during which we spoke on a daily basis.'

'And what do you make of him?'

'I do think he has some unusual powers. I can't tell if all the stories are real, but I think some of them are,' he confided.

'What about the sexual abuse allegations; what do you make of them?'

Haraldsson looked down at me (he is quite a tall man) and shrugged.

'Well, he's obviously a gay man ...'

I stared at Haraldsson and said nothing. We stayed quiet for a moment and then changed subject.

Violence comes in many shapes. Sexual abuse is one of the most difficult forms of violence to confront; often the abuser is a powerful figure, either within a family or an organization. Spiritual organizations are not immune to this. The recent scandal of sexual abuse among the Roman Catholic clergy has stirred waves in the Western world, but Buddhist monks in the East, including leading priests, have also been found guilty of this. Recently in the USA Sasaki, a revered Zen priest known to be Leonard Cohen's Buddhist teacher, has been accused of sexual abuse by a number of female followers. On various occasions Sasaki asked women to show their breasts, and explained that this was part of a Zen *koan* or a way of showing non-attachment. Another woman complained that the master massaged her breasts during a private session and was asked to massage his genitals[55]. The accusations against Sai Baba were very similar, but the target of the abuse was at the time a young male adolescent. I thought again of what Carlos do Carmo Silva, the philosopher, had said: the holiest man on earth can also be the most selfish. I also remembered German psychologist Harold Wallach telling me that he had met advanced meditators who were 'assholes'. As hard and paradoxical as it sounds, it is very likely that no human being is immune to being cruel or taking advantage of others at times, no matter how spiritually evolved.

By the time I'd uncovered all this material, I was feeling disillusioned and somewhat nauseated. The old aphorism 'the road to hell is paved with good intentions' played loudly in my mind. Meditation and spiritual teachers are coloured with a sweetened aura that distorts the reality of individuals, societies and history. The unrealistically positive ideas associated with meditation only make people more vulnerable to either the adverse psychological effects or its enlightened-amoral teachers. The other danger was that the cover up about the dark aspects of meditation, implicitly or explicitly endowed by scientists studying its effects, could destroy the good it had to offer. I painfully understood Koestler's feelings of disillusion at the end of his chapter on Japanese Buddhism:

'For a week or so I bargained with a Kyoto antique dealer for a small bronze Buddha of the Kamakura period; but when he came down to a price that I was able to afford, I backed out. I realized with shock that the Buddha smile had gone dead on me. It was no longer mysterious but empty.' (p.274)

But I also realized, with a sense of relief and humility, that meditation need not be a panacea to cure every ill, nor a tool to moral perfection; perhaps we shouldn't treat it very differently from prayer, which can quiet our minds, give us some comfort, and lead us towards a deeper place where we can explore who we are or be closer to God. Perhaps meditation was never supposed to be more than a tool to help with self-knowledge; one that could never be divorced from a strong ethical grounding, who we are and the world we live in. In Patanjali's *sutras*, when he describes the various aspects of yoga, meditation is only one of them[56]. The first one, the very basis of a healthy and eventual selfless being is self-restraint (*yama*), which he defines as 'non-violation, truthfulness, non-stealing, containment, and non-grasping' (p.119). And to be sure that these are the definite and non-debatable foundations he adds:

'These restraints are not limited by birth, time or circumstance; they constitute the great vow everywhere.' (p.120)

Only with this strong foundation, can the other limbs of yoga (as Patanjali calls them) emerge, including the *asanas*, *pranayama*, meditation and the blissful experiences of unity with the ground of being.

FIGHT WITH EVERYTHING YOU'VE GOT!

Re-reading this chapter I felt unhappy not to finish on a more hopeful note. Despite its dark side and the limitations of the current scientific research, I still think meditation is a technique with real potential for personal change, if properly guided and taught within a larger spiritual-ethical framework. I was also aware that read on its own, religious extremists and proselytizers could use it to belittle Buddhism and Hinduism. I thought of looking for someone who, coming from the West, had embraced the Eastern meditation tradition without denying its darker side. I found that person in Swami Ambikananda, a South African woman who took religious Hindu vows and who teaches meditation and yoga, while also running a charity in the southwest of England. She has translated a number of Indian sacred texts from the Sanskrit; I'd read her clear and poetic translation of the *Katha Upanishad*, which has the very first recorded teaching on yoga[57].

She welcomed me at her house in Reading, about an hour west of London. It felt odd to call her Swami Am-bi-ka-nan-da, seven full syllables of a name; her direct and expansive personality seemed to require no more than two. I wondered what birth name she'd been given, but it felt odd to ask. She was dressed in the orange cloth of the Indian ascetics, but her way of speaking and gesticulating was definitely Western feminine. We walked into her living room and she invited me to sit down on a cushion on the floor.

'We have no chairs here,' she explained. 'I hope you don't mind.'

'I don't. Is it okay if I write down some notes?'

She offered me tea. I was happy to see her again. We'd first met at the day course on the psychology of meditation I gave with Catherine Crane (see pp.109–110). Her questions and comments stood out, very much like her orange garment. When I told her I was writing this book and looking into the potential dark side of meditation, she asked whether I had heard of Aaron Alexis; I hadn't yet.

'There is a new dogma about meditation: when it fails its limitations are never questioned,' she told me. 'We are told that they weren't doing it right. But it may be neither the practice nor the person that is wrong. The truth about our human condition is that no one thing works for everyone. The spiritual journey is about the unmasking of oneself, being more authentically "self" and whatever path leads us there is grand for each of us, but that particular path is not necessarily good for all of us.'

She was aware of the dangers of contemplative practice and open about it. I asked how she had become interested in meditation and Indian spirituality.

'My father was a Marxist atheist and my mum a devout Catholic. This was confusing but not too much, until I turned 11 or 12. Then, I heard about the doctrine of limbo – I don't think the Catholic Church believes in it anymore – you know, this place where the souls of unbaptized children were supposed to go and stay for eternity. That was it for me; I became an atheist. I didn't think too much about the soul or religion for a while, until I had twins and then became depressed. One day a friend thought it was a good distraction to take me to a lecture by a *swami*, so I went. The people there were very serious – try lighting a cigarette in a yoga lecture like I did! – but there was something I liked about Swami Venkatesananda and kept meeting him. But I only got to the yoga and meditation later.'

'How did that happen?'

'I was visiting Swami Venkatesananda in Mauritius and had bought a pile of books on Indian spirituality and philosophy. One day he told me he needed some help in clearing up some junk and pointed at a ravine where people threw all kinds of stuff – old fridges, cars, you name it. I said, yes, I'll help you. He then picked up the whole pile of books I had just bought and threw them down the ravine. "Why did you do that?" I asked him. He told me the time had come to stop reading and to try out yoga and meditation. That's how I started.'

I asked Ambikananda whether or not she believes meditation can change a person, and, if she does, how much meditation it would take to change. She told me about meeting Krishnamurti, the Indian-born writer who was heralded as the New World messiah by the Theosophical Society, but eventually walked away from the movement to become a kind of spiritual free thinker.

'He told me two minutes a day was enough. I laughed; it takes me two hours of meditation to get two worthwhile minutes! But he was right that it's not only about meditation; your intention counts. My teacher used to tell me: "Hunt down the self ruthlessly; this isn't for the faint hearted." There is an acknowledgment in all religious traditions – whether it's the spiritual work of Ignatius of Loyola or the process of St Theresa of Avila, or the Way of the Buddha, or the yoga path of Patanjali – that you need more than meditation to change.'

'What do you mean?' I asked.

'To start with, you need to have a healthy ego; what kind of self are you surrendering if you don't have a stable sense of who you are?'

'What about the clinical use of mindfulness to treat depression and anxiety? I suppose you don't have a healthy sense of self there ...'

'I'm uncertain about the exact value of mindfulness,' Ambikananda told me. 'Since it has moved out of the monastic environment into the wider secular world, meditation is being sold as that which will not only make use feel better but will make us better people – more successful, stronger, convincing ...'

I interrupted her. 'But are you aware that some researchers are claiming that mindfulness meditation *per se* can turn you into a better, more compassionate person?'

'No, no, no,' she stressed. 'Meditation needs to be embedded in its context, there are moral and emotional guidelines to be followed; Patanjali spells them out clearly in his work on yoga.'

'But the whole purpose of meditating – isn't it meant to make you an enlightened and deeply moral individual; moral in the sense of unselfish and compassionate. Isn't that was happens?'

'Morality can be divorced from spirituality. My ego can dissolve while I meditate, but when I get up it's reconstructed. You can meditate 22 hours a day, but in those two hours you have left, you are a human being living in matter, and this aspect of reality' (she touched the ground) 'doesn't care too much if you're enlightened or not.'

I told Swami Ambikananda about the evidence I'd uncovered concerning the adverse aspects of meditation and its violent history in the East; she simply nodded. Even the claims of sexual abuse by some spiritual teachers didn't surprise her. 'I had one of the few truly celibate Indian spiritual teachers,' she admitted. Ambikananda then told me the story of once travelling through the Himalayas in search of a levitating holy man. She was staying at the ashram of her teacher in Rishikesh, at the foot of the Ganges, when a friend told her about a flying hermit, who lived in a cave only a day's journey away.

'It took us about three days, walking in the Himalayas to find him. We were going in the wrong direction for more than a day. But we managed to find our way and met the flying *baba*. He asked for some rupees and went into a trance state. After a few minutes I couldn't believe my eyes: he was really lifting off the ground! I felt rather irritated; this is *not* supposed to happen. I got some branches from a nearby tree and moved them beneath and above him to make sure it was not a trick. I couldn't see the trick and asked him to do it again; he did it and still I couldn't see how. When I asked if he could also do it standing, he said he couldn't; he had to be sitting down. I wanted to see him doing it a third time, but he refused. He said he'd teach me if I stayed for a few days and gave him some more rupees.

'And did you?' I asked.

'I wouldn't stay alone with that man for anything in this world!' she said laughing. 'He made it very clear that besides money he wanted sexual favours.'

After our talk Swami Ambikananda gave me a lift to Reading railway station. I thanked her for her time and asked again about Aaron Alexis, the man who was a regular meditator and killed 12 people.

'Do you think it had anything to do with meditation?'

'I don't know. I don't dispute that he had serious mental health problems; but meditation probably didn't help him either. Meditation is about looking into the abyss within, it wasn't created to make you or me happy, but to help us fight the illusions we have and find out who we truly are. My teacher used to tell me: "This is your battle, you fight it with everything you've got." He also used to say that we shouldn't take ourselves too seriously. I certainly do my best,' she said, laughing.

Meeting this lively and grounded South African woman turned Hindu priest made me feel less pessimistic about the use of meditation and yoga in the West. If we admit its frailties and limits, that it takes other things for these techniques to make real positive change – the right intention, a good teacher and moral framing – they can still prove effective engines of personal change. I wanted to test the effects on a population who might not often get the chance to try out yoga and meditation practice, but who might need the benefits more than your average person. Back in Oxford I rang the director of the Prison Phoenix Trust. 'Sam, let's go ahead with the research project. If you provide the yoga and meditation classes to prisoners, I'll handle the science part.'

CHAPTER 7

BEHIND BARS

It's 8am on a freezing January morning and I'm standing in the gate lodge of a Midlands prison, wishing I'd brought a coat. It's the first day of what will be six weeks of driving across the Midlands to seven prisons to interview prisoners who have volunteered to participate in our yoga and meditation research study. I've had both my passport and driving licence checked, had my photograph taken, and obtained a visitor badge. I'm now waiting for a prison officer to collect me and escort me inside.

Finally, a tall middle-aged man shows up and fishes his keys from his belt pouch to unlock the heavy iron gate. 'You here about the yoga?' he asks. 'Come this way.'

Once inside I'm taken through security; my bag needs to be scanned and searched, as do I. Once sufficiently frisked to check I have no mobile phones, drugs, chewing gum, or other banned items, I'm escorted through the prison to the room where I will be spending the next few days interviewing prisoners.

***

The 'interview room' turned out to be a small chaplain's office situated at the end of the prison chapel. My escort unlocked the door for me and left. As this was a Category C prison, security had not deemed it necessary for me to carry an alarm, although I noticed a panic button nearby on the wall to call for help if something went wrong. I sat down in the chair nearest the door and arranged my materials on the desk: a battery of questionnaires that would enable me to gain measures of mood, level of aggression, impulsivity, and so on; information sheets, consent forms and visual rulers. The latter were intended to do pretty much what they said on the tin – large rulers with numbers on them representing the range of possible responses participants can give to a particular questionnaire item (such as, 'How sad have you felt over the last week, on a scale of one to seven?').

There was a knock on the door; I looked up to see a man's face at the glass window. 'Come in,' I said, expecting my first participant of the day. The door opened.

'Hi,' said a short, shaven-headed man in his thirties, dressed in blue prison clothes. 'Would you like a tea or coffee?'

I thanked him and minutes later, he returned with a cup of coffee in a plastic beaker. He explained that this is his job; he is a chapel orderly, and one of his tasks is making tea and coffee for staff. He sat back down at his table in the corner of the chapel, stacking Bibles.

A couple of minutes later, there was another knock on the door. This time it *was* my first participant. The man entered, looking a little wary.

I introduced myself and we shook hands. I started by explaining the study and what the interview would involve. I told him that if he took part, he would be randomly allocated into either the 'yoga' group, the members of which would take part in a weekly yoga and meditation class, or the control group.

'What day will the yoga classes be on?' he asked.

I told him I wasn't entirely sure – we were yet to hear from the prison authorities what day of the week would work best in terms of fitting around the regime (although as an officer wryly remarked to me, 'it probably doesn't matter; every day here is a bit like Groundhog Day'). What I did know was it would most likely be an afternoon class. I asked him if that would be okay.

'Oh yeah. I can do afternoons. I used to work in the kitchen, but I don't anymore.' I asked him what he did instead.

'Nothing,' he replied. 'I usually just stay in my pad most of the day. It's boring ... that's why I want to do the yoga. To give me something to do.'

Over the past few years, I have interviewed around a couple of hundred prisoners (both men and women), including lifers, sex offenders and young offenders. While there is a lot of variation in experience, between both prisons and prisoners, certain themes are common: a depressing sense of frustration, boredom and futility, of endless, meaningless time, of life being on hold or even over. Many prison governors and staff make a real effort to engage prisoners in meaningful activities that extend far beyond menial work tasks – education, art, music and drama, psychological therapy, befriending, and even outside work. However, budget limitations, risk issues, and varying levels of motivation or ability to engage mean that such activities are not available to or appropriate for many. Therefore, some prisoners may spend much of their time in a small cell – potentially up to 23 hours a day – doing nothing more stimulating than watching the soaps.

MONASTIC CELLS

Yet, there are numerous prisoners across the world who spend their time engaged in a practice they believe not only helps them to cope with captivity, but will change them for the better. In the first chapter of this book, I introduced the notion that a prison cell can be conceived of as an ashram, or a monastic cell. I discussed how the asceticism of prison life – though imposed, rather than desired – bears certain similarities to that of monks' lives, and how prisoners might have an increased opportunity for self-reflection, personal growth and even spiritual development. The notion that incarceration could be reconceived of as an 'opportunity' to develop and better the self, through the use of meditation, was

even espoused by one of the greatest political figures of
our time. Nelson Mandela, former president of South Africa,
spent 27 years in prison because of his fight against apartheid.
During his imprisonment he wrote the following in a letter to his
wife, Winnie, who was also in prison:

'The cell is an ideal place to learn to know yourself, to search
realistically and regularly the process of your own mind and
feelings. Internal factors may be even more crucial in assessing
one's development as a human being. Honesty, simplicity,
humility, pure generosity, absence of vanity, readiness to serve
others – qualities that are within the reach of every soul – are
the foundation of one's spiritual life. Development in matters
of this nature is inconceivable without knowing yourself, your
weaknesses and mistakes. At least, if for nothing else, the cell
gives you the opportunity to look daily into your entire conduct.
Regular meditation, say about 15 minutes a day before you turn in,
can be very fruitful in this regard. You may find it difficult at first...
but the tenth attempt may yield rich rewards.'

Thinking of incarceration as 'opportunity' rather than
punishment requires quite a shift in perspective, a shift that for
Mandela was facilitated through deep reflection and meditative
practice. Although those of us on the outside may well feel certain
benefits through doing yoga or meditation, regular practice can
be hard to fit it into our busy lives.

Prisoners are a demographic who have that opportunity;
while they are deprived of their liberty, they are rich in time.
In the absence of the distractions of the outside world, they
may be able to immerse themselves in it in a way the rest of us
might only be able to experience on a retreat, or by ditching
our nine-to-fives to become yoga teachers ourselves. Even for
prisoners who practise less frequently, yoga and meditation may
accrue a value that they never had during life on the outside.
Prisoners are often so desperate for relief from negative emotions
and the frustrations of prison life, they will try anything that might

provide it – be that drugs, self-harm, or perhaps yoga and meditation.

But how strong is the rationale for offering these techniques to individuals who have committed crimes, and are behind bars in order to be punished? Over the course of this book, I have discussed the various psychological benefits of meditation in 'normal' populations and considered their potential to change us for the better. But are these practices, with their associations of peace and spirituality, really suited to prison life? Can the so-called 'worst of society' gain genuine benefit? Or, given meditation's dark side, might it increase their emotional disturbance?

Prison yoga across the world

Yoga and meditation classes are increasing in prisons throughout the UK – and elsewhere, too. Given the origins of yoga, it is unsurprising that India is one of the countries most accepting of yoga in prisons. In 2010 a prison program in the Indian state of Madhya Pradesh caused a flurry of media attention, when it was reported that prisoners could be freed early if they completed courses of yoga. A BBC report detailed that for every three months offenders spent practising yoga, they could reduce their jail time by fifteen days[1]. The authorities believed that the yoga classes helped to improve prisoners' self-control and reduce their aggression.

In the USA a number of different charitable organizations, including Bo Lozoff's Prison Ashram Project (see p.14) and James Fox's Prison Yoga Project, founded over a decade ago in California, exist to provide yoga classes in prisons. Prison yoga classes also occur throughout Scandinavian countries. In Sweden yoga has become an integral part of the prison service, which employs a yoga co-ordinator and trains some of its prison staff as yoga instructors. Vipassana meditation classes – and even retreats – have also been offered in several prisons in India, the USA and New Zealand.

But do yoga and meditation classes really offer prisoners any meaningful benefit, or do they simply represent an hour a week of out-of-cell relaxation? While acceptance of the provision of yoga and meditation classes in prisons has been increasing, quality scientific research into this area has been relatively limited. Later in this chapter I will discuss the scientific evidence that does exist for the effectiveness of these techniques to bring about measurable change in prisoners. However, while the scientific evidence may provide the 'proof', it is the accounts of prisoners who testify to having experienced meaningful changes that really brings to life the potential of yoga and meditation as catalysts for personal change, and justifies the scientific research in the first place.

DRUG SMUGGLER TURNED YOGI

Around the time I began writing this chapter, my partner arrived home one evening from a business meeting with a potential investor, looking rather pleased with himself.
'Did the meeting go well?' I asked.

'Yes,' he said. 'I think he likes my idea. But also,' he grinned, 'Turns out he knows someone you might want to speak to for your book. A guy called Nick. He used to be a drug smuggler and now he's a yoga instructor! He's a friend of his – he pointed out his studio in Notting Hill as we were walking to our meeting.'

Seizing the moment I quickly wrote an email to be passed on to Nick, explaining a bit about the book and why I'd like to speak to him.

The next day I checked my emails ten times, keen to hear back. No response. The days passed. Nothing. I started to guess that ex-drug smugglers aren't so keen on sharing their life stories with curious, book-writing psychologists. Ah, well. But it made me start to wonder ... if this Nick person had undergone such a transformation, surely there would be others; ex-prisoners who had turned their lives around through yoga, to the point of even becoming yoga instructors themselves. If anyone was going to know such a person, I thought, it would be Sam Settle, the director of the Prison Phoenix Trust. I gave Sam a call. He said he had someone in mind; he would check with them and get back to me.

A few days later Sam called me back. He had heard from his contact, who would love to speak to me. 'Who is he?' I asked. 'A very interesting person,' said Sam, evenly. 'I believe he used to be an international drugs smuggler, and now he's a yoga instructor.'

The coincidence! I thought to myself. What are the chances that the only two ex-prisoner-turned-yoga instructors I've ever heard of were both notorious in the drug underworld? 'His name's Nick,' said Sam.

And so it was that I finally got to meet Nick Brewer. Nick emailed to say that he would be happy to meet me, but that he was soon to leave for a three-week spiritual retreat in the Philippines. He offered a couple of potential dates he could meet in the following week, which I had to turn down, somewhat sheepishly admitting that I would myself be departing for a week in Las Vegas (I could not help but feel a chasm between the seeming morality of our trips). When finally we found a day, shortly before I was due to leave, there was no discussion about where we would be meeting – Nick's email was succinct: 'You will have to come to me. I am very busy.'

Reading his words I couldn't help but imagine he had used such phrases many times before, in the context of slightly more illicit arrangements.

A couple of days after our initial correspondence, I got off the tube at Notting Hill Gate and wandered off in search of the deli where Nick had instructed me to meet him. Taking a few wrong turns and walking down a seemingly never-ending, tree-lined street, I was aware that I'd possibly underestimated how long it would take me to get there. I started to pick up my pace – was he likely to be the kind of man who would take kindly to being kept waiting? By the time I located the deli, in the heart of affluent Notting Hill, I was a little flustered – and 10 minutes late. Only then did I realize that I had no idea what Nick looked like. I noticed three men standing on the street nearby, talking animatedly to one another. I looked at them hopefully. One of them, a shaven-headed man in his forties, caught my eye and walked towards me: 'Hi, I'm Nick.'

He greeted me with a warm handshake and we went inside, where he ordered a freshly squeezed juice and bought me a cappuccino. It was warm and busy, but we managed to find a sofa to sit down at. It was quite loud with the chatter from nearby tables, and I realized I wouldn't be able to record our interview on my Dictaphone, as I had hoped. When I shared this observation with him, his smile dropped for a second: 'I don't think I'd be up for being recorded,' he said.

Nick was charismatic and engaging in conversation and he seemed keen to ask me about myself. Initially, I couldn't decide whether this was out of politeness or genuine interest, or as a means to try to suss out what my motives might be – perhaps to decide how much he should divulge. If the latter were true, it would make sense. Much of Nick's 'success' in his criminal activities would have depended on his ability to determine whom he should and should not trust. Over the course of our conversation, however, I found him surprisingly open when it came to talking about his life events. When I offered to anonymize his name for this book, he told me there was no need – the majority of his yoga clients already knew about his criminal past, and he suspected that some of them may have chosen to practise with him not in spite of it, but *because* of it.

Amid the hustle and bustle of the café, Nick revealed a fascinating tale. The son of a policeman, he was raised in east London and enjoyed a stable upbringing. At 11 years old he went skiing for the first time. He proved to be a natural and threw himself into his new hobby with a single-minded passion. Driven to be the best, Nick secured sponsorship at just 15 years of age, leaving his family home for the French Alps to train full time with the England junior skiing team. His commitment to skiing was such that his daily life, and moreover his whole identity centred on this one true talent. As a teenager he had a lifestyle envied by his peers, with a future that looked nothing but golden. He was set to become a champion professional skier, nurturing dreams of Olympic glory.

Then, in one devastating moment, his charmed life fell apart. A jump on the slopes went badly wrong and he fell, fracturing his back in two places. Coming round in hospital, doctors told him he was lucky; his spinal cord was intact and he would make a full recovery – in terms of being able to walk. But his competitive skiing days were over. The consequence of his injury devastated him; he could no longer do the thing he loved. He had felt destined to be a sporting hero. What was he to do now? Who *was* he now? 'I felt like nothing,' he told me. 'And I had nothing, financially.'

This was a pivotal point in Nick's life, which led to a drastic change in his worldview. Overnight, he had gone from being a young sportsman full of potential, with an exciting career ahead of him, to a nobody. Wanting to escape his life, he hitchhiked to Antibes, where he lived rough on the beach for several months. There in the south of France, the policeman's son met a group of people who took him under their wing – and recruited him into drug smuggling, offering him an apparent escape from his then-depressing life. Learning their trade gave him not only an income, but a sense of purpose and identity; and so his life as a career criminal began. At twenty, he moved to southwest Spain, where he became involved with a gang and began smuggling cannabis. However, a year later Nick got caught with a large cannabis haul at the docks in Dover, Kent, and was sentenced to prison, serving 18 months at HMP Maidstone.

'Getting sent to prison then was the worst thing that could

ever have happened to me,' Nick explained. 'Not because it was a heavy punishment – it was a short sentence. But because it gave me an education in how to be a better drugs smuggler.'

While in prison Nick made a lot of influential contacts and learned more about methods of smuggling. On his release he moved to South America, turning his attentions to the more lucrative drug of cocaine. He was good at his new 'job' and began to make a name for himself in the drug-smuggling underworld, which proved quite a boost to his ego: 'I was able to become someone after being nobody.'

Taking on the alias 'The Kid', Nick's game of choice was logistics and container shipping; smuggling huge quantities of cocaine from South America to be distributed across Europe. His drug trafficking made him a millionaire and he spent most of the 1990s living a high-octane playboy lifestyle in Marbella. He successfully evaded the law for 13 years, until in 2004 he was arrested in Argentina, having been caught in possession of 200 kilograms of cocaine, a mere fraction of a 1,000 kilograms consignment he had been waiting for. Nick was sentenced to ten years in Devoto, Buenos Aires, one of South America's toughest maximum-security prisons. Corrupt and rife with violence, he found Argentinian prison to be wildly different to his 'educative' incarceration in the UK: 'It was a hell hole where every day was a battle for survival; where cons would quite happily slit your throat for your shoes or a phone card.'

Initially, Nick was unrepentant and spent his first year in the prison trying to continue his involvement in smuggling, liaising with contacts from the inside. But one day he happened to come across a book on yoga belonging to a fellow prisoner. Flicking through it, the content struck him as vaguely interesting, but he thought little more of it. Shortly afterwards, however, he was put into solitary confinement for his own safety. In an attempt to alleviate his increasing boredom, he borrowed the book and began studying the pictures of the *asanas*; soon, he was practising yoga every day.

Over the next few months, Nick began to notice some gradual changes in himself. He felt calmer, less aggressive, less impulsive – was there something in this? He asked his parents back in London to send some more yoga books. After six months Nick was released from solitary confinement, but continued practising yoga on a daily basis in his cell. His practice began to foster in him a renewed sense of ability and potential, like he had felt all those years ago on the slopes: 'It was like I had come back full circle to being that young kid again.'

As he immersed himself in yoga, he began to feel a restoration of hope and a recapturing of lost innocence. He began to feel that he was worth something – a something that was unrelated to the quantity of drugs he could smuggle, the money he could make, or the flashy lifestyle he could sustain. This led him to look at his past with a new perspective.

'After a year or two of regular practice of *asanas* and spending time sitting and observing the breath, I became aware of a definite shift in my consciousness. My thought processes changed. I found myself re-evaluating my past criminal behaviour; I'd never previously questioned the morality of it before.'

Slowly it dawned on Nick that he no longer wanted to be involved with crime. He stopped identifying with the other prisoners in the jail, so he began distancing himself from them, spending most of his time alone. He finally came to a life-changing conclusion: 'I realized that at this point in my life, I *needed* to be in prison. Not because I felt I had a debt to pay to society, nor because I deserved to be punished – but because I needed to be rehabilitated. And the rehabilitation I found was through yoga.'

In 2010, six years into his sentence, Nick was released and expedited back to England. By this point he felt 'completely alienated to crime – I was done with it'. Arriving back on home soil for the first time in over a decade, he was ready to start over from scratch. Gone were the millions; all he had to his name was a criminal record and £300 in his pocket. He moved back in with his mum and dad and started planning the way forwards.

Applying the same single-mindedness that had made him a skiing champion and a rich drug smuggler to his new passion for yoga, within a year Nick had trained as an instructor, found a flat to rent, and turned his front room into a yoga studio. There, he began to teach on a one-to-one basis, picking up clients through word-of-mouth. He quickly gained popularity in the local area, where he now teaches up to 100 private lessons a month. Yoga students don't avoid Nick, pariah-style, because of his criminal past; in fact he considers that his past may be a factor that actually attracts some clients. In the context of his teaching in bourgeois-bohemian Notting Hill, where many of his students are businessmen or hedge-fund managers, I can imagine it lending a certain frisson of excitement, a little edge, to be able to slip into dinner party conversation that your yoga instructor is a somewhat infamous ex-convict.

As we talked about the inner peace he felt and his love of yoga, the idea that the smiling, affable man I was chatting to was the same person who headed up a drugs empire and spent more than half a decade in an Argentinian prison seemed somewhat incongruent. Nick and 'The Kid' seemed like two completely different people. And perhaps Nick picked up on my thinking, as he suddenly changed tack in our conversation and, looking me straight in the eyes, said: 'You're probably sitting here thinking, oh, Nick's a really nice guy – and I am that guy, but I *did* do all of those things. I am *still* that person.'

I asked him to elaborate. Despite his radical transformation from drug smuggler to yogi, I discovered that Nick does not attribute yoga as producing any lasting personality change. Rather, he believes it instilled in him a renewed sense of self-belief and self-worth, enabling him to find a non-deviant way to direct his ambitious, driven streak. He drew a comparison to his dedication and discipline in learning and teaching yoga to the way in which he ran his drug-smuggling empire; getting up at

5am every day to practise. Despite the significant changes it had brought about in his perspective and lifestyle, he by no means saw it as a magic cure ridding him of criminal impulses. He was quite upfront about this; admitting that if he goes a few days without doing yoga, he starts to feel edgy and unsettled, and notices some of his 'old thoughts' creeping back into consciousness.

Although yoga may have proven effective at keeping 'The Kid' at bay, it has not banished his alter ego altogether. While Nick was somewhat hesitant to term his experience as being a 'spiritual' transformation ('What does that really even mean?' he asked me), his practice of yoga certainly brought about considerable, meaningful change, radically transforming his lifestyle, priorities and ambitions. But, he told me, the journey isn't over yet; the key to Nick's personal transformation lies in the discipline of his on-going practice.

'It's no quick fix,' he said, with a half smile as we concluded our meeting. 'Yoga is my lifetime AA.'

LETTERS FROM INSIDE

Nick's story of transformation is one of the more unusual I've come across, yet there are myriad testimonies of prisoners experiencing meaningful personal change through yoga or meditation. In Chapter 11 described the Prison Phoenix Trust headquarters, in Summertown, Oxford, where an entire room is filled with wall-to-wall filing cabinets, brimming with letters from prisoners. Sifting through the correspondence, I found myself quite amazed not only at the sheer quantity, but at the significance seemingly attributed to the benefits that prisoners were experiencing. Many common themes appeared in the letters. Often, prisoners described a reduction in stress:

'I have started to use meditation mainly when extremely stressed. I was sentenced last week and was really uptight. After 10 to 15 minutes of meditation in the holding cell, I was relaxed. It works. Not tried many yoga poses yet even though I recognize a few from the Wii Fit games.' (G.M. at HMP Nottingham)

Others wrote vivid descriptions of a sense of increased peace, kindness and compassion:

'My body has never felt so good and my mind is at ease. I wrote in a letter to a fellow Christian friend this week "all my life I've been lost or so caught up in my own self-centredness, it's like my whole life I've been in prison. And now I'm actually in prison, I feel so free, so calm, and at ease with life ..." ' (N.T. at HMP Forrest Bank)

Some described a decrease in difficult emotions, such as anger and irritability:

'It's been a few months now since you sent me the book on meditation and yoga and for me it's been great. It's been a struggle because I never had much patience and I was always quick to anger but I'm learning so much now and I'm able to help others; I'm not fighting everything.' (R.T. at HMP Lowdham Grange)

Many described improved mood and increased sense of positivity:

'I have never been satisfied with my own company or ever been comforted with myself before, but now that my life has turned around, the TV hardly ever goes on, I'm always full of life and energy, and most of all the bad days don't seem that bad anymore ... I've already got three other people doing yoga on my wing and I'm noticing the difference in them too. If only more people realized how they would benefit from yoga in prisons, the prison system would be a whole lot more relaxed and calm.' (K.P. at HMP Swaleside)

Others described a shift in perspective and a re-evaluation of what was important to them:

'I have been practising yoga now for about three months and have noticed a huge difference in my general health and wellbeing, both externally and internally. Rising early, meditating! Yoga! Keeps me in tune to everything in and around me. It doesn't manifest overnight but the rewards are deep and fulfilling. The prison routine can really cause depression and a feeling of hopelessness and despair. But going inside helps with the daily goings on outside. It's like being in the prison but *not of* the prison.' (J.D. at HMP Usk)

Some of the most moving stories told simply of feeling more able to cope in difficult circumstances:

'This is my second life sentence. A past life of profound psychological pain and torment that I tried to blot out with alcohol which only made my situation worse. My emotions erupted like a volcano with consequences to family, victims, friends and anyone associated with me. I feel all of us prisoners wear a mask when the cell door opens. We give the impression we are fine, we can cope, nothing bothers us. Then when that cell door is slammed shut incarcerating us in a small concrete box, that sound of the door and lock, removing the mask and many times the emotional and psychological pains and torments start, our minds begin to spin, our breathing increases, tears of anger, pity, sorrow and regret may run. What then? Crack up, explode, smoke a joint, drop a pill, even though we know this is not the solution as these methods do not deal with the problem.

I have only concentrated on yoga and meditation for a short period of time. I previously hardly breathed through my nose. Now I make the effort to always breathe through my nose and fully concentrate on the *asanas* in my daily life. I can concentrate on a dirty rough piece of wood, saw it, plane it, sand it and eventually reveal a lovely smooth grained item. This is how I see myself. The yoga is what takes the roughness away and gives me a tranquillity I have not felt in a long time.' (J.N. at HMP Frankland)

'Not so long ago I hit an all time low. I've always managed to keep my head together in prison; then my wife fell ill. She was seven months pregnant and there was a race to save her and the baby. This was possibly the worst time in my life ever. They both survived, being fighters, but I took a hell of a bashing emotionally and while I was thankful that everything turned out right I felt drained. I hadn't slept all week. I didn't tell anyone in case they put me on suicide watch. I had put my name down for yoga some months before and the timing was most welcome. Our teacher was an inspiration. Thanks to him I had already learnt enough to know that if nothing else yoga makes you feel better and it was free, something to do in your cell when the door shuts. I now start every morning with Sun Salutations (gone is my back pain) and when I am in my pit at night and the demons raise their ugly heads I empty my mind and concentrate on my breathing and destroy the demons.' (T.D. at HMP Kennet)

The above extracts from prisoners' letters represent just a tiny fraction of the vast body of anecdotal evidence attesting to the benefits gained from yoga and meditation in prison. However, while such testimonies may be moving or inspiring, and taken together in their thousands appear quite convincing, they represent the subjective personal experiences of individuals who felt touched by yoga and meditation. How robust are these effects if we look at them in a controlled way?

WHAT CAN SCIENCE TELL US?

Most of the published research has focused primarily on the use of meditation with prisoners. So far, there have been some promising results, with studies reporting that meditation leads to improved psychosocial functioning[2], reduced substance abuse[3], and lowered rates of recidivism[4]. There is also evidence indicating that deficits in executive function – in particular those relating to impulsivity[5] – are linked to difficulties in controlling violent behaviour[6]. Executive function is an umbrella term for various high-level cognitive processes and subprocesses in the frontal lobe, which control and regulate abilities such as attention, memory, inhibition and problem-solving. Research has shown that some forms of meditation may enhance cognitive-behavioural control, yielding benefits in sustained attention (maintaining focused attention over prolonged periods of time) and response inhibition (the ability to suppress actions that are inappropriate in a particular context)[7]. Such findings may suggest that meditation could therefore be useful as a means to manage disinhibited and criminal behaviours[8].

Less is known, however, about the benefits of yoga in prisons. In part this may be owing to its comparative complexity as an 'intervention', given that it incorporates breathing techniques, poses (*asanas*), relaxation and meditation. However, there have been an increasing number of studies investigating the effects of yoga in the general population. Practising yoga is associated with improvements in mood[9], life satisfaction and emotional function[10], as well as reductions in anger, aggression and anxiety[11]. Furthermore, the use of yoga with vulnerable and clinical samples has shown it to be effective in reducing negative affect, anxiety and depression[12], and in improving emotional wellbeing[13]. These findings suggest that yoga may have considerable utility for a prison population, where mental health difficulties, anger and aggression are particularly prevalent.

While the majority of studies have focused on the physical or mental health benefits of practising yoga, rather than the psychological processes that it might stimulate, recent work has also enabled some understanding of the underlying effects of yoga on cognitive processes, including improved memory[14], enhanced attention[15], and a range of improvements in cognitive functioning in patients affected by major depression[16]. In addition, a recent brain-imaging study[17] has shed some light on the neural underpinnings of the effects of yoga on emotion and cognition. Its findings suggested that yoga may activate mental processes and brain regions that are involved in our ability to become aware of and control emotions and behaviours[18].

Reading through the research on the benefits of yoga, we had reasons to be hopeful about its use in prison populations – particularly in reducing anxiety and aggression and improving behavioural control. Yet, there was the need to put these ideas to the test, which is what we did.

THE OXFORD STUDY

Planning research is like designing a new building: despite some basic constraints (such as materials or measures), on paper you imagine the perfect plan. Ours was simple: we wanted to randomly allocate prisoners to either a yoga or a control group for ten weeks. Those in the yoga group would take part in a once-weekly class and be asked to keep a diary record of any in-cell practise they did. Those in the control group went on a waiting list (they would also have ten weeks of yoga after our study was finished) and would keep diaries of their physical activity to compare with those in the yoga group. As I explained in previous chapters, it's far from ideal having a control group that is not doing a novel activity that matches that of the yoga group. We did things this way because no one had ever tried a randomized controlled trial on the effects of yoga in prisons before – we first needed to check that yoga worked better than doing nothing. Our hypothesis was that yoga practice would lead to improved mood and psychological wellbeing, and decreased stress and aggression. We were also interested to see whether yoga might enhance self-control in prisoners.

Putting theory into practice

While the idea seemed relatively straightforward, the process was not. Getting into prisons is not an easy process, especially when doing research. We first needed to get ethical approval for our proposed study from the National Offender Management Service (NOMS) and the Ministry of Justice. Our initial plan was that, as well as using questionnaires and cognitive tasks, before and after ten weeks of yoga, we would also take a quick saliva swab of the inside of our participants' cheeks to enable us to measure levels of cortisol, a biological marker of stress. But it was not to be. The Ministry of Justice was very concerned that we could use the saliva samples to do genetic analyses of prisoners, which would have dire political and ethical implications. It had never crossed our minds to do any genetic analysis, we tried to argue – but we failed to change the Ministry's view. Approval of our study required us to drop our saliva plans.

Finally, two years after its initial inception, the study began. We had a short six-month period in which to collect all our data, driving back and forth to seven prisons in the heart of England, in the West Midlands. The participating prisons themselves varied considerably: one prison (HMP Hewell) was housed in a grand country estate with sprawling acres of grounds. A Category D, or 'open' prison, it allowed prisoners free movement and enabled them to take part in educational courses and outside work in the community, with some even parking their cars outside the prison so they could drive home for weekend visits. In contrast another (HMP Shrewsbury) was situated near a town centre and was much more secure (Category B/C), housing a very high proportion of sex offenders. HMP Drake Hall was a women's prison, while HMP Dovegate was a private-sector prison.

The process of getting in and out of the prisons also varied considerably. On arrival at the open prison HMP Hewell, an impressive Grade-II listed manor house, I simply opened the huge wooden front door and walked in – as a prisoner in jeans casually ambled out past me, on his way to work. In most of the other prisons, on the other hand, my bag was scanned, my laptop was whisked off to security for clearance, and I was thoroughly searched. A couple of the prisons even took the added precaution of asking me to sit on a chair that would scan me internally for illicit substances; another used passive drugs dogs. In one particular prison a security officer was so thorough in the search for any banned items that I was checked not only under my trouser waistband, but also under my tongue.

Once inside the prisons we faced the challenge of actually managing to access the prisoners who were interested in participating, and finding a place to interview them. We encountered obstacles such as staffing shortages (meaning

no one could escort our participants to the interview rooms)
and prisons going into lockdown (meaning no movement –
prisoners could not come to us and we could not leave the prison).
Availability of rooms for our research interviews was often quite
limited. Over the course of the study, I ended up interviewing
prisoners in chaplains' offices, education blocks, chapels, and on
one occasion even in a storage room for gym kit. Nevertheless, we
were able to interview a total of 167 prisoners across these seven
prisons, over a six-week period. Our sample was very varied,
including both men and women who ranged in age from 21 to
68 years old. They had been imprisoned for a wide range of index
crimes and there was a significant variation in sentences – while
some faced less than a year inside for relatively minor crimes,
several had life sentences.

After the first round of interviews, the participants from each
prison were randomly allocated to either the yoga group or
the control group. Those in the yoga group began a ten-week
yoga course, consisting of a once-weekly yoga class. They were
encouraged to do their own practise between classes. Different
yoga teachers taught the classes across the prisons, but the
classes all followed the same format: a standardized set of
hatha yoga postures and stretches, with the final 20 minutes of
each class spent doing meditation that focused on the breath.
Teachers kept an attendance record in order to check how many
of the participants in the yoga group came to each session. The
prisoners were also given practice diaries in which to record how
often they practised yoga in between the classes, and for how
long. Those in the control group were asked simply to continue
with whatever they normally did with regard to their usual social
life and physical exercise activities. After the ten weeks, we
returned to each of the prisons to re-interview our participants.

DOWNWARD DOG WITH DEVIANTS

The interview process was quite full on: keen to get as many participants as we could, I would often interview several prisoners a day. The majority of the interviews went very smoothly. All the prisoners were taking part voluntarily, and all of them wanted to get to do the yoga, so it's probably not surprising that they were generally co-operative. Many also seemed to be pleased to have the opportunity to speak to a human being who wasn't a prison officer or another prisoner, even if the conversations we had mostly involved me asking them about 200 closed questions regarding their mood and behaviour.

Only a couple of times did I find myself in an uncomfortable situation. Once, I had to halt an interview midway. All was going well until the prisoner thought that the question 'How guilty have you felt over the last week, on a scale of one to five?' implied that he was guilty of his offence. His response was aggressive, raising his voice and slamming his hands down on the table. When he had calmed down enough to give his answer, it was a very emphatic '1' ('not at all'). We continued for about three more questions, until I had to ask: 'How ashamed have you felt over the last week?' The response this time was an angry tirade of denial and fury at the criminal justice system – and it was the only time during the interviews that I found myself eyeing the nearest panic button.

While there were no other outbursts relating to prisoners' perceptions of their own guilt or innocence in relation to their offences, the notion of criminality was a common theme that arose during the weeks of interviewing. Often prisoners would tell me that they were 'not really a criminal', 'not like these other low-lifes', or that they personally were 'not criminally minded'. One man insisted on telling me at the outset of the interview about the nature of his index offence – fraud – and how this was totally different to 'actual crime', which he defined as 'mugging someone or hurting someone'. Another referred to his religious beliefs as evidence of his separateness from other criminals incarcerated for similar violent offences to his own: 'I'm not like them; I'm a Buddhist.' It seemed to me that the vast majority of criminals were dead set on distinguishing themselves from 'the criminals'. On more than a couple of occasions, prisoners expressed seeming concern for my safety while in the prison: 'Be careful – there are criminals in here,' advised one prisoner in his late fifties, pointing out the panic button on the wall.

All in one room

Given that one prisoner on his or her own can sometimes be challenging to manage, what, I wondered, would it actually be like to teach yoga to a roomful of robbers and rapists, or rowdy young offenders? Speaking to several yoga teachers, though, challenged my assumptions. I had imagined that classes might require a bit of crowd control or that there might even be issues of inappropriate behaviour towards the teachers. What I discovered through my conversations, however, was that this was rarely the case. While not all yoga teachers would share Sandy Chubb's belief that 'prisoners are all perfect' (see p.20), those I spoke to seemed to find the classes a pleasure to teach and a meaningful experience both for the prisoners and themselves.

To try to understand this better, I arranged to meet with Pollyanna Stokoe, an experienced yoga teacher who taught for six years at HMP Wandsworth and currently teaches at HMP Wormwood Scrubs, both in London. 'The Scrubs', as it is commonly known, is a local category-B prison for adult male offenders. It detains prisoners who are both sentenced and on remand and has been frequently referenced in popular culture, mentioned in a number of well-known films, books and songs – including Pete Doherty's 'Broken Love Song', about his time inside. Such·references, along with a history of riots, escapes, violent protests and damning reports by both prisoners and staff, have given the place a certain notoriety. In the 1980s its own governor condemned it as a 'penal dustbin'.

Since then conditions are said to have improved significantly, but the Scrubs hasn't quite lost its controversial edge, and is now flagged up for overcrowding. In 2013 an official watchdog report warned that Wormwood Scrubs was on a 'knife edge' owing to a combination of staff cuts and increasing violence and gang-related activity. It was reported that there was a 50 per cent increase in officers' use of force and restraint as a means of trying to control prisoners. Knowing all that I was keen to talk to Pollyanna to find out what it is like to teach yoga in such a hostile environment.

Expansion, not contraction

We agreed to meet the following week at a small café in Acton, west London. Pollyanna was a slim, middle-aged woman, who was well spoken and articulate. We ordered two coffees and sat down to talk about her experiences of teaching behind bars.

'It's made me appreciate my freedom to make decisions about my life, such as choosing what to eat for lunch. It's made me appreciate just how thin the line is between inside and outside, how easily people can slip up. It's made me feel very grateful and aware of the line, and very sad that some people haven't had the support, the skills to stay on the "right" side.'

As Pollyanna talked I gained a sense of a non-judgmental person with a notable absence of an 'us-and-them' attitude, which seemed in keeping with the general ethos associated with yoga, the notion of connectedness with others. This was in marked contrast to attitudes prevalently held about prisoners, who are so often seen as 'other' or 'less than' or simply a 'bane of society'. Pollyanna demonstrated this herself, giving an example of being told by a friend of hers in the corporate world, 'I don't know why you bother, they were all born evil.'

Speaking to Pollyanna, and other yoga teachers like her, I realized there are two essential beliefs in those who teach yoga in prisons. First, a belief in the idea that people *can* change; second, a belief in the idea that yoga can be a catalyst for this change. In Pollyanna's experience personal change through yoga isn't just possible – it's inevitable.

She admitted, however, that it can take some time to reap the benefits – perhaps even years. I learned she was unconvinced by the advertised promises of transformation during weekend retreats. The changes that yoga brings about in prisoners may at first seem very small, she argued, but they are by no means inconsequential.

'The reward for me is seeing how yoga helps to create change in prisoners' lives,' she said, 'even if it's only small. It at least facilitates a good night's sleep. But the real highlight is when you start to see the pennies drop.'

And what were the pennies that were dropping? Apparently, prisoners' sense of connectedness to their own bodies, as well as to others or to a religious or spiritual faith (if they have one), and a sense of being able to gain some control and calmness. Depression, anxiety, stress and sleep difficulties are all common among prisoners. Prisons are often volatile environments where those within may find themselves constantly on 'red alert'. Pollyanna explained that she felt yoga classes could benefit prisoners by imparting techniques that, as she had seen first hand, may increase their sense of self-control and reduce their impulsive reactivity.

'Through practice, they learn to use the breath to help calm the mind,' she told me. 'So they can hopefully afford a breath before reacting. Learning yoga and meditation helps to lengthen the fuse.'

It strikes me that the idea of this is reminiscent of the 'stop-and-think' principle. This is central to CBT and CBT-informed offending behaviour programs targeted at reducing impulsivity, including impulsive aggression and violence, among prisoners. Could yoga be an alternative way to effectively achieve the same results as traditional therapeutic techniques?

As we concluded our meeting, Pollyanna left me with some final food for thought about what yoga can offer prisoners, above and beyond improving sleep, and reducing stress and impulsivity: 'I think it gives them a sense of expansion, rather than contraction.'

Her words echo the sentiment of the idea of an ashram in a prison cell – the notion that yoga and meditation can enable a sense of freedom in confined spaces. I wonder if this might be the most pertinent benefit of all.

'I LOVE EVERYONE WHILE I'M MEDITATING, BUT …'

After our yoga group of prisoners had completed the ten-week yoga courses, we returned to the prisons to carry out the second round of interviews. This time the interview format was a little different. Each participant began the assessment by completing a computerized task called 'Go/No-Go' using a small laptop computer. We asked the prisoners to watch the screen and to press the space bar when an 'x' appeared (a 'Go' trial), and to *not* press it when an 'o' appeared (a 'No-Go' trial). Because the 'x' appears much more frequently (about 80 per cent of the time), the trickiest part is to withhold your impulse to press the space bar when the 'o' flashes up. This task allows us to measure how quickly people respond and the percentage of correct answers. Getting the 'x' stimuli right and quickly is an indicator of being able to hold your attention, while getting the 'o' stimuli right shows that you can inhibit your impulses.

Statistical analysis of the data showed that the prisoners who had been doing the yoga course reported significantly improved mood, decreased stress, and reduced psychological distress, compared to the control group[19]. Furthermore, we found that participants in the yoga group had a greater accuracy on the computer 'Go' trials, indicating that yoga may enhance prisoners' ability to sustain attention and concentration. Their performance was also better than the control group on the 'No-Go' trials. This suggests that yoga may help prisoners to inhibit automatic responses and improve their capacity for cognitive control[20].

Meaning in the findings

Taken together, our findings, which were published in the *Journal of Psychiatric Research* (2013), provide the first robust scientific evidence that yoga has beneficial effects on wellbeing, mental health and self-control in a prison population. These findings aren't just scientifically interesting, they have implications for prison environments. Previous research has linked antisocial behaviour, which is common among prison populations, with impairments in cognitive control[21]. It may therefore be that, through facilitating self-control, yoga practice has the potential to reduce violent and antisocial behaviour among prisoners.

Our results also have implications for policy-making. To date, research and policy surrounding rehabilitative interventions in prisons have predominantly focused on psychological and group treatments. Prisoners often view psychosocial interventions (such as offending-behaviour or substance-misuse programs) as stigmatizing and undesirable; while individual treatment provided by psychologists or psychiatrists is expensive, which limits prisoners' potential access to it. Yoga, on the other hand, is less intrusive and less stigmatizing and might represent a more socially acceptable alternative to some prisoners. It also has the potential to be used effectively as a supplement to other rehabilitation programs. Yoga is also cost effective: running a weekly yoga class with a trained instructor costs a prison less than £50 a week.

However, there was a less positive side to our findings. We had hypothesized that if yoga improved cognitive control and reduced impulsivity, it might also lead to reduced aggression. While we found that yoga did improve attentional control and inhibition, we discovered that, statistically, it didn't make a difference when it came to levels of aggression or how prisoners behaved towards others. So, despite the other positive results, there were no real changes in how aggressive prisoners felt.

In the previous chapter we saw that meditation practice can bring about a number of unexpected, sometimes difficult-to-manage, emotional reactions – perhaps yoga can do the same. This is reportedly what happened at Ringerike, a high-security prison near Oslo, Norway. In 2005 some prisoners taking part in a trial of a yoga program became more agitated, aggressive and irritable and had difficulty sleeping[22]. The prison dropped the program on the grounds that it did not have the resources to treat the emotions that were being 'unleashed' by the yoga practice.

In psychological therapy the path of personal change or recovery is often far from linear. Individuals entering therapy may often get worse before they get better, as they finally address difficulties they had previously ignored, or they come to terms with difficult truths. Might the same not also be true for embarking on yoga practice? In the Norwegian study, like in ours, the intervention was of a brief duration – mere weeks. In light of this, is it really that surprising that prisoners might initially find themselves experiencing stronger emotions, or simply becoming more aware of them, perhaps as the practice of yoga enables them to become more in touch with themselves and heightens their awareness of their feelings? Talking to yoga teacher Pollyanna about the possibility of increased negative emotions after starting yoga, she did not seem remotely fazed. 'We aim to get in there and rattle the cage a bit,' she smiled. 'Yoga can bring things to the surface that were previously buried.'

Just as recovery from mental illness or addiction can be a long and slow process, requiring commitment from an individual over a period of time and a solid support network, so it seems too that meaningful, lasting change through yoga or meditation might require much longer than a ten-week intervention. A prisoner learning these new, unfamiliar techniques might require additional emotional support and guidance as he or she begins this new journey of self-exploration. In our study we also found that the more yoga classes prisoners attended, the greater their psychological wellbeing. The likelihood is also that continued benefit would require continuing practice.

However, while continued practice may keep the inner enemy at bay – think of the desire for power in ex-druglord Nick (see p.188–195) – it may not be truly transformational. If people stop their practice, they may revert back to their former selves. This is what the South African woman turned swami and charity director in Reading meant when she confided that, while you are doing meditation or yoga, you may be full of bliss or even enlightened. However, the moment the door bell rings and you have to get up, you are thrown back into everyday reality – and this reality seems to care little about your feelings of connection to God. The following letter from a prisoner at HMP Frankland pertinently illustrates how transient and volatile the mental and emotional states acquired during yoga and meditation may be:

'I am re-establishing contact after quite a few years of madness. I have recently begun again to search for myself and to find true peace and spirituality. I started this process before but despite experiencing massive changes, I let it slip. I fell back into drugs and crime and came back to prison, despite my best intentions. For the four months before I was released from my last sentence, I meditated and did *pranayama*, and I found such peace and happiness. I unfortunately didn't keep up my practices and it has taken five years of dillydallying to find them again! ... So for four weeks now, no medz, and I have stuck to a strict routine of diet, exercise, meditation, yoga and *pranayama*. I am writing because I would like to have contact with someone who can help me to understand my spiritual path. I have so many questions, and while I know all the knowledge is within me, I feel I need help to unearth it. While I understand principles, I find it hard implementing them. I love everyone while I'm meditating, but as soon as my door opens, I find my ego, pride, judgments and anger cloud things, and I slip.'

CHAPTER 8

CAN MEDITATION CHANGE YOU?

'How can I be substantial without casting a shadow? I must have a dark side too if I am to be whole; and by becoming conscious of my shadow I remember once more that I am a human being like any other.'

C.G. Jung[1](p.59)

The first time I came across a critical remark about the effects of meditation was where I'd have least expected it – at a Sufi gathering. I'd just finished my psychology undergraduate degree and travelled with friends by train from Lisbon to Turkey. One of us had learned about a renowned Sufi group, the longest-established in Istanbul, and we went to visit. The members met in a small mosque in the eastern part of the city. Their music, chanting and dancing were vibrant, even ecstatic. In the upper gallery of the small mosque, some women entered into a trance, their bodies swaying back and forth to the rhythm of the music.

They were welcoming to visitors and we stayed to eat and take part in a sort of 'Questions and Answers' session with the *effendi* (the elected leader of the group). A Bulgarian man, who had been initiated into Sufism only a few months earlier, offered a cigarette multipack to the *effendi*, which he opened. The *effendi* thanked the man and asked about his spiritual practice. The man replied that he was progressing fast.

'I do have a question, however,' he said in English. 'How long will it take before I reach the state of unattachment to emotions and cravings that Buddhists talk about?' Someone sitting close to the *effendi* translated into Turkish. Before responding, the *effendi* lit a cigarette.

'The state of being that Buddhists reach in their meditation,' he said, pausing to puff, 'is, for Sufis, only the first stage.' All Sufis in the room laughed loudly at hearing this.

A Sufi sitting next to me explained that the *effendi* was not mocking Buddhist meditation as such, but the man's otherworldly desire to get rid of emotions and cravings. Sufis believe both spirit and body, with all pleasures and sufferings, are to be cherished as a divine gift. They looked at that man's spiritual goal as misguided, not too different from what Buddhist scholar Robert Sharf referred to as a 'meditation sickness'. Jung, a psychologist who was sympathetic towards yoga and meditation long before they became widely known, suggested that trying to live without suffering was a fool's errand. For him personal healing and transformation meant achieving not 'an impossible state of happiness' but a 'balance between joy and sorrow' (p.81). Although much of this sounds like common sense, it needs to be reinforced in the face of the expectations and claims that many people, including scientists, have about meditation's effects.

SEVEN MYTHS ABOUT MEDITATION

As we entered the final stages of writing this book, Catherine and I struggled to make sense of all the evidence we'd gathered, and of the range of contradictory emotions we felt – surprise, tiredness, angst, joy and confusion – over the course of writing it. The truth is that neither of us had ever expected to find so many frailties with the scientific literature, and much less to encounter a dark side of meditation. But these faults don't lie with the technique itself; it's much more likely that it's our heightened expectations and unguided meditation practice that are dangerous. For the secularized mind meditation fills a spiritual vacuum; it brings the hope of a better, happier individual and the ideal of a peaceful world. That meditation was primarily designed not to make us happier but to destroy our sense of individual self – who we feel and think we are most of the time – is often overlooked in the science and media stories.

To remind us of what has been covered in this book, let's now review what we found out about the personal changes meditation can bring about, by juxtaposing the myths with the scientific evidence.

Myth 1 *Meditation produces a unique state of consciousness that we can measure scientifically.*
Research on Transcendental Meditation published in the early 1970s claimed that meditation produced a state of consciousness different from sleep, waking or hypnosis, and that scientists could assess this state in a person's physiology or brain activity. Claims about the unique effects of meditation are not something of the past: emerging neuroscience studies on the effects of meditation sometimes argue that mindfulness or compassion meditation regulates emotion in a unique way (an example of this, described in Chapter 5, is the idea that compassion meditation can activate a unique neural marker for altruism[2]).

Fact 1
Meditation produces states of consciousness that we can indeed measure using various scientific instruments. However, the overall evidence is that these states are not physiologically unique.

Furthermore, although different kinds of meditation may have diverse effects on consciousness (and on the brain), there is as yet no scientific consensus about what these effects are.

Myth 2 *If everyone meditated the world would be a much better place.*
Meditation researchers, both from the Hindu-based TM and Buddhist-based mindfulness traditions, have claimed that meditation can reduce aggression and increase compassionate feelings and behaviours. Various studies have been produced on this topic, from sociological studies on the reduction of crime to brain-imaging research on the increase of positive emotions.

Fact 2

All world religions share the belief that following their particular practices and ideals will make us better individuals. So far, there is no clear scientific evidence that meditation is more effective in making us more compassionate or less aggressive than other spiritual or psychological practices. Research on this topic has serious methodological and theoretical limitations and biases. Most of the studies have no adequate control groups; they also generally fail to assess the expectations of participants or to acknowledge the potential association between meditation and aggression.

Myth 3 *If you're seeking personal change and growth, meditating is as or more efficient than having therapy.*
Mindfulness as a mental health intervention is becoming more popular. Healthcare services, city councils and universities offer eight-week courses on mindfulness-based stress reduction (MBSR) and mindfulness-based cognitive therapy (MBCT). A number of clinical trials have shown that mindfulness can help people with mental health problems such as recurrent depression.

Fact 3

There is very little evidence that an eight-week mindfulness-based group program has the same benefits as those of being in conventional psychological therapy – most studies compare mindfulness with 'treatment as usual' (such as seeing your GP), rather than individual therapy. Although mindfulness interventions are group-based and most psychological therapy is conducted on a one-to-one basis, both approaches involve developing an increased awareness of our thoughts, emotions and way of relating to others. But the levels of awareness probably differ. A therapist can encourage us to examine conscious or unconscious patterns within ourselves, whereas these might be difficult to access in a one-size-fits-all group course, or if we were meditating on our own.

Myth 4 *Meditation can benefit everyone.*

Meditation, including mindfulness, is popularly presented and endorsed as a technique for improved wellbeing, inner peace, and happiness that works for any individual. Packaged and sold in an increasingly super-charged, secularized way as a magic pill for anyone feeling the pressures and stresses of 21st-century life, modern meditation is being widely touted as today's cure-all. With some exceptions[3], scientists who study this technique have seldom challenged this view of meditation as a panacea.

Fact 4

The idea that meditation is a cure-all – and *for* all – lacks scientific basis. 'One man's meat is another man's poison' reminds Arnold Lazarus when writing about meditation (see p.146). Although there has been relatively little research looking at how individual circumstances – such as age, gender, or personality type – might play a role in the value of meditation, there is a growing awareness that meditation works differently for each individual. For example, it may provide an effective stress-relief technique for individuals facing serious life problems (such as being unemployed), but have little value for low-stressed individuals[4]. Or it may benefit depressed individuals who suffered trauma and abuse in their childhood, but not other depressed people[5]. There is also some evidence that – along with yoga – it can be of particular use to prisoners, for whom it improves psychological wellbeing and, perhaps more importantly, encourages better control over impulsivity.

We shouldn't be surprised about meditation having quite variable benefits from person to person: after all, the practice wasn't intended to make us happier or less stressed, but to assist us in diving deep within and challenging who we believe we are.

Myth 5 *Meditation has no adverse or negative effects. It will change you for the better (and only the better).*
There is an expectation that meditation leads to self-discovery and healing, or even produces a highly moral compassionate character, and has no ill effects.

Fact 5
On the surface of things, it's easy to see why this myth might come to light. After all, sitting in silence, focusing on your breathing, would seem like a fairly innocuous activity with little potential for harm. Before writing this book we weren't aware of the dark side of meditation either. Discussing this with Swami Ambikananda (see p.177), she nodded, saying, 'The way I like to explain it is: when you cook the scum rises to the surface.' When you think how many of us when worried, or in difficult life circumstances, may cope by keeping ourselves very busy *so that we don't think*, it isn't that much of a surprise that sitting without distractions, with only ourselves, might lead to disturbing emotions rising to the surface.

However, many scientists have turned a blind eye to the unexpected or harmful consequences of meditation. With TM, this is probably because many of the researchers were personally involved in the movement; with mindfulness, the reasons are less clear because it is presented as a secular technique. Nevertheless, there is emerging scientific evidence from case studies and surveys of meditators' experience, as well as from historical studies, to show that meditation can be associated with stress, negative effects, mental health problems, and violence.

Myth 6 *Science has unequivocally shown how meditation can change us and why.*
When scientists started studying meditation in the 1960s, the practice was surrounded in an aura of exoticism. Many thought it was unworthy of scientific attention. Since then thousands of studies have shown that it produces various kinds of measurable psychobiological effects.

Fact 6
Meta-analyses show there is moderate evidence that meditation affects us in various ways, such as increasing positive emotions and reducing anxiety. However, it is less clear how powerful and long-lasting these changes are. Some studies show that meditating can have a greater impact than physical relaxation[6], although other research using a placebo meditation[7] (see p.55) contradicts this finding. We need better studies but, perhaps as important, we also need models that explain *how* meditation works. For example, with mindfulness-based cognitive therapy (MBCT), we still can't be sure about what is actually the 'active' ingredient. Is it the meditation itself that causes positive effects, or is it the fact that the participant learns to step back and become aware of his or her thoughts and feelings in a supportive group environment?

There simply is no cohesive, overarching attempt to describe the various psychobiological processes that meditation sets in motion. Unless we can clearly map the effects of meditation –

both the positive and the negative – and identify the processes underpinning the practice, our scientific understanding of meditation is precarious, and can easily lead to exaggeration and misinterpretation.

Myth 7 *We can practise meditation as a purely scientific technique with no religious or spiritual leanings.*
The origins of the practice of meditation lie in religious traditions. However, scientists have cut away religion from the technique, so that we can use it therapeutically in a secular environment.

Fact 7

In principle it's perfectly possible to meditate and be uninterested in meditation's spiritual background. However, research shows that meditation leads us to become more spiritual[8], and that this increase in spirituality is partly responsible for the practice's positive effects[9]. So, even if we set out to ignore meditation's spiritual roots, those roots may nonetheless envelop us, to a greater or lesser degree. Overall, it is unclear whether secular models of mindfulness are fully secular.

MEDITATION IS ONLY THE FIRST STEP

When we started writing this book, we'd envisaged that towards the end it would be a good idea to visit a Buddhist monastery and talk to one or more of the monks about what we had found. 'We might as well visit a Catholic monastery, don't you think?' Catherine suggested. 'Just to get a balance: we'd have both an Eastern and a Western religious view.'

We chose a Benedictine monastery. Benedictines are known for their simple and austere way of life, which includes seven services of daily contemplation, prayer and singing, beginning at 5am. We met with a monk named Father Nicholas in the Abbey of Quarr, a beautiful red-bricked, Moorish-looking building that you can see as you approach the Isle of Wight by ferry. As the guest master of this monastery, part of Father Nicholas's role is to look after visitors who come for retreats. (Hospitality is an important part of the Benedictine tradition, which still follows the rules originally laid down by St Benedict more than 1,500 years ago.) Father Nicholas grew up as an Anglican and entered the Anglican Benedictines in his twenties. Years later he felt something was spiritually missing and he moved into the Catholic Benedictine order at its monastery on the Isle of Wight.

We sat down at the guesthouse with Father Nicholas. He offered us tea and told us he'd had meetings with Buddhist monks to discuss the role and value of meditation in religious life.

'Meditation is only the first step. It's preparing you for contemplation, where your mind and heart are focused on Christ,' he told us. 'Meditation itself cannot change the individual or the world; only if it is a Christ-centred meditation and, even then, only if Christ comes. You can toil the earth, prepare the soil for the plants to grow – but you can't make the rain come.'

We told Father Nicholas about some of the darker aspects of meditation we had found, how it can unleash deep emotional material, possibly leading to violent or unethical behaviour. Can the same happen with a Christian monk who prays and meditates a number of hours per day?

'Yes and no,' he answered. 'If you're a monk it is your duty to open those boxes where you keep hidden aspects of yourself. But the only way to do this safely is to admit one's limitations and that you're in need of God. That's why monks have fled to the desert: to find in solitude their absolute need of God. You can find people that help you confront the hidden or darker aspects of yourself – even a good therapist – but only God can give you the key to control all aspects of yourself.'

'Are you're saying that you can't really change yourself?'
'No, no, you can; I have certainly seen a few conversions in my lifetime. But they're only possible through God's power. Other people are important; God can act through other people. But as a monk

So - solo hike

I think that if you want to see real change, being around people is usually unhelpful – it masks who you truly are. You're acting in a different way than you would if you were totally on your own, completely alone and receptive to God's grace. In the end what you want is to be open to God for only God's grace can change you.' Father Nicholas stopped talking and smiled, looking down.

'Perhaps it's not as much about change but integration,' Catherine said; Father Nicholas looked up at her. 'I mean, it's not as much about erasing in you the desire for power, aggression or sex, but knowing that all these exist and can have their place, but they're integrated with the whole of your being, so you know who you are and can choose your action. In other words, although he chooses not to, even a saint could be capable of murder – isn't that always a possibility?'

'It's true that sin always exists,' said Father Nicholas, 'always, while we're alive. So if you are in meditation, contemplation or prayer 22 hours a day, there are still two hours where you have to act and are open to sin. But psychological integration is not enough – only God allows you to be in real control of your actions; only God can disperse evil.'

'What do you mean by evil?'

'Oh, it's very un-PC to talk about it these days, but Catholics do believe that evil is real; that angels and demons exist. Psychology and psychiatry don't explain all our behaviours, do they?'

We smiled at Father Nicholas. I was about to say something when he looked at his watch and jumped up.

'Oh dear Lord! I have to do the community's wash up.'

A BUDDHA PILL

When I typed up the interview, I was struck to notice that a Benedictine monk had used almost exactly the same words as a Hindu ascetic – Swami Ambikananda had also mentioned that we could meditate for 22 hours a day but that during those two remaining hours all kinds of un-enlightened selfish actions were possible. (It also brought to mind a prisoner I'd met who told me that he had been a Buddhist for years and meditated daily – but was nevertheless in prison for recently committing a violent armed robbery.) I liked their no-nonsense, pragmatic approach to the spiritual life. Neither of them believes in magical solutions to personal change – rather, they believe it takes persistence, hard work, as well as an element of luck, fortune and, for the Benedictine monk, God's grace. This realization is at odds with our culture of wanting instant results, which some people hope to get through meditation.

Is meditation then a Buddha pill? *No*, it isn't in the sense that it does not constitute an easy or certain cure for common ailments (if we conceptualize depression as the common cold of the mental health world). However, *yes*, in the sense that, like medication, meditation can produce changes in us both physiologically and psychologically, and that it can affect all of us differently. Like swallowing a pill, it can bring about unwanted or unexpected side-effects in some individuals, which may be temporary, or more long-lasting. Some of us might notice feeling different quite quickly; others may need a bigger dosage to bring about the desired effect. Certain individuals may find they feel no different at all; others may suffer quite a strong reaction, possibly an irreversible one. Some may find the effect lasts only for the specific time they are 'taking the pill' (that is, the actual 20 minutes, or however long, that they spend in meditation), and then quickly wears off. Others may be surprised to notice themselves feelings more spiritually minded (which is the 'Buddha' part of the pill)[10]. Which of these parameters and effects apply to you will depend on your motivation to try out meditation, the time you spend doing it and the guidance you have during your practice.

So if you're a therapist and your client asks you about using meditation – of any kind – what should you say? I would want to know what my client believes he or she will get from the practice. Is the client looking to feel less stressed, or are aspirations somewhat higher. Perhaps, for example, he or she is expecting a fast-track route to increased insight or better relationships with others?

I'd be more favourably inclined to encourage a client to try meditation if he or she wanted to use it for stress relief than for relational issues. And, as a rule of thumb, it's probably a good idea to tell your client that there is no guarantee that meditation will have any impact on shifting the cognitive or behavioural patterns that underpin or maintain the difficulties he or she is already having. Realistically, stories of enduring personal change are far less common than stories of 'becoming relaxed' or 'feeling more centred'. Writing this, I'm reminded of something a personal trainer once told me, about what often happens when he encourages new female clients to move away from pure cardio and to start lifting weights.

'I don't want to get too big and muscly!' they exclaim, as if putting on 7 kilograms of toned muscle was something that could happen overnight, from a few quick swings of a kettlebell. As the trainer liked to put it, not lifting weights because you're worried about getting 'too big', is like not driving your car because you're afraid you'll become the next Lewis Hamilton. As anyone who has radically transformed his or her body will tell you, that kind of change does not happen overnight. It takes commitment, determination, a tailored diet, and hours of hard work in the gym.

Just as there's no risk you'll wake up a bodybuilder against your will if you lift a few weights, it is unlikely you'll find your mind wildly altered if you try a bit of meditation – unless your mind works like David Lynch's. Change, for most of us, is a long, slow and uneven process, very much like a small child's language development – weeks go by in which a child may utter no new words, but then, suddenly, within a couple of days, he or she speaks a whole sentence.

Don't forget the dark side

And remember, there is, of course, a less benign side to the Buddha pill, especially where it concerns mental health. Pressure from health services to come up with more effective interventions in terms of time and cost, as well as treatment outcome, for mental health problems means that more people are exposed to meditation than ever before. Mindfulness-based interventions, such as MBCT and MBSR, are cheap because they run as groups over a mere eight sessions. However, although this is brief in terms of learning to meditate, for some people an eight-session intervention is not considered brief enough.

In 2013 I was on a panel of interviewers looking for a new lecturer in psychology. One of the candidates argued that eight therapy sessions in the National Health Service were far, far too expensive. She had come up with a much better plan: the secret was to use a cognitive enhancing pill that quickens your capacity to think analytically and to combine it with a one-off CBT session. The pill would allow you to process and consolidate faster how to deal with your dysfunctional thoughts. I felt my blood chill as this woman schematically presented her stupendous idea for fast-forwarding the process of emotional healing in a pre-packed and neat one-hour session. This is not how we function; we might live in the age of a budget-restricted NHS, but there are no quick fixes when it concerns our inner life.

A VISIT TO THE VIHARA

We arrived late for the beginning of the meditation session. Catherine had been stuck in a traffic jam on the way from London. We took our shoes off and walked into the room of the Burmese Buddha Vihara monastery in Oxford to find it was packed. People were sitting cross-legged on the floor on cushions, knee-to-knee, chanting. This was Catherine's first visit to a Buddhist temple – I noticed her expression of surprise as we entered. She had been expecting a quiet meditation session in a bare room. I motioned to her to sit down next to me and join in with the chanting.

'That little room was filled with statues of Buddha,' she remarked to me afterwards, somewhat incredulously. 'For a religion that isn't meant to have a god, that was more religious imagery than I've ever seen in a local church.' Having never experienced it first-hand before, she was also a little surprised by the focus of the chanting – on the praises of the Buddha and his many triumphs – and by having to repeatedly bow down on her knees, to a near prostrate position, to the eight Buddhas. I rather enjoyed the chanting: the text was full of colourful images of how the Buddha fought demons and sexual temptation. A 40-minute meditation followed. After this there was a question-and-answer session with one of the monks, Venerable Dhammasi.

It turned out that Dhammasi was a trustee of the Oxford Mindfulness Centre and was well acquainted with a number of mindfulness researchers – I'd forewarned him about our mindfulness-based therapy questions, so that he could come prepared.

'Mindfulness is nothing but an introduction to Buddhism; Mark Williams [see p.87] has told me that himself, though he won't write it in his books. But it's not enough; eight weeks of mindfulness only touches the surface of what is needed for personal development.'

'But can these secular mindfulness programs actually change people?' I asked.

'Their purpose is to reduce stress or to prevent relapse of depression. It's designed to help with a certain issue. Whether or not it transforms them...' the monk hesitated for a moment, 'you'd need to see from research. It's a beginning, just a beginning. If you read the Buddhist teachings, mindfulness doesn't come alone, you need the other parts – right thinking, right action...'

'Excuse me, can I say something?' a woman interrupted. 'Some weeks ago a monk from New Zealand visited this centre and he told us that mindfulness on its own can teach soldiers to kill more effectively; you need to follow the eight-fold path of Buddha to live your life in a transformed way.'

'That's right,' Dhammasi said. 'You can visit the Pentagon website and learn how they're also using mindfulness with soldiers.'

Catherine raised her eyebrows at me and pointed to one of the questions on our list. 'Some studies suggest that mindfulness might be more effective on people who are more psychologically vulnerable – for example, those who suffered trauma and abuse at an early age. Do you have any ideas on why that may be?'

'People are using a manual, a program and trying to tick all the boxes. Mindfulness is not meant to be used in this way – with a manual; the effect will be limited. The skill and experience of the teacher is the main thing – someone who doesn't rely on ticking the boxes.'

At the end of the session, after most people had left the room, I went up to and thanked the monk. I couldn't resist asking one last question: 'Is an enlightened individual still able to commit imperfect actions?'

Dhammasa smiled at me. 'You're asking me about enlightenment, but what is that? It's just ticking one more box; it's ideology,' he stated; then he added, 'I'm sorry if that's not the answer you were looking for.'

FROM MENTAL HYGIENE TO INNER EXPLORATION

The monk's frankness was disarming. We tend to think of meditation as a rocket that will thrust us deep into inner space and, as we move closer to the centre of our own inner universe (our inner sun, if you like), we get enlightened. Once we're there all is well. But, as the monk said, that's just a mental category, the ticking of a box of how we think advanced meditators ought to feel and behave.

Increasingly, we've been buying into exotic ideas of personal change. This is partly because meditation has been marketed to us very well. Along with yoga, meditation continues to grow in popularity. Once viewed as hippyish, meditation and yoga are now simply 'hip'. Greater numbers of people are jumping on this fashionable, money-making bandwagon, with companies finding ever-more ways to create something modern out of something ancient, to seize the imagination of the self-improvement generation. This has led to a flurry of emerging new yoga and meditation trends over the last few years – some good, some bad, some rather wacky.

For the purposes of research, Catherine briefly explored the wacky side. While celebrating her birthday in Las Vegas, she attended a yoga class at the Mirage hotel. The practice room was small, fitting only half a dozen mats, and it would have been utterly unremarkable were it not for the fact that it was underwater and had floor-to-ceiling windows that looked out into a dolphin enclosure. The instructor, a blonde American named Willow, explained that 'yoga with dolphins' was not just a Vegas gimmick, but that it had a scientific rationale – being around the dolphins leads to a release of oxytocin, the 'cuddle chemical', possibly augmenting the benefits we might already feel from a yoga class. She also went on to say that the dolphins appeared to express a preference (by rubbing up against the windows of the room) for certain types of music played during the yoga classes; in particular, they seemed to be fans of Radiohead.

And it's not just Vegas involving animals in yoga practice. Back in London Catherine saw an advert for a yoga class designed for dogs. In these classes you are the yogi, your dog is the dogi and together you create – you guessed it – Doga. Promising to extend the benefits of yoga from human to dog, in these classes, your instructor will teach you how to incorporate man's best friend into your yoga practice, using postures, massage and meditation. Originating in the USA in 2002, Doga classes are on the rise. London-based yoga/Doga instructor Mahny Djahanguiri, who has taught classes all over the capital, including at Harrods' Pet Spa, explains on her website that 'the parasympathetic nervous system and the sympathetic nervous system of a dog work the same way as a human. These govern sleep, digestive systems and the flushing of toxins. Calming your dog down with Doga can have huge benefits for them.' Be that as it may, the bemused reaction of Catherine's two dogs to her attempts to haul them into the air in a Sun Salutation, before using them as balancing props for Warrior II, suggests that they'd probably rather reap their health benefits through a good old-fashioned walk in the park.

But what is the problem if you want your dog to try out yoga or meditation – it can't hurt, can it? Why not treat meditation as simple mental hygiene: 'Think about it, you shower every day and clean your body, but have you ever showered your mind?' asks Ema Seppälä, the Associate Director of the Center for Compassion and Altruism Research and Education at Stanford University[11]. If we look at meditation in this way, should we not be welcoming it as part of our children's school day? Shouldn't good, responsible parents start enforcing daily 'mind hygiene' on their kids in the same way they do dental hygiene – brush your teeth for 3 minutes, meditate for 10, then off to bed?

There is something very misleading about this idea: meditation *isn't* the same thing as brushing your teeth. If you don't ever brush your teeth, they'll rot and fall out. If you don't ever meditate? Well, your mind is not going to decay or fall out. The mental hygiene view of meditation trivializes this ancient technique, tries to portray it as being like a 'mental shower'. By 'hygienizing' meditation we water it down, limiting its purpose and richness as a tool for deep inner exploration.

Throughout this book we have aimed to be fully transparent about our own journey in teasing out the facts, about meditation's ability to propagate personal change, from the fiction. Meditation and yoga are not a panacea; nevertheless, they can be powerful techniques for exploring the self. Probably more important than the type of practice is the choice of teacher and knowing *why* you want to put time aside to meditate every day or try out a weekend retreat. Be realistic about what you're trying to get out of it. Personality may also play its part. Extraverts will struggle more on silent retreats, while introverts may cringe in yoga classes that ask you to find a partner and assist each other with poses. You may find that the method that is 'right' for you is one where you and your instructor have a lot in common, personality-wise.

Can meditation change you? Of course it can. Anything you invest time and effort into is likely to impact you in some way. It's just that the impact may not necessarily be in the ways you may expect or predict. Meaningful personal change isn't a destination, it's a journey; and usually one that is far from linear. If, like us, you still have hope that contemplative techniques can help you change or explore yourself, don't forget to stay open to what happens along the way. Each and every practice, the classes we choose to attend, the books we read and especially the people we meet will change you – perhaps more significantly than the technique itself.

ENDNOTES

introduction

1   Cited in p. 2, Broad, W. (2012). *The Science of Yoga: The Risks and the Rewards.* New York: Simon & Schuster.
2   Lutz, A., Greischar, L., Rawlings, N.B., Ricard, M., Davidson, R.J. (2004). Long-term meditators self-induce high-amplitude synchrony during mental practice. *Proceedings of the National Academy of Sciences,* 101: pp.16369–16373.
3   Teasdale J., Segal Z. V., Williams J. M. G., Ridgeway V. A., Soulsby J. M., & Lau M. A. (2000). Prevention of relapse/recurrence in major depression by mindfulness-based cognitive therapy. *Journal of Consulting and Clinical Psychology,* 68: pp.615–623.
4   Cramer, H., Lauche, R., Langhorst, J., & Dobos, G. (2013). Yoga for depression: A systematic review and meta-analysis. *Depression and Anxiety,* 30: pp.1068–1083.
5   Hickey, W. (2010). Meditation as medicine: A critique. *Crosscurrents,* June issue, pp.168–184.
6   Mascaro, J., Rilling, J. Tenzin, L, & Raison, C. (2013). Compassion meditation enhances empathic accuracy and related neural activity. *Social Cognitive and Affective Neurosciences,* 8(1): pp.48–55.
7   Du Boulay, S. (2005). *The Cave of the Heart: The life of Swami Abhishiktananda.* Maryknoll, New York: Orbis Books.
8   Ranganathan, N., Bohet, A., & Wadhwa, T. (2008). Beyond the prison walls: Reforming through silence. *Psychological Studies,* 5(1): pp.54–63.

chapter 1

1   http://www.ru.org/society/seven-ways-to-fix-the-criminal-justice-system.html

2   Hardy, A. (1975). *The Biology of God: a Scientist's Study of Man the Religious Animal*. London: Cape.

3   Dass, R. (1978). *Be Here Now*. New Mexico: Hanuman Foundation.

4   Lozoff, B. (1985). *We're All Doing Time – A Guide for Getting Free*. Human Kindness Foundation.

5   Squires, N. (2011). 'Harry Potter and yoga are evil', says Catholic Church exorcist. *Daily Telegraph*, 25 November.

6   *The Fires That Burn* (documentary) http://www.telefilm.ca/en/catalogues/production/fires-burn

7   http://www.ascentmagazine.com/articles aspx?articleID=192&issueID=30

8   Abrams, A.I. & Siegel, L.M. (1978). The Transcendental Meditation® Program and Rehabilitation at Folsom State Prison A Cross-Validation Study. *Criminal Justice and Behavior*, 5(1): pp.3–20.

9   Allen, D. (1979). TM At Folsom Prison: A Critique of Abrams and Siegel. *Criminal Justice and Behavior*, 6(1): pp.9–12.

10   Samuelson, M., Carmody, J., Kabat-Zinn, J., Bratt, M.A. Mindfulness-based stress reduction in Massachusetts correctional facilities (2007). *The Prison Journal*, 87: pp.254–68.

11   Bowen, S., Witkiewitz, K., Dillworth, T. et al (2006). Mindfulness meditation and substance use in an incarcerated population. *Psychology of Addictive Behaviors*, 20: pp.343–7.

12   Rainforth, M., Alexander, C. & Cavanaugh, K. (2003). Effects of the transcendental meditation program on recidivism among former inmates of Folsom prison. *Journal of Offender Rehabilitation*, 36: pp.181–203.

13   McGuire, J. (2006). General offending behaviour programs: Concept, theory, and practice. *Offending behaviour programs: Development, application, and controversies*, pp.69–111.

chapter 2

1 James, W. (1890/2007). *Principles of Psychology*, 1: p.121. Cosimo.

2 Aristotle (1907). *De Anima*. Cambridge University Press.

3 Watson, J. (1924/1930). *Behaviorism*. University of Chicago Press.

4 Huxley, A. (1932). *Brave New World*, Ch. 2. London: Chatto & Windus.

5 Eysenck, H. (1947). *Dimensions of Personality*. London: Routledge & Kegan Paul.

6 Costa, P.T., Jr. & McRae, R.R. (1988). Personality in adulthood: A six-year longitudinal study of self-reports and spouse ratings on the NEO Personality Inventory. *Journal of Personality and Social Psychology*, 54: pp.853–863. And, Costa, P. T., Jr. & McRae, R.R. (1994). Set like plaster? Evidence for the stability of adult personality. In T. Heatherton & J. Weinberger (eds) *Can Personality Change?* pp.21–40. Washington: American Psychological Association.

7 Jacobson, E. (1929). *Progressive Relaxation: a Physiological and Clinical Investigation of Muscular States and their Significance in Psychology and Medical Practice*. University of Chicago Press.

8 Roberts, B.W., Walton, K.E. & Viechtbauer, W. (2006). Patterns of mean-level change in personality traits across the life course: A meta-analysis of longitudinal studies. *Psychological Bulletin*, 132(1): pp.1–25.

9 Roberts, B.W. & Mroczek, D. (2008). *Personality trait change in adulthood. Current Directions in Psychological Research*, 17(1): pp.31–35.

10 McAdams, D. (1994). A psychology of the stranger, *Psychological Inquiry*, 5(2): pp.145–148.

11 Miller, W. & c'de Baca, J. (1994). Quantum change: Toward a psychology of transformation. In Heatherton, T. & Weinberger,

J. (eds) *Can Personality Change?* pp.253–280. Washington, D.C.: American Psychological Association.

12 Sargant, W. (1969). The physiology of faith. *British Journal of Psychiatry*, 115: pp.505–518.

13 James, W. (1902/1929). *The Varieties of Religious Experience. A Study in Human Nature.* New York: The Modern Library.

14 Russell, B. (1945/1976). *A History of Western Philosophy, Book One*, pp.123–4. New York: Simon and Schuster.

15 Pahnke, W. (1966). Drugs and mysticism. *International Journal of Parapsychology*, 8: pp.295–315.

16 Grof, S. (1975). *Realms of the Human Unconscious: Observations from LSD Research.* New York: Viking Press.

17 United Nations (1971). *Convention on Psychotropic Substances.* Available online at: https://www.unodc.org/pdf/convention_1971_en.pdf

18 Griffiths, R., Richards, W., McCann, U. & Jesse, R. (2006). Psilocybin can occasion mystical-type experiences having substantial and sustained personal meaning and spiritual significance. *Psychopharmacology*, 187(3): pp.268–83.

19 MacLean, K., Johnson, M. & Griffiths, R. (2011). Mystical experiences occasioned by the hallucinogen psilocybin lead to increases in the personality domain of openness, *Journal of Psychopharmacology*, 25(11): pp.1453–1461.

chapter 3

1 Bainbridge, W. & Jackson, D. (1981). The rise and decline of Transcendental Meditation. In Wilson, B. (ed), *The Social Impact of New Religious Movements*. New York: The Unification Theological Seminary.

2 Orme-Johnson, D. & Farrow, J. (1977). *Scientific Research on the Transcendental Meditation Program. Collected Papers, Volume 1.* Maharishi European Research University Press.

3 Maharishi Mahesh Yogi (1969). *Maharishi Mahesh Yogi on the Bhagavad-Gita: A New Translation and Commentary.* Baltimore, Maryland: Penguin.

4 Chesterton, G.K. (1909). *Orthodoxy*, pp.242–43. London, New York: John Lane Company.

5 Lynch, D. (2006). *Catching the Big Fish: Meditation, Consciousness, and Creativity.* New York: Jeremy Tarcher/ Penguin.

6 Allison, J. (1970). Respiratory chances during Transcendental Meditation. *The Lancet*, 295(7651): pp.833–34.

7 Wallace, Robert K. (1970). Physiological effects of Transcendental Meditation. *Science*, 167(3926): pp.1751–1754.

8 One article claimed that with TM you can achieve a 17 per cent reduction of oxygen consumption after only 5–10 minutes of meditation; it usually takes 6–7 hours of sleep to achieve a 15 per cent reduction. Wallace, R., Benson, H, & Wilson, A. (1971). A wakeful hypometabolic wakeful state. *American Journal of Physiology*, 221(3): pp.795–99.

9 Wallace, R. & Benson, H. (1972). The physiology of meditation: Is the meditative state that is achieved by yogis and other Far-Eastern mystics accompanied by distinct physiological changes? A study of volunteer subjects in the USA indicates that it is. *Scientific American*, 226: pp.84–90.

10 Another problem is that mental states, including what Maharishi calls cosmic consciousness, need not have a corresponding set of *unique* biological characteristics. Many psychologists and philosophers would argue that our mental lives can never be completely reduced to the firing of brain cells, or molecular processes.

11 These were adrenaline and noradrenaline. Michaels, R., Huber, M. & McCann, D. (1976). Evaluation of Transcendental Meditation as a method of reducing stress. *Science*, 192(4245): pp.1242–4.

12 Pagano, R, Rose, R., Stivers, R. & Warrenburg, S. (1976). Sleep during Transcendental Meditation. *Science*, 191(4224): pp.308–310.

13 An interesting 1977 article by Donald Morse and colleagues (A physiological and subjective evaluation of meditation, hypnosis, and relaxation, *Psychosomatic Medicine*, 39(5): pp.304–24) contrasted meditation with hypnosis and relaxation techniques, including a condition where, instead of repeating a Sanskrit mantra, they used the word 'one'. There were no differences between the meditation, hypnosis and relaxation groups on all physiological measures, except for muscle activity which was lower for the meditation group. Curiously, it made no difference repeating the Sanskrit mantra or the word 'one'. Krishnamurti, another Indian spiritual teacher living in the USA and Europe, had already suggested in 1969 that repeating 'coca-cola, coca-cola' or 'OM' had the same effect (see *Freedom from the Known*, Ch.15. London: Gollancz).

14 Benson, H. & Klippler, M. (1975). *The Relaxation Response*. New York: Morrow.

15 Otis, L. (1974). If well-integrated but anxious, try TM. *Psychology Today*, 7(11): pp.45–46.

16 See the section on 'Development of Personality' in Volume 1 of the TM collected papers (see note 1), which includes 15 articles.

17 Bono, J. Jr. (1984). Psychological assessment of transcendental meditation. In Shapiro, D. & Walsh, R. (eds), *Meditation: Classic and Contemporary Perspectives* (pp.209–217).

18 Smith, J. (1976). Psychotherapeutic effects of Transcendental Meditation with controls for expectation of relief and daily sitting. *Journal of Consulting and Clinical Psychology*, 44(4): pp.630–37.

19 Smith, J. (1984). Meditation research: Three observations on the state-of-the-art. In Shapiro, D.H. & Walsh, R. (eds), *Meditation: Classic and Contemporary Perspectives* (pp.677–78).

20 Orme-Johnson, D. & Farrow, J. (1977). *Scientific Research on the Transcendental Meditation Program. Collected Papers, Volume 1, Part V*: The TM-Sidhi Program. Maharishi European Research University Press.

21 Patanjali (2009). *The Wisdom of Patanjali's yoga sutras: A new translation and guide*. Translated by Ravi Ravindra. Adyar, Chennai, India and Wheaton, IL, USA: Theosophical Publishing House.

22 Orme-Johnson, D., Clements, G., Haynes, C. & Badaoui (1977). Higher states of consciousness: EEG coherence, creativity, and experiences of the sidhis. In Orme-Johnson, & David, Farrow, John (1974). Scientific Research on the *Transcendental Meditation Program. Collected Papers, Volume 1, Part V*: The TM-Sidhi Program, pp.705–712. Maharishi European Research University Press.

23 Radin, D. (2013). *Supernormal: Science, yoga, and the evidence for extraordinary psychic abilities*. New York: Deepak Chopra Books, Random House.

24 Bainbridge, W. & Jackson, D. (1981). The rise and decline of Transcendental Meditation. In Wilson, B. (ed), *The Social Impact of New Religious Movements*. New York: The Unification Theological Seminary.

25 See note 20; cited in p.704.

26 When I interviewed him in 2013, Dr Alex Hankey was the Dean of Academic Studies at the Institute of Ayurveda and Integrative Medicine in Bangalore.

27 Barnett, R. & Sears, C. (1991). *JAMA* gets into an Indian herbal jam. *Science*, 254: pp.188–89.

28 Sharma, H., Triguna, B. & Chopra, D. (1991). Letter from New Delhi: Maharishi Ayur-Veda: Modern insights into ancient medicine. *Journal of the American Medical Association*, 265(20): pp.2633–37.

29 Skolnick, A. (1991). Maharishi Ayur-Veda: Guru's marketing scheme promises the world eternal 'perfect health'. *Journal of the American Medical Association*, 266(13): pp.1741–50.

30 Skolnick, A. (1991). The Maharishi caper: Or how to hoodwink top medical journals. *The Newsletter of the National Association of Science Writers*, Fall issue. Retrieved from http://www.aaskolnick.com/naswmav.htm.

31 See note 5.

32 Booth, W. (2005). Yogi bearer; dark films aside, David Lynch brims with the light of Transcendental Meditation. *Washington Post*, 2 December.

33 Orme-Johnson, D., Alexander, C., Davies, J., Chandler, H. & Larimore, W. (1988). International peace project in the Middle East: The effects of the Maharishi Technology of the Unified Field. *Journal of Conflict Resolution*, 32: pp.776–812.

34 Goodstein, L. (1993). Karmic convergence, the sequel; TM faithful return to district to try again for peace through group meditation. *The Washington Post*, 9 June.

35 Haegelin, J., Rainforth, M., Orme-Johnson, D., Cavanaugh, K., Alexander, C., Shatkin, S., Davies, J., Hughes, A. & Ross, E. (1999). Effects of group practice of the Transcendental Meditation program on preventing violent crime in Washington, D.C.: Results of the National Demonstration Project, June–July 1993. *Social Indicators Research*, 47: pp.153–201.

36 Goodstein, L. (1993). Meditators see signs of success; more harmony, less crime claimed as project ends. *The Washington Post*, 30 July.

37 Park, R. (2000). *Voodoo Science: The Road from Foolishness to Fraud*, pp.29–30. Oxford University Press.

38 'After removing the outlier of June 22, Poisson regression analysis indicated there was no significant difference in the level of homicides in June and July 1993 from the remainder

of the year.' Published online at: http://istpp.org/crime_
prevention/voodoo_bookreview.html#fn1

39 Castaneda, R. (1994). Fighting crime by meditation. *The
Washington Post*, 7 October.

40 Hatchard, G., Deans, A., Cavanaugh, K. & Orme-Johnson, D.
(1996). The Maharishi Effect: A model for social improvement.
Time series analysis of a phase transition to reduced crime in
Merseyside metropolitan area. *Psychology, Crime & Law*, 2(3):
pp.165–174.

41 See http://hk.tm.org/social-benefits

42 See https://www.youtube.com/watch?v=438UKM1Av1g

43 Sieveking, D. (2010). *David wants to fly*. Produced by Lichtblick
Film.

44 Seldmeier, P., Eberth, J., Schwarz, M., Zimmermann, D., Haarig,
F., Jaeger, S. & Kunze, S. (2012). The psychological effects of
meditation: A meta-analysis. *Psychological Bulletin*, 138(6):
pp.1139–1171.

45 Brook, R., Appel, L., Rubenfire, M. Ogedegbe, G., Bisognano,
J., et al (2013). Beyond Medications and Diet: Alternative
Approaches to Lowering Blood Pressure: A Scientific
Statement from the American Heart Association. *Hypertension*,
61: pp.1360–83.

chapter 4

1 Falkenström, F., Granström, F. & Holmqvist, R. (2013).
Therapeutic alliance predicts symptomatic improvement
session by session. *Journal of Counseling Psychology*, 60(3):
pp.317–328.

2 Horvath, A. O., Del Re, A. C., Flückiger, C. & Symonds, D. (2011).
Alliance in individual psychotherapy. *Psychotherapy*, 48(1):
pp.9–16.

3 Arnow, B.A. & Steidtmann, D. (2014). Harnessing the potential of the therapeutic alliance. *World Psychiatry*, 13(3): pp.238–240.

4 Khaneman, D. & Tversky, A. (1979). Prospect theory: an analysis of decision under risk. *Econometrica*, 47(2): pp.263–291.

5 Vohs, K.D. & Luce, M.F. (2010) *Judgement and decision making*. In Baumeister, R.F. & Finkel, E.J. (eds) *Advanced Social Psychology: the State of the Science*, p.736iii. New York: Oxford University Press.

6 Larkin, P. (1974). *This Be the Verse: Collected Poems of Phillip Larkin.*

7 The theory that there are 'stages of change' was first developed by James Prochaska in 1997; he called it the trans-theoretical model of behaviour change. The model is designed to enable one to assess a person's readiness to change and to guide them through the different stages: in the contemplation stage you may be wondering about what's going on; things only start happening by the time you move on to the preparation stage, when you share with friends or family your motivation to seek change. The last stages are those of action, maintenance and termination. To move through the latter stages, you have to increase your awareness that the 'pros' of changing outweigh the 'cons', thereby increasing your motivation to translate intention into sustained action. Prochaska, J.O. & Velicer, W.F. (1997). The transtheoretical model of health behavior change. *American Journal of Health Promotion*, 12(1): pp.38–48.

8 Principe, J. M., Marci, C. D., Glick, D. M. & Ablon, J. S. (2006). The relationship among patient contemplation, early alliance, and continuation in psychotherapy. *Psychotherapy: Theory, Research, Practice, Training*, 43(2): p.238.

9 Paley, G. & Lawton, D. (2001). Evidence-based practice: Accounting for the importance of the therapeutic relationship in UK National Health Service therapy provision. Counselling and Psychotherapy Research, 1(1): pp.12–17.

10 Bowlby, J. (1958). The nature of the child's tie to his mother. *International Journal of Psychoanalysis*, 39(5): pp.350–373.

11 Wilson, T. D., Reinhard, D. A., Westgate, E. C., Gilbert, D. T., Ellerbeck, N., Hahn, C. & Shaked, A. (2014). Just think: The challenges of the disengaged mind. *Science*, 345(6192): pp.75–77.

12 Williams, M. & Penman, D. (2011). *Mindfulness: a practical guide to finding peace in a frantic world*. London: Piatkus.

13 Miller, S.D. & Duncan, B.L. (2004). *The outcome and session rating scales: Administration and scoring manual*. Chicago: Institute for the Study of Therapeutic Change.

14 NICE (2009) Depression: the Treatment and Management of Depression in Adults (Update). NICE clinical guideline 90. Available at www.nice.org.uk/CG90

15 http://www.slideshare.net/scottdmiller/supershrinks-an-interview-with-scott-miller-about-what-clinicians-can-learn-from-the-fields-most-effective-practitioners

16 Ricks, D.F. (1974). Supershrink: Methods of a therapist judged successful on the basis of adult outcomes of adolescent patients. In Ricks, D.F. & Roff, M. (eds), *Life History Research in Psychopathology*. Minneapolis: University of Minnesota Press, pp.275–297.

17 Wampold, B.E. & Brown, G.S.J. (2005). Estimating variability in outcomes attributable to therapists: a naturalistic study of outcomes in managed care. *Journal of Consulting and Clinical Psychology*, 73(5): pp.914–923.

18 Miller, S. D., Duncan, B. & Hubble, M. (2008). Supershrinks: What is the secret of their success? *Psychotherapy in Australia*, 14(4): pp.14–22.

19 Vollmer, S., Spada, H., Caspar, F. & Burri, S. (2013). Expertise in clinical psychology. The effects of university training and practical experience on expertise in clinical psychology. *Frontiers in psychology*, 27(4): p.141.

20 See note 18.

21 Colvin, G. (19 October 2006). What It Takes to Be Great. *Fortune.*

22 Ericsson, K.A. (2006). *Cambridge Handbook of Expertise and Expert Performance.* Cambridge University Press.

chapter 5

1 *Yoga Journal*, December 5th 2012. http://www.yogajournal. com/uncategorized/new-study-finds-20-million-yogis-u-s/

2 Quilty M., Saper R., Goldstein R., Khalsa S.B. (2013). Yoga in the real world: Motivations and patterns of use. *Global Advances in Health and Medicine*, 2(1): pp.44–49.

3 Sharma, M. (2014). Yoga as an alternative and complementary approach for stress management: A systematic review. *Journal of Evidence-Based Complementary and Alternative Medicine*, 19(1): pp.59–67.

4 Descilo, T., Vedamurtachar, A., Gerbarg, P., et al. (2010). Effects of a yoga breath intervention alone and in combination with an exposure therapy for post-traumatic stress disorder and depression in survivors of the 2004 South-East Asia tsunami. *Acta Psychiatrica Scandinavica*, 121(4): pp.289–300.

5 Van der Kolk, B. (2009). Interview: Yoga and Post-Traumatic Stress Disorder. *Integral Yoga Magazine*, pp.12–13.

6 Cramer, H., Lauche, R., Langhorst, J. & Dobos, G. (2013). *Yoga for depression*: A systematic review and meta-analysis. *Depression and Anxiety*, 30: pp.1068–1083

7 Cramer, H., Lauche, R., Langhorst, J. & Dobos, G. (2013). Yoga for schizophrenia: A systematic review and meta-analysis. *Biomedical Central Psychiatry*, 13:32.

8 Hickey, W. (2010). Meditation as medicine: A critique. *Crosscurrents*, June Issue, pp.168–184.

9 Bunting, M. (2014). Why we will come to see mindfulness as mandatory. *The Guardian*, 6 May.

10 World Health Organisation (2011). *Mental Health Atlas*. Geneva: WHO Press. Also available online at http://www.who.int/ mental_health/publications/mental_health_atlas_2011/

11 Post, R. (1992). Transduction of psychosocial stress into the neurobiology of recurrent affective disorder. *American Journal of Psychiatry*, 49: pp.999–1010.

12 Wiech, K. & Tracey, I. (2009). The influence of negative emotions on pain: Behavioral effects and neural mechanisms. *Neuroimage*, 47: pp.987–994.

13 Toneatto, T. & Nguyen, L. (2007). Does mindfulness meditation improve anxiety and mood symptoms? A review of the evidence. *La Revue Cannadienne de Psychiatrie*, 52(4): pp.260–266.

14 Piet, J. & Hougaard, E. (2011). The effect of mindfulness-based cognitive therapy for prevention of relapse in recurrent major depressive disorder: A systematic review and meta-analysis. *Clinical Psychology Review*, 31: pp.1032–1040.

15 Teasdale J., Segal Z.V., Williams J.M.G., Ridgeway V.A., Soulsby J.M. & Lau M.A. (2000). Prevention of relapse/recurrence in major depression by mindfulness-based cognitive therapy. *Journal of Consulting and Clinical Psychology*, 68: pp.615–623.

16 Moyers, B. (1993). *Healing and the Mind*. Public Broadcasting System. Available for free at: http://www.mindfulnesscds.com/ pages/bill-moyers-special

17 Williams, M., Crane, C., Barnhofer, T., et al (2014). Mindfulness-based cognitive therapy for preventing relapse in recurrent depression: a randomized dismantling trial. *Journal of Consulting and Clinical Psychology*, 82(2): pp.275–86.

18 National Institute for Health and Care Excellence Guidelines [CG90] (2009). Depression in adults: The treatment and management of depression in adults. https://www.nice.org.uk/ guidance/cg90/chapter/key-priorities-for-implementation

19 Marchant, J. (1994). Can meditation help prevent the effects of ageing? BBC, 1st July. http://www.bbc.com/future/story/20140701-can-meditation-delay-ageing

20 Jacobs, T., Epel, E., Lin, J, Blackburn, E., et al (2011). Intensive meditation training, immune cell telomerase activity, and psychological mediators. *Psychoneuroendocrinology*, 36: pp.664–681.

21 Creswell, J., Pacilio, L., Lindsay, E. & Brown, K. (2014). Brief mindfulness meditation training alters psychological and neuroendocrine responses to social evaluative stress. *Psychoneuroendocrinology*, 4: pp.1–12.

22 Jacobs, T., Shaver, P., Epel, E., et al (2013). Self-reported mindfulness and cortisol during a Shamatha meditation retreat. *Health Psychology*, 32(10): pp.1104–9.

23 Hickey, W. (2010). Meditation as medicine: A critique. *Crosscurrents*, June Issue, pp.168–184.

24 Purser, R. (2013). Beyond McMindfulness. *Huffington Post*, 1 July. http://www.huffingtonpost.com/ron-purser/beyond-mcmindfulness_b_3519289.html

25 Schumpeter (2013). The mindfulness business. *The Economist*, 16 September, p.73.

26 http://www.mindful.org/mindfulness-practice/mindfulness-and-awareness/search-inside-yourself

27 Wallace, A. & Bodhi, B. (2006). The nature of mindfulness and its role in Buddhist meditation: A Correspondence between B. Alan Wallace and the Venerable Bhikkhu Bodhi. http://shamatha.org/sites/default/files/Bhikkhu_Bodhi_Correspondence.pdf

28 It could be argued that Buddhism and other spiritual traditions also value this inner aspect. However, these traditions have developed ways of critically examining the inner experience.

29 'And I am appalled at what happens in these days – namely, when some soul with the very smallest experience of meditation, if it be conscious of certain locutions of this kind in some state of recollection, at once christens them all as coming from God, and assumes this is the case, saying: "God said to me…"; "God answered me…"; whereas it is not so at all, but, as we have said, it is for the most part they who are saying these things to themselves.' (II, 29, 4). Cross, J. of the (2000). *Ascent of Mount Carmel* (translated by William Whiston). Grand Rapids: Christian Classics Ethereal Library.

30 Sharf, R. (1995). Buddhist modernism and the rhetoric of meditative experience. *Numen*, 42: pp.228–83.

31 Sharf, R. (2013). Mindfulness or mindlessness: Traditional and modern Buddhist critiques of 'bare awareness'. https://www. youtube.com/watch?v=c6Avs5iwACs

32 Kitayama, S. & Cohen, D. (2007). *Handbook of Cultural Psychology*. New York: Guildford Press.

33 Hutcherson, C., Seppala, E. & Gross, J. (2008). Loving-kindness meditation increases social connectdness. *Emotion*, 8(5): pp.720–4.

34 Mascaro, J., Rilling, J., Negi, L. & Raison, C. (2013). Compassion meditation enhances empathic accuracy and related neural activity. *Social Cognitive and Affective Neuroscience*, 8(1): pp.48–55.

35 Kang, Y., Gray, J., Dovidio, J. (2014).The nondiscriminating heart: Lovingkindness meditation training decreases implicit intergroup bias. *Journal of Experimental Psychology: General*, 143(3): pp.1306-1313.

36 Weng, H., Fox, A., Shackman, A. et al. (2013). Compassion training alters altruism and neural responses to suffering. *Psychological Science*, 24(7): pp.1171–1180.

37 Sedlmeier, P., Eberth, J., Schwarz, M., et al. (2012). The psychological effects of meditation: A meta-analysis. *Psychological Bulletin*, 138(6): pp.1139–1171.

38 Goyal, M., Singh, S., Sibinga, E., et al (2014). Meditation programs for psychological stress and wellbeing. *Journal of*

the *American Medical Association: Internal Medicine*, 174(3): pp.357–68.

39 Ki-duk, K. (2003). *Spring, Summer, Fall, Winter... and Spring.* Sony Picture Classics.

40 Fjorback, L., Arendt, M., Ornbol, E., Fink, P. & Walach, H. (2011). Mindfulness-based stress reduction and mindfulness-based cognitive therapy – a systematic review of randomized controlled trials. *Acta Psychiatrica Scandinavica*, 124: pp.102–119.

41 This can be generalized to a vast range of psychological problems that can't be 'meditated away'. Recently, a Tibetan priest told me that she had been an alcoholic for twenty years and she meditated regularly throughout that period. In the end what helped her overcome the addiction was the group support from *Alcoholics Anonymous*.

chapter 6

1 Media reports on 16–17 September 2013 by *The New York Times* and the *Daily Telegraph*. See http://www.nytimes. com/2013/09/17/us/shooting-reported-at-washington-navy-yard.html?pagewanted=all&_r=0 and http://www.telegraph. co.uk/news/worldnews/northamerica/usa/10314585/Aaron-Alexis-Washington-navy-yard-gunman-obsessed-with-violent-video-games.html

2 Szalavitz, M. (2013). Aaron Alexis and the dark side of meditation. *Time*, 17 September. http://healthland.time. com/2013/09/17/aaron-alexis-and-the-dark-side-of-meditation/

3 Buddhists and violence, *Wildmind Buddhist Meditation Blog*, 17 September 2013. http://www.wildmind.org/blogs/on-practice/buddhists-and-violence

4   Yorston, G. (2001). Mania precipitated by meditation: A case report and literature review. *Mental Health, Religion & Culture*, 4(2): pp.209–213.

5   Shapiro, D. (1992). Adverse effects of meditation: a preliminary investigation of long-term meditators. *International Journal of Psychosomatics*, 39: pp.62–67.

6   Otis, L. (1984). Adverse effects of Transcendental Meditation. In Shapiro, D.H. & Walsh, R. (eds), *Meditation: Classic and Contemporary Perspectives* (pp.201–208). New York: Aldine.

7   Lazarus, A. (1976). Psychiatric problems precipitated by Transcendental Meditation. *Psychological Reports*, 39: pp.601–602.

8   Ellis, A. (1984). The place of meditation in cognitive-behavior therapy and rational-emotive therapy. In Shapiro, D.H. & Walsh, R. (eds), *Meditation: Classic and Contemporary Perspectives* (pp.671–2673). New York: Aldine.

9   Razzaque, R. (2014). *Breaking Down is Waking Up: Can Psychological Suffering be a Spiritual Gateway?* London: Watkins Publishing.

10   Grof, S. & Grof, C. (eds) (1989). *Spiritual Emergency: When Personal Transformation becomes a Crisis.* New York: Jeremy Tarcher/Putnam.

11   American Psychiatric Association (1994). Diagnostic and statistical manual of mental disorders: DSM-IV. Washington, DC: American Pyschiatric Association.

12   Sierra, M. & Berrios, G. (2000). The Cambridge Depersonalisation Scale: a new instrument for the measurement of depersonalisation. *Psychiatry Research*, 93(2): pp.153–164.

13   Lukoff, D. (1998). From spiritual emergency to spiritual problem: the transpersonal roots of the new DSM-IV category. *Journal of Humanistic Psychology*, 38(2): pp.21–50.

14   Lukoff, D. (n.d.). *DSM_IV: Religious and spiritual problems.* http://www.spiritualcompetency.com/dsm4/dsmrsproblem.pdf

15 St John of the Cross (2013). *The Dark Night of the Soul*. Godalming: Elam Publications.

16 Testimonies and advice for the Dark Night. http://thehamiltonproject.blogspot.co.uk/2010/12/testimonies-of-dark-night.html

17 http://www.buddhistgeeks.com/2011/09/bg-231-the-dark-side-of-dharma/

18 http://www.buddhistgeeks.com/2011/09/bg-232-the-dark-night-project/

19 The US National Centre for Alternative and Complementary Medicine considers that meditation is safe, unless you have a psychiatric problem; it does not acknowledge that healthy people may suffer from its practice. http://nccam.nih.gov/health/meditation/overview.htm#sideeffects

20 https://www.deepakchopra.com/blog/view/1557/intense_emotional_release_in_meditation

21 https://twitter.com/marwilliamson/status/269092321100972032

22 Graham, J. & Haidt, J. (2010). Beyond beliefs: Religions bind individuals into moral communities. *Personality and Social Psychology Review*, 14(1): pp.140–150.

23 Hamlin, J., Wynn, K. & Bloom, P. (2007). Social evaluation by preverbal infants. *Nature*, 450: pp.557–560.

24 Hunsberger, B. & Jackson, L. (2005). Religion, meaning and prejudice. *Journal of Social Issues*, 61(4): pp.807–826.

25 Tikhonov, V. & Torkel, B. (2013). *Violent Buddhism: Militarism and Buddhism in modern Asia*. Abingdon: Routledge.

26 Gospel of Luke, 6:29, New International Version.

27 Cited in the Introduction by Tikhonov, V. In Tikhonov, V. & Brekke, T. (eds) (2013). See note 25.

28 This and the next two citations are from Yu, Xue (2013). Buddhism and the justification of war with focus on Chinese Buddhist history. Tikhonov, V. & Brekke, T. (eds) (2013), pp.194–208. See note 25.

29 Strathern, A. (2013). Why are Buddhist monks attacking Muslims? BBC News, 2 May. http://www.bbc.co.uk/news/magazine-22356306

30 See note 27.

31 See note 28.

32 Greene, J.D., Sommerville, R.B., Nystrom, L.E., Darley, J.M., Cohen, J.D. (2001). An fMRI investigation of emotional engagement in moral judgment. *Science*, 293: pp.2105-2108

33 Gleichgerrcht E., Young L. (2013) Low Levels of Empathic Concern Predict Utilitarian Moral Judgment. *PLoS ONE*, 8(4): e60418.

34 See note 28.

35 Faure, B. (2010). Afterthoughts. In Jerryson, M. & Juergensmeyer, M. (eds), *Buddhist Warfare* (pp.224-238). New York: Oxford University Press.

36 Kleine, C. (2006). Evil monks with good intentions? Remarks on Buddhist monastic violence and its doctrinal background. In Zimmermann, M., Chiew, H. & Pierce, P. (eds), *Buddhism and Violence* (pp.65-98), *Lumbini: Lumbini International Research Institute*.

37 Maher, D. (2010). Sacralized warfare: The fifth Dalai Lama and the discourse of religious violence. In Jerryson, M. & Juergensmeyer, M. (eds), *Buddhist Warfare*, pp.90-103. New York: Oxford University Press.

38 Wallace, V. (2010). Legalized violence: Punitive measures of Buddhist Khans in Mongolia. In Jerryson, M. & Juergensmeyer, M. (eds), *Buddhist Warfare*, pp.104-116. New York: Oxford University Press.

39 See note 35.

40 Satha Anand, S. (2013). The question of violence in Thai Buddhism. Tikhonov, V. & Brekke, T. (eds), pp.175-193. Referenced in note 25.

41 Cited in epigraph to Victoria, B. (2003). *Zen war stories*. London: RoutledgeCurzon

42 Koestler, Arthur (1960). *The Lotus and the Robot*. London: Hutchinson & Co. LTD.

43 Suzuki, Daisetz (1959). *Zen and Japanese Culture*. London: Routledge and Kegan Paul.

44 Victoria, Brian (1997). *Zen at War*. New York: Weatherhill.

45 Victoria, Brian (2010). A Buddhological critique of 'Soldier-Zen' in wartime Japan. In Jerryson, M. & Juergensmeyer, M. (eds), *Buddhist Warfare*, pp.118–143. New York: Oxford University Press.

46 See note 45.

47 See note 45.

48 Longerich, P. (2012). *Heinrich Himmler*. Oxford University Press.

49 Jalon, A. (2003). Meditating on war and guilt, Zen says it's sorry. *The New York Times*, January 2011.

50 Avila, T. de (1962). *Life of Saint Teresa: Written by herself*. London: Burns & Oates.

51 There used to be a Sai Baba community in Glastonbury that I visited around 2001. After the morning chanting, they offered some of these holy ashes flown straight from the guru's ashram in India. Seeing that the other people ate them, I did the same: they tasted like ash! I was even less pleased about that tasting experience when, months later, a friend who had been reading up on Sai Baba explained that the ashes were actually made from Sai Baba's dried excrements – literally, holy shit.

52 Silva, C. do C. (2007). Marga absolvido ou caminho da Cruz? Budismo / Cristianismo iluminação, nirvana e kenosis cristã. [Absolved Marga or way of the Cross? Buddhism / Christianity – enlightenment, nirvana and Christian kenosis]. *Revista Lusófonoa de Ciências das Religiões*. 6(11): pp.39–66.

53 Hardy, E. (director) (2004). *Secret Swami*. BBC 2, broadcast on 17 June.

54 Haraldsson, E. (1987). 'Miracles are my visiting cards': An investigative report on the psychic phenomena associated with Sathya Sai Baba. London: Century.

55 Oppenheimer, M. & Lovett, I. (2013). Zen groups distressed by accusations against teacher. *The New York Times*, February 2011.

56 Patanjali (2009). *The wisdom of Patanjali's yoga sutras: A new translation and guide*. Translated by Ravi Ravindra. Adyar, Chennai, India and Wheaton, IL, USA: Theosophical Publishing House.

57 Sarawasti, Swami A. (translator) (2001). *Katha Upanishad*. London: Frances Lincoln Limited.

chapter 7

1 http://news.bbc.co.uk/1/hi/8472762.stm

2 Chandiramani, K., Dhar, P.L. & Verma, S. K. (1998). Psychological effects of Vipassana on Tihar jail inmates; Samuelson, M., Carmody, J., Kabat-Zinn, J. & Bratt, M.A. (2007). Mindfulness-based stress reduction in Massachusetts correctional facilities. *The Prison Journal*, 87(2): pp.254–268.

3 Bowen, S., Witkiewitz, K., Dillworth, T.M., Chawla, N., Simpson, T. L., Ostafin, B. D. & Marlatt, G. A. (2006). Mindfulness meditation and substance use in an incarcerated population. *Psychology of addictive behaviors*, 20(3), pp.343–347.

4 Rainforth, M.V., Alexander, C.N. & Cavanaugh, K.L. (2003). Effects of the transcendental meditation program on recidivism among former inmates of Folsom Prison: Survival analysis of 15-year follow-up data. *Journal of Offender Rehabilitation*, 36(1–4): pp.181–203.
Bleick, C.R. & Abrams, A.I. (1987). The Transcendental Meditation program and criminal recidivism in California. *Journal of Criminal Justice*, 15(3): pp.211–230.

5   Band, G.P.H. & Van Boxtel, G.J.M. (1999). Inhibitory motor control in stop paradigms: review and reinterpretation of neural mechanisms. *Acta Psychologica*, 101(2), pp.179–211.

6   Munro, G.E., Dywan, J., Harris, G.T., McKee, S., Unsal, A. & Segalowitz, S.J. (2007). Response inhibition in psychopathy: the frontal N2 and P3. *Neuroscience Letters*, 418(2): pp.149–153.

7   Chiesa, A., Calati, R. & Serretti, A. (2011). Does mindfulness training improve cognitive abilities? A systematic review of neuropsychological findings. *Clinical Psychology Review*, 31(3): pp.449–464.

8   Walton, K.G. & Levitsky, D.K. (2003). Effects of the transcendental meditation program on neuroendocrine abnormalities associated with aggression and crime. *Journal of Offender Rehabilitation*, 36(1–4): pp.67–87.

9   Shapiro, D. & Cline K. (2004). Mood Changes Associated with Iyengar Yoga Practices: A Pilot Study. *International Journal of Yoga*, 14: pp.35–44.

10 Hartfiel, N., Havenhand, J., Khalsa, S.B., Clarke, G. & Krayer, A. (2011). The effectiveness of yoga for the improvement of well-being and resilience to stress in the workplace. *Scandinavian Journal of Work, Environment & Health*, 37(1): pp.70–76.

11 Yoshihara, K., Hiramoto, T., Sudo, N. & Kubo, C. (2011). Profile of mood states and stress-related biochemical indices in long-term yoga practitioners. *BioPsychoSocial Medicine*, 5(1): pp.1–8.

12 Michalsen, A., Grossman, P., Acil, A., Langhorst, J., Lüdtke, R., Esch, T. & Dobos, G. (2005). Rapid stress reduction and anxiolysis among distressed women as a consequenceof a three-month intensive yoga program. *American Journal of Case Reports*, 11(12): pp.555–561.
Woolery, A., Myers, H., Sternlieb, B. & Zeltzer, L. (2004). A yoga intervention for young adults with elevated symptoms of depression. *Alternative Therapies in Health and Medicine*, 10(2): pp.60–63.

13 Moadel, A.B., Shah, C., Wylie-Rosett, J., Harris, M.S., Patel, S.R., Hall, C.B. & Sparano, J.A. (2007). Randomized controlled trial of yoga among a multiethnic sample of breast cancer patients: effects on quality of life. *Journal of Clinical Oncology*, 25(28): pp.4387–4395.

14 Rocha, K.K.F., Ribeiro, A.M., Rocha, K.C.F., Sousa, M.B.C., Albuquerque, F.S., Ribeiro, S. & Silva, R.H. (2012). Improvement in physiological and psychological parameters after 6 months of yoga practice. *Consciousness and Cognition*, 21(2): pp.843–850.

15 Sheela, H.R.R.N. & Ganpat, T.S. (2013). Efficacy of Yoga for sustained attention in university students. Ayu, 34(3): p.270.

16 Sharma, V.K., Das, S., Mondal, S., Goswami, U. & Gandhi, A. (2006). Effect of Sahaj Yoga on neuro-cognitive functions in patients suffering from major depression. *Indian Journal of Physiology and Pharmacology*, 50(4): p.375.

17 Froeliger, B.E., Garland, E.L., Modlin, L.A. & McClernon, F.J. (2012). Neurocognitive correlates of the effects of yoga meditation practice on emotion and cognition: a pilot study. *Frontiers in Integrative Neuroscience*, 6:48.

18 When research participants lying in the brain scanner were presented with unpleasant pictures, yoga practitioners exhibited less reactivity in the right dorsolateral prefrontal cortex, as compared to a control group.

19 Bilderbeck, A.C., Farias, M., Brazil, I.A., Jakobowitz, S. & Wikholm, C. (2013). Participation in a 10-week course of yoga improves behavioural control and decreases psychological distress in a prison population. *Journal of Psychiatric Research*, 47(10): pp.1438–1445.

20 Band, G.P.H. & Van Boxtel, G.J.M. (1999). Inhibitory motor control in stop paradigms: review and reinterpretation of neural mechanisms. *Acta Psychologica*, 101(2): pp.179–211.

21 Ogilvie, J.M., Stewart, A.L., Chan, R.C. & Shum, D.H. (2011). Neuropsychological measures of executive fucntion and antisocial behaviour: a meta-analysis. *Criminology*, 49(4): pp.1063–1107.

22 http://news.bbc.co.uk/1/hi/world/europe/4743741.stm

chapter 8

1 Jung, C. (1954/1993). *The Practice of Psychotherapy: Essays on the Psychology of the Transference and other Subjects.* London: Routledge.

2 Weng, H., Fox, A., Shackman, A., Stodola, D., Caldwell, J., Olson, M., Rogers, G. & Davidson, R. (2013). Compassion training alters altruism and neural responses to suffering. *Psychological Science*, 24(7): pp.1171–1180.

3 Shapiro, D.H. & Walsh, R. (eds) (1984), *Meditation: Classic and Contemporary Perspectives.* New York: Aldine.

4 Creswell, J.D. & Lindsay, E. (2014). How does mindfulness training affect health? A mindfulness stress-buffering account. *Current Directions in Psychological Science*, 23(6): pp.401–407,

5 Williams, M., Crane, C., Barnhofer, T., et al (2014). Mindfulness-based cognitive therapy for preventing relapse in recurrent depression: a randomized dismantling trial. *Journal of Consulting and Clinical Psychology*, 82(2): pp.275–86.

6 Sedlmeier, P., Eberth, J., Schwarz, M., et al. (2012). The psychological effects of meditation: A meta-analysis. *Psychological Bulletin*, 138(6): pp.1139–1171.

7 Smith, J. (1976). Psychotherapeutic effects of Transcendental Meditation with controls for expectation of relief and daily sitting. *Journal of Consulting and Clinical Psychology*, 44(4): pp.630–37.

8   Carmody, J., Reed, G., Kristeller, J. & Merriam, P. (2008).
    Mindfulness, spirituality, and health-related symptoms. *Journal
    of Psychosomatic Research*, 64(4): pp.393–403.
9   Greeson, J., Webber, D., Smoski, M., Brantley, J., Ekblad,
    A., Suarez, E. & Wolever, R. (2011). Changes in spirituality
    partly explain health-related quality of life outcomes after
    Mindfulness-Based Stress Reduction, *Behavioral Medicine*,
    34(6): pp.508–18.
10 Carmody, J., Reed, G., Kristeller, J. & Merriam, P. (2008).
    Mindfulness, spirituality, and health-related symptoms. *Journal
    of Psychosomatic Research*, 64(4): pp.393–403.
11 Fulfilment Daily, 30 December 2014, http://www.
    fulfillmentdaily.com/20-science-based-reasons-make-
    meditation-new-years-resolution/

GLOSSARY

Bold oblique indicates a word or term that also appears
in this glossary.

Advaita Vedanta A system of Indian spirituality that presupposes
there is only one undivided reality (*atman*), and that our individual
selves are nothing more than an illusion.

autogenic therapy A physical relaxation technique developed by
German psychiatrist Johannes Schultz.

behaviourism A school of psychology founded by psychologist
John Watson, based on the premise that behaviours can be
measured, trained and changed.

biofeedback training The use of physiological indicators, such as
a heart-rate monitor, to help with increasing awareness of and
changing of your mental, emotional and physiological states.

Chi-Gong A Chinese martial art involving slow movements or
moving meditation that aims to balance the body and mind.

clairvoyance Perceiving an event that is happening at a distance
which you can't access through your five senses.

cognitive psychological education In *MBCT*, learning how to
become aware of your thoughts, feelings and sensations, without
involving meditation.

cognitive behavioural therapy A talking therapy that aims to help
clients manage their problems by changing the way they think
and behave. Commonly used in the treatment of anxiety and
depression.

conditioning A process in which a stimulus that was previously neutral comes to evoke a particular response.

meta-analysis A statistical technique that analyzes the results of various studies to ascertain the strength of the effects of a clinical intervention or technique.

mindfulness A Buddhist-based technique of meditation during which you cultivate a state of non-judgmental awareness. Mindfulness is usually practised sitting down, but it can also be practised while walking.

Mindfulness-based cognitive therapy (MBCT) An eight-week psychological therapy group program developed by John Segal, Mark Williams and John Teasdale, which uses *mindfulness* techniques and cognitive therapy to treat the relapse of depression.

Mindfulness-based stress reduction (MBSR) An eight-week group program founded by Jon Kabat-Zinn. Initially designed to help people with pain through the use of mindfulness techniques.

Non-duality The Indian spiritual system of *Advaita Vedanta* explains that reality is non-dual – all the beings and things in the universe are part of the same undivided essence.

parapsychology The scientific study of psi phenomena, which violate the conventions of time, space or physics (such as, having a vision of a future event).

peak experience A term originally coined by US psychologist Abraham Maslow, referring to transient feelings of great happiness and connectedness to the universe or God.

precognition To have a vision of an event that is yet to happen.

progressive muscle relaxation Originally developed by US physician Edmund Jacobson, a relaxation technique in which you intentionally contract and then relax specific muscle groups.

psychoanalysis A theory of the mind and a therapeutic school founded by Austrian neurologist Sigmund Freud. This approach emphasizes the influence of the unconscious mind on human behaviour.

psychodrama A form of therapy created by Austrian–American psychiatrist Jacob Moreno in which self-exploration takes the form of acting events, usually from your past.

psychodynamic psychotherapy A school of therapy that focuses on revealing unconscious processes in order to promote insight and self-understanding.

psychokinesis Being able to move an object or influence matter by mental effort.

psychosocial Relating to the interaction between the social environment and psychological processes.

quantum theory A branch of theoretical physics, developed in the early twentieth century, that aims to explain the atomic and subatomic levels of reality.

recidivism The repetition of a criminal behaviour after having received sanctions (such as, imprisonment) for a previous crime.

Tai-Chi Similar to *Chi-Gong*, a Chinese slow-moving martial art comprising a defined set of movements which aim to balance your mind and body.

telepathy To hear what another person is thinking without any outward conversation taking place.

TM-sidhi techniques A set of practices associated with transcendental meditation that were expected to unleash your spiritual potential and lead to the development of unusual abilities such as flying.

Transcendental Meditation (TM) A Hindu-based form of meditation popularized in the West by Maharishi that consists of focusing your mind on a mantra (a Sanskrit holy word).

Upanishads The holy scriptures of Hinduism.

zazen Seated meditation in *Zen Buddhism*.

Zen Buddhism Developed in Japan, a form of Buddhism that cultivates meditation and other techniques with the aim of achieving a state of enlightenment *(satori)*.

INDEX

ACKNOWLEDGMENTS

Our agent, Caroline Hardman, and Jo Lal at Watkins, have been tireless in their support throughout the writing process: thank you for your encouragement. We are also grateful to Judy Barratt, for the careful editing, and Vicky Hartley and Francesca Yarde-Buller for organizing the book promotion. The BIAL Foundation has supported our work for many years, including the research on yoga and meditation in prisons. This work was carried out in collaboration with Amy Bilderbeck and the Prison Phoenix Trust: we are particularly indebted to Sam Settle, Sandy Chubb and John Dring. A number of people who remain anonymous have nonetheless played an important role: thank you to all those in prison we interviewed and the therapy clients we worked with. Of the people we mention by name in the book, we are particularly grateful to Swami Ambikananda, for her insights on the difficulties one may encounter when meditating, and to Nick Brewer for speaking so openly about his experiences.

Miguel: I would like to thank Gillian Johnson, Nicholas Shakespeare, Mansur Lalljee, Tony Cross and John O'Connor for tea and dialogue on the various topics of the book. Gareth Bloomfield and Meg Bartlett for their invaluable advice on the writing process. The conversations I had over a decade ago with philosopher Carlos do Carmo Silva on mystical experience (East and West) have been a continuous source of inspiration. I am deeply grateful to my parents, and to Pedro Soares and Tiago Santos, for introducing me to and sharing my enthusiasm for the study of meditation and spirituality; to Soheila for being there all along; to my son António, for never tiring of asking 'Have you finished the book?', and to Romara for her love, enthusiasm and companionship.

Catherine: I would like to thank my husband, Jens, for his unwavering love and support, and most of all for keeping me company on so many evenings in during the writing process! I'm ever grateful to my parents: Cathy, for being my constant and my role model; and Tony, for instilling in me a love of books. Thank you both for all your support and encouragement. Thanks also to James Stroud, Kerin Barry, Abi Nancarrow, and Francesca Sawer for the valuable feedback on chapter drafts.

ABOUT THE AUTHORS

Dr Miguel Farias has pioneered brain research on the pain-alleviating effects of spirituality and the psychological benefits of yoga and meditation in prisoners. He was a postdoctoral researcher at the Oxford Centre for the Science of Mind and a lecturer at the Department of Experimental Psychology, University of Oxford. He currently leads the Brain, Belief and Behaviour Group at the Centre for Research in Psychology, Behaviour and Achievement, Coventry University. His research has been reported by the BBC, *New Scientist* and *National Geographic*.

Catherine Wikholm read Philosophy and Theology at St Peter's College, University of Oxford, before going on to do a Masters degree in Forensic Psychology. She was employed by HM Prison Service, where she worked with young offenders. She now works in the NHS and is currently in the final year of her doctoral training in Clinical Psychology at the University of Surrey. Miguel and Catherine worked together on a research study that looked at the psychological effects of yoga and meditation in prisoners.

WATKINS

Sharing Wisdom Since
1893

The story of Watkins Publishing dates back to March 1893, when John M. Watkins, a scholar of esotericism, overheard his friend and teacher Madame Blavatsky lamenting the fact that there was nowhere in London to buy books on mysticism, occultism or metaphysics. At that moment Watkins was born, soon to become the home of many of the leading lights of spiritual literature, including Carl Jung, Rudolf Steiner, Alice Bailey and Chögyam Trungpa.

Today our passion for vigorous questioning is still resolute. With over 350 titles on our list, Watkins Publishing reflects the development of spiritual thinking and new science over the past 120 years. We remain at the cutting edge, committed to publishing books that change lives.

DISCOVER MORE ...

Read our blog

Watch and listen to
our authors in action

Sign up to
our mailing list

JOIN IN THE CONVERSATION

 WatkinsPublishing   @watkinswisdom

▶ WatkinsPublishingLtd   8+ +watkinspublishing1893

Our books celebrate conscious, passionate, wise and happy living.
Be part of the community by visiting

www.watkinspublishing.com